Decision Making for Library Management

by
Michael R.W. Bommer
and
Ronald W. Chorba

Knowledge Industry Publications, Inc.

Professional Librarian Series

Decision Making for Library Management

Library of Congress Cataloging in Publication Data

Bommer, Michael R.W.
    Decision making for library management.

    (The Professional librarian)
    Bibliography: p.
    Includes index.
    1. Library administration—Decision-making.
I. Chorba, Ronald W. II. Title. III. Series.
Z678.B65   025.1   81-17160
ISBN 0-86729-001-3   AACR2
ISBN 0-86729-000-5 (pbk.)

Printed in the United States of America

10   9   8   7   6   5   4   3   2   1

Table of Contents

List of Tables and Figures

Preface

This book is the result of efforts to explore the feasibility of developing a comprehensive approach to decision support for managers of academic and special libraries. Faced with the prospect of ever-tightening budgets, it is increasingly necessary for library managers to plan and allocate resources in the most effective manner in concert with the objectives of the institution with which the library is affiliated. The library manager must be able to identify problems, needs and trends, and then must respond with decisions and programs that apportion resources appropriately.

At the same time, the library manager is confronted with the increasing availability and employment of technological systems in library operations such as circulation, acquisition, cataloging, interlibrary loan and bibliographic search. Automation in each of these areas provides data concerning utilization activities and available materials resources. The availability of these operating and transaction type data provides a new opportunity to support management decisions. However, these data are only available as a by-product of the operational activities from which they originate, and as yet, little attempt has been made to organize this data base in a manner responsive to the real needs of management. Further, most of these data reflect only the manifest demand for library services and the status of the collection. There still remains a definite lack of direct, objective data concerning the needs of the client community and benefits imported by various services.

Our examination of the literature revealed a considerable body of research on the relationship between user needs and library services. With few exceptions, this body of research employed means of assessing user needs that would not be practical in a continuous day-to-day tracking. In this day and age library management requires continuing feedback. In addition to providing information on library operations and user needs, further data concerning the institutional environment affecting the library are required.

The challenge we confronted in preparing this study was to develop a comprehensive approach to decision support combining data about user productivity and activities, use of library resources and availability of library materials. The organization of and access to this data base should be well-matched to the decisions faced by library managers. Furthermore, in view of current budget restrictions, the resulting system should be parsimonious

1

in its use of resources. Thus, one thrust of our efforts was to address the questions of what kinds of data should be captured to provide sufficiently valid information and how the data should be captured from the standpoint of efficiency. We feel that our study has been successful in identifying a framework and a feasible evolutionary path for the development of such a system. We look forward to developing a prototype system in the future.

- - - - - - - -

This book is a product of the efforts of many individuals and organizations who generously assisted the authors with their time and expertise.

First, we would like to express our appreciation to the Division of Information Science and Technology, the National Science Foundation, which provided support for a major portion of this study. The usual disclaimer applies in that any opinions, findings and conclusions or recommendations expressed in this publication are those of the authors and do not necessarily reflect the views of the National Science Foundation.

We would like to thank Dr. Walter Grattidge who provided valuable insights as a consultant on the NSF Grant. At the time of the grant, Dr. Grattidge directed the design and development of Clarkson College's new Educational Resource System while he was on leave from his position as manager of Technical Information, General Electric Corporate Research and Development.

We would also like to thank Janice Treggett, Ann Black and Margaret Rohdy, research librarians on the project, and Gail Santimaw, who provided editorial assistance.

Valuable assistance and comments were offered by: Ottilie Rollins, Head Librarian, and her staff at Clarkson College Library; Mahlon Peterson, University Librarian, and his staff at St. Lawrence University Library; Richard Talbot, Director of Libraries, and his staff at the University of Massachusetts Library; Selby Gration, Library Director, and his staff at the SUNY Cortland Library; and the late Donald Streeter, Director of Technical Communications, and the staff of the IBM Technical Library at White Plains.

We also would like to acknowledge the members of the advisory committee for Clarkson College's new Educational Resources System, who acted as an advising committee during the early stages of this project. Finally, we would like to thank Virginia Smith and Mary Veglahn, who worked long hours on short notice to type the many tasks associated with this project.

1

Introduction

The collection, storage and transfer of human knowledge in academic libraries is becoming increasingly dependent on technically sophisticated systems. Computerized cataloging networks have become essential for classifying and cataloging a library's collection. These same systems are now being extended to provide electronic communication and computer-controlled interlibrary loan services. Many libraries employ or subscribe to vendors for automated materials acquisition systems. Automated circulation systems for controlling the location and use of materials are becoming commonplace. Libraries are rapidly moving in the direction of computer-on-microform and online catalog access of holdings. A catalog listing reserve room reading material associated with various courses in academic libraries is often automated. Computer-aided searches of bibliographic data bases are supplementing, and, in some cases, replacing traditional manual searches. These systems are also being used to provide selected dissemination of information (SDI) services in response to generated profiles for particular users or user groups on a periodic basis. All of these library support systems represent a wealth of untapped information for potential use in the planning and management of library resources and services.

While all this information-gathering is taking place in libraries, the administration of the parent institution is at the same time also collecting and processing a wealth of information relevant to the planning and management of the library. At many academic institutions, computer-based systems are being used to schedule classes, track student progress and chart enrollment patterns. Information on textbook usage, course descriptions and faculty assignments for courses each semester is now contained in data bases. Academic administrators are compiling data on faculty-generated research proposals, grant awards, publications and papers presented at conferences. Information on new program developments, changes in the emphasis of existing programs and changing pedagogical trends as related to institutional goals and objectives is often available. Likewise, a wealth of relevant information appropriate to the planning and management of special libraries is also being collected and stored. Awareness of the parent institution's goals and objectives is an important determinant for special library decision making. New research projects, sponsored contracts, programs, as well as departmental activities of the institution, all provide valuable information. Finally, trends in the production of knowledge and societal priorities represent further sources of planning and management information for both special and academic libraries.

It can be anticipated that library management will continue to be faced with providing increased access to a volume of knowledge that is expanding at a dramatic rate. Rising inflationary costs for providing materials and service, coupled with increasing and more sophisticated demands by users, further intensify the situation. At the same time, institutional financial and personnel resources are becoming severely constrained and resource allocation for the library is in competition with other institutional activities and operations. Gore (1976) predicts that further growth of the local library will not be the solution to information problems while Schmidt documents the existence of a declining acquisition rate among research libraries during a time when the rate of knowledge output is increasing.*

CHALLENGES AND OPPORTUNITIES

To meet the challenge of providing patrons with increased access to a knowledge base that is growing at an alarming rate, it is vital that the library's resources—human, material and financial—be used in the most effective and efficient manner. A study conducted by Booz, Allen & Hamilton Inc. targeted four major areas for managerial improvement in the 1980s. These areas, identified as the strategic areas which will yield the greatest degree of benefits or output as a result of improvements in management design and action, are shown in Figure 1.1.

Recently, much attention has been focused on office support cost reductions. New advances in equipment design, especially those making use of computer capabilities, are increasing the productivity of secretarial staff. Word processing capabilities, computerized filing and retrieval systems, office activity scheduling, routine monitoring, etc., are becoming commonplace. While these advances are offering improvements in the productivity of secretarial staff, significant future increases in the office support area are not expected to occur in the same magnitude as increases in the other areas. Future gains in productivity in the office area are expected to be modest in comparison to opportunities in other areas because of the current high state of technology of office equipment and the disproportionately smaller amount of expenditures for and in support of office staff as compared with professional and managerial staff. In contrast, the potential gains from improvements in productivity and decision making with regard to the professional and managerial staff are significantly greater.

New forms of organizational design will emerge which will develop and use human resources more effectively at all levels. The classic pyramid structure of early American organizations was forged by powerful social values of individualism, conservation, competition and property rights. Technology, services and client needs were relatively stable during this period. Since employees often were relatively uneducated, lacked transferable skills and were in oversupply, organizations evolved which stressed specialization, conformity and centralization of authority and decision making. In recent years, the traditional pyramid structure has eroded as a new set of values and circumstances has evolved. The

---

*Citations for these studies and for others noted throughout this book are given in the Bibliography.

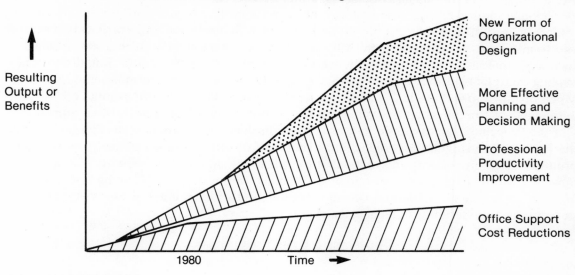

**Figure 1.1 Resulting Output or Benefits
Over Time as a Function of Management Evolution**

Source: Booz, Allen & Hamilton Inc.

social ethic and professional management came into being. Workers developed higher skills, education, mobility and expectations of reward. Technology, services and client needs changed rapidly. As a result, organizations began to embrace more cooperative endeavors with decision making and authority becoming more decentralized and transferred to lower levels. The pyramid structure thus became more rectangular in shape.

In the course of the 1980s, new forms of organizations will evolve to cope with changing values and to increase the effectiveness of human resources at all levels. New forms of design will be used to motivate individuals and groups, to facilitate communication among groups performing interdependent activities and to provide a common direction with explicit, agreed-upon goals for all to work toward. In future organizations, work loads will be more balanced, work support services more accessible and there will be greater emphasis on the needs and merits of individual employees.

Productivity of members of the professional staff will be enhanced through the application of advances in computer and communications technology and through more effective use of their own time. Computer-aided searches of bibliographic data bases, computerized cataloging systems, computerized interlibrary loan services, etc., have all significantly increased the effectiveness of librarian professionals. Innovations in these and other areas will continue to improve the productivity of these staffs. At the same time, professional librarians will be called upon to manage their time more effectively. Chronic time wasters such as inefficiently run staff meetings, inefficient retrieval of previously read information, seeking a particular person, tracking assigned tasks, interruptions, etc., will be reduced.

Staff training efforts will play a significant role in developing the capability of each individual professional to manage his/her time more effectively.

Finally, improved decision making and planning will be required to use the library's resources most effectively. The library manager must be able to identify problems, needs and trends, and then must respond with decisions and programs that direct resources in such a manner as to best support the overall objectives of the institution. Sound decision making and planning, however, require appropriate management information and models. Much of this information is available from existing data bases, as a by-product of automated or computerized operating systems or can be captured from various sources.

All four above areas are important to the improvement of library effectiveness during the 1980s: office support cost reduction; new forms of organizational design; professional productivity improvement; and more effective planning and decision making. This book, however, will focus primarily on one of these areas—more effective planning and decision making. In particular, a framework will be examined for designing a decision support system (DSS) to aid library management.

STRUCTURE OF THIS BOOK

The purpose of this book is to identify and analyze parameters and indicators important to the design of a decision support system (DSS) for academic and special libraries. The development of an information-based DSS seems particularly appropriate at this time. This development is stimulated by the need for such management information in the decision-making and planning processes and the potential availability of such information as a by-product of the various library automated operating systems. These efforts are intended to provide a basis for a library decision support system which will provide management with ongoing performance evaluation and support for planning, budgeting and control decisions. This book attempts to synthesize a number of concepts and ideas, presently extant, into a coherent system of variables and relationships for performance assessment of a library system.

Information on many of the day-to-day library services and operational transactions, as well as institutional and environmental activities, can be obtained and processed for use in a decision support system. This prospect becomes increasingly feasible as more and more transactions are monitored or controlled by computerized systems. Similarly, information on user need profiles can often be gleaned from research activity reports, program descriptions, student enrollment patterns, course offerings, library transactions, bibliographic searches and selected dissemination of information (SDI) activity. Information pertaining to library use can be obtained from circulation transactions, reserve room transactions, interlibrary loans and bibliographic searches. Document availability can be ascertained from catalog entries, interlibrary loan transactions and circulation transactions. User activity or productivity can be measured by research project involvement, publication endeavors, patent activity, course offerings, and recognitions, honors and awards. Information on institutional and environmental factors can be obtained from written statements of institutional goals and objectives, publishing industry reports and an awareness of societal trends.

Thus, the objective of this study is to develop an integrated system for identifying, collecting and analyzing those measures and data which are critical in making effective management decisions and plans. Further, this system will provide a basis for linking various survey and research study results with resource allocation decisions. (As previously noted, citations for studies and other publications mentioned throughout the book are listed in the Bibliography.)

Decision support concepts are developed in Chapter 2. Library managers with varied educational backgrounds, experiences, personalities, values, etc., will require different kinds of information in a variety of forms to arrive at their decisions; this diversity is recognized and dealt with. Similarly, the types of decisions faced by library managers vary widely. A framework for mapping out various types of decisions is developed along four dimensions: degree of structure; function area; decision level; and decision stage. Degree of structure can be used to describe the level of complexity and uncertainty involved in a decision. Decisions can also be categorized according to the functional area in which they apply within the organization. The organizational level (strategic, managerial or operational) at which decisions are made serves to further distinguish types of decisions. Finally, the decision-making process can be defined according to the various stages of the decision-making process including intelligence, design and choice activities. Chapter 2 concludes with a description of and design considerations for a decision support system.

Chapter 3 considers overall library objectives, resource allocation concepts and assessment measures, along with decision tasks and management information needs. The chapter emphasizes the need for clearly defined library objectives which are congruent with and supportive of the objectives of the parent institution. A set of clearly stated objectives also provides a necessary context of guidance and direction in making decisions at all levels of library management. Decision tasks and related management information needs are also identified and mapped out in Chapter 3.

An overview of the more important decision models developed and management information elements identified relating to the collection is presented in Chapter 4. This overview is performed for each of the decision tasks identified for the collection development and technical services functional areas.

Chapter 5 provides a similar overview for user services. It discusses decision models and management information elements relating to the decision tasks in Reference and Bibliographic Service, Collection Access, Interlibrary Loan and Physical Facilities functional areas.

Given the decision environment of the library, Chapter 6 develops an organized, conceptual view of this environment. The objective is to produce a data model of relevant entities and activities in the library and its parent institution. This data model will constitute the foundation of the generalized decision support system. Rather than collecting and storing data for specific reporting applications, the data base approach provides a general, overall method of operation which can accommodate changing needs and timely response.

To implement the data base model in a cost-effective fashion, the authors investigated a number of possible operational approaches. Field trials were conducted to identify inexpensive yet valid procedures for capturing data essential to the model. This was especially important with respect to information about user and organizational activities. Chapter 7 discusses the results of these field trials.

A detailed discussion of a framework for management reporting is presented in Chapter 8. A generalized reporting system must be capable of retrieving data from the data base in a variety of forms and modes. The complete discussion of these capabilities provides a basis for designing the reporting system or for evaluating existing systems available on the market. An example of the use of such a reporting system is presented within the context of our data base model.

Finally, Chapter 9 offers recommendations for implementing a complete decision support system. Consideration is given to the level of existing technology in the library as well as the potential effect of forthcoming hardware and software developments in the computer field. Emphasis is placed on developing a sound, logical approach to decision support which can develop and evolve with organizational demands and constraints independent of existing technology.

2

Decision Support Concepts

Libraries are increasingly using computer applications for many technical processing activities and user services. The computer's contribution to the management of libraries, however, has not been significant to date. Some commercially available automated circulation systems provide summary statistics on circulation activity; however, this appears to be a peripheral contribution of these systems. Dranov (1977) has surveyed users of automated circulation systems and found that these statistics have not been used in the management process.

The recurring criticism of management information systems reported by DeGennaro (1978) is that they contribute little to the really important decisions of upper-management or even middle-management levels. Such decisions require managerial judgment and consideration of unquantifiable factors which cannot be accomplished by computers. Simon (1965) characterizes these decisions as "unstructured." Structured decisions are those which can be programmed or automated, and often a single "best" solution can be identified. An unstructured decision may require consideration of qualitative factors, ethical judgments or simply personal taste. Unstructuredness may also be the result of the decision maker's inability to fully comprehend a structure in a complex situation.

The operations research and systems approach to a decision problem is to discover and exploit the underlying problem structure. These methods usually require considerable investment of time and money spent in developing a formal decision model. Many problems, however, are difficult to structure without ignoring important qualitative features. To date, operations and systems research models have been successful only in dealing with the more structured, routine, repetitive problems for which definite and specific procedures can be applied (see Bommer, 1975). Many of the important, unstructured decisions must be made without reliance on formalized models and tools.

The quality of decision making in libraries depends largely upon the availability and timeliness of appropriate management information. Information, however, is not the sole component for good decision making and planning. The experience and judgment brought to the problem by the decision maker are also critical ingredients. Ackoff (1967) discusses the need for managers to develop an adequate mental model of a decision problem. Mintzberg found that managers collect and piece together various scraps of information until patterns begin to emerge in their minds. These patterns combine to form mental models which describe various aspects of a problem. What would appear to be needed then is a decision support system which assists the manager in supporting and developing these models. Such a system would extend the powers of the decision maker in dealing with these unstructured problems. At the same time the system should be tailored to the cognitive style and idiosyncrasies of the decision maker.

Critical to the development of a decision support system is the identification of a link between the decision-making process and the information elements necessary to support the decision process. Specification of the informational elements to be included in the support system is a function of the types of decisions to be made and the decision process employed by the manager. Lucas states that the identification of "the type of decision involved and the informational requirements for each decision type are essential in the design or analysis of an information system." Ackoff (1967) concurs with this view stating that "for managers to know what information is needed, they must be aware of each type of decision and have an adequate model for each decision." As a first step in identifying informational needs, the decision process for academic libraries must be analyzed and delineated. A systematic "mapping out" of the decision process would provide a basis for identifying informational needs and designing a decision support system.

This chapter develops a framework for mapping out the decision process within academic and special libraries. The dimensions of the framework include (1) key functional areas (2) managerial level (3) degree of structure and (4) decision stage. These dimensions provide a basis for identifying informational requirements within the decision process when designing an overall decision support system. A discussion of the concept of a decision support system as an extension of a manager's decision-making capabilities as well as system design considerations is also included in this chapter.

DIMENSIONS OF DECISION MAKING

One system for classifying decisions is according to key library functions. Goals and objectives for several libraries were surveyed and analyzed to identify these key functional areas. Objectives most frequently cited and judged to involve significant decisions regarding current and future library directions were identified. The objectives that emerged were classified according to the manner in which library managers view library services and operations. This is an important consideration since incompatibility between the decision maker's problem-solving method and the format of the support systems results in its not being used, as documented by Churchman and Schainblatt. To be truly effective, a decision support system should mesh with the cognitive structure of the users.

The key functional decision areas for libraries (in no particular order) identified and used in this study are as follows:

- Collection Development
- Technical Services
- Reference and Bibliography Service
- Collection Access
- Access by Interlibrary Loan
- Physical Facilities

(A seventh area, encompassing staff development activities, will not be considered, since this study is focused primarily on users and services.)

Other logical systems for structuring library services and operations have been proposed by Hamburg et al. (1974), Orr et al. (1968) and Strauss et al. (1972). However, the system presented here seems to be most congruent with the manner in which library managers organize their decision-making processes, as evidenced by articulated statements of objectives and by interviews with selected library managers.

A second dimension of decision classification is borrowed from Anthony and distinguishes decisions made at different organizational levels, as illustrated in Figure 2.1. Decisions in strategic planning relate to the selection of objectives, objective priorities, changes in objectives and resource selection. Management control decisions involve policies and objectives developed in the strategic planning process. These decisions encompass program development, staffing levels, funding levels, trade-off resolution, etc., with respect to appropriate objectives and goals. Operational control decisions assure that specific tasks are performed in an effective and efficient manner. While these categories are not strictly mutually exclusive, they provide useful guidelines for analyzing differing informational needs. This book focuses primarily on the strategic planning and management control levels, particularly those relating to planning and resource allocation activities.

Figure 2.1   Decision Levels

Level	Examples
1. Strategic Planning	Setting objectives; negotiating interlibrary agreements; adopting major technological innovations; expanding facilities.
2. Management Control	Allocating funds among subject areas; identifying staff development needs; assessing program performance with respect to strategic objectives; determining hours of library service; developing weeding policy; purchasing equipment and services; settting standards for operations.
3. Operational Control	Monitoring daily operations and activities with respect to standards, corrective actions, scheduling, response to complaints, coordinating special requests and projects. Decisions made in performing cataloging, shelving, acquisitions, weeding, circulation, reference, etc.

Another useful dimension for classifying decisions, proposed by Simon (1960), is by the degree of structure inherent in the decision to be made. Decisions are classified as structured or unstructured, depending upon the degree to which the decision process can be described in detail. Decisions are unstructured as a result of lack of knowledge, need for value judgments, complexity of the problem, uniqueness of the problem, etc. The distinction between structured and unstructured decisions is not always precise. In fact, decisions generally lie on a continuum between these two extremes. Nonetheless, this classification scheme is helpful in designing the information support system.

An example of how decisions might be categorized according to the degree of structure and decision level is shown as Figure 2.2.

In the past, most management information systems have been designed to support the more routine, repetitive, structured decisions and those for which definite procedures can be applied. Recently, through advances in technology and increased knowledge of the decision-making process, impressive strides have been made in industry to develop decision support systems that can assist managers in less structured decision-making situations. In the library environment many, if not most, of the decisions are of the less structured type. To date, information support systems have only been sparingly applied to decision-making in libraries.

Figure 2.2   Decision Classification

Degree of Structure	Decision Level		
	Operational Control	Management Control	Strategic Planning
Structured	Control of new acquisitions	Staffing of circulation desk	Policy on level of cataloging
Unstructured	Online bibliographic search procedure	Allocating funds to subject areas	Collection development goals

Finally, a fourth dimension of decision making also proposed by Simon (1965) is the perception of the distinction between various stages in the decision-making process itself. The most generally accepted view of these stages labels them as: identifying problems and opportunities (intelligence); developing and analyzing alternatives or courses of action (design); and selecting and implementing a course of action (choice). These three decision stages of intelligence, design and choice are illustrated in Figure 2.3.

The decision process can be viewed as a continuous flow from intelligence to design and then to choice. At any stage, however, the flow may be stopped and the decision maker may return to a previous stage. For example, all courses of action may be rejected in the choice stage requiring the decision maker to return to the design stage to develop additional alternatives; or, after a choice is made, the decision maker may monitor the result by returning to the intelligence stage. A schematic of this process appears in Figure 2.4.

Figure 2.3   Stages of Decision Making

Stage	Examples
1. Intelligence: Searching for Problems and Opportunities	Complaints; identifying documents which circulate infrequently; measuring adequacy of collection for specific programs; forecasting future needs; identifying potentially useful technological innovations; comparing performance to expectations.
2. Design: Defining and Analyzing Alternative Actions	Data gathering, modeling and parameter estimation to further understand problem structure; identifying contributing factors; creative generation of possible solutions; discovery of relationships between variables.
3. Choice: Selecting and Implementing a Course of Action	Forecasting implications of alternative actions; evaluating outcomes; dealing with behavioral and technical problems in implementation.

Figure 2.4　Flowchart of the Decision Process

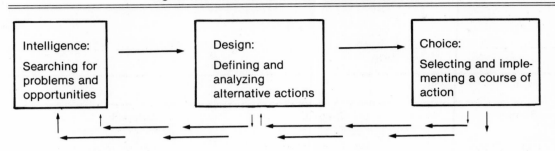

Library managers can think of their jobs as being composed of many decision-making tasks, each characterized along the four dimensions of function, level, structure and stage. The support requirements of any such decision task are dependent on these four attributes. Characteristics of data reported to management such as accuracy, timeliness, source, scope, detail, format and currency must be compatible with the dimensional attributes. The use of mathematical models, statistical tools and the body of research findings about effective library operations must also be invoked with the dimensional attributes in mind.

DECISION SUPPORT SYSTEMS

A decision support system (DSS) can be viewed as a natural progression from an electronic data processing system (EDP) and a management information system (MIS) as depicted in Figure 2.5.

In Stage I, the computer was primarily used as a data processor for transactions and record keeping. Clerical activities were automated with the principal benefit being that data collection and tabulation were performed faster and more efficiently. In Stage II, data were converted to information for management use. This was the phase wherein MIS played a dominant role and in which standardized reports were provided to support the more routine, repetitive, structured decisions. In Stage III, the process is extended to provide information and models which support specific decision processes. These systems are designed to conform to the unique style and needs of a manager so as to assist him in determining the solutions to all problems. The man-machine (manager-computer) system operates interactively to provide a high degree of synergism in the decision-making and planning process.

Decision support systems have evolved for several reasons: the apparent failure of structured management information systems and operations research techniques to aid management in solving partly structured or unstructured problems; the recognition of the unique decision-making styles and needs of different managers; and recent advances in computer technology. Unlike traditional management information systems and operations research techniques, decision support systems rely on the decision maker's insights and judgment at all stages of problem solving: problem identification and formulation; choosing the relevant data to work with; selecting the approach to be used in generating solutions; and evaluating the solutions presented to the decision maker. Decision support systems help the manager improve the quality of decisions by providing more insight into all phases of the problem-solving process.

Figure 2.5   Information System Progression

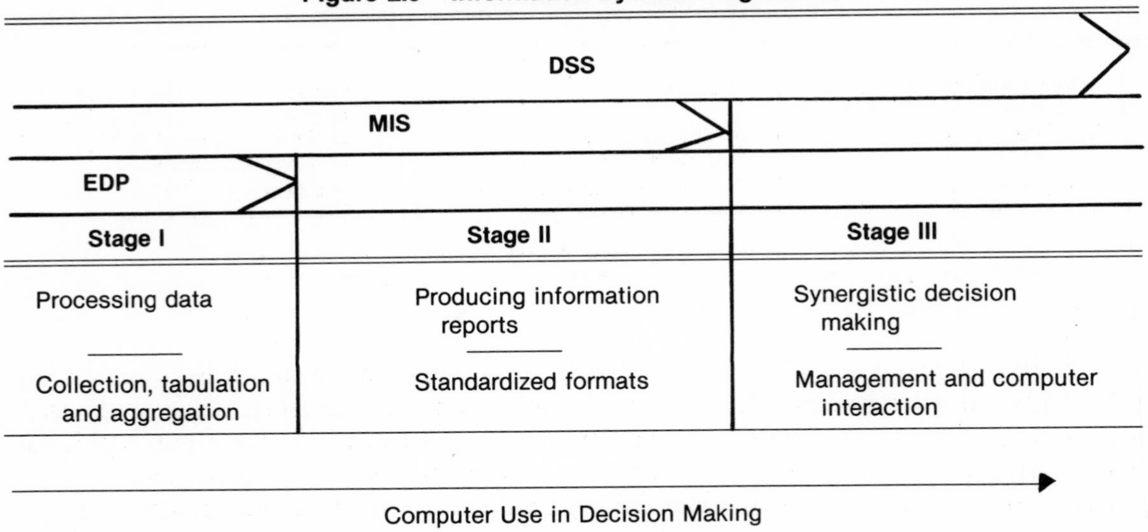

DSS		
MIS		
EDP		
Stage I	**Stage II**	**Stage III**
Processing data	Producing information reports	Synergistic decision making
Collection, tabulation and aggregation	Standardized formats	Management and computer interaction

Computer Use in Decision Making

Since the critical element in solving nonstructured problems is the human decision maker whose judgment is required to identify data requirements and formulate solutions, the design of a support system should carefully consider how the decision maker acquires and uses information. The system should be tailored to complement the cognitive style of the manager in every way possible. Mason and Mitroff conclude that "what is information for one type of decision maker will definitely not be information to another. Thus, as designers of MIS, our job is not to get or force all types to conform to one, but give each type the kind of information he/she is psychologically attuned to and will use most effectively."

Decision support capabilities would therefore have to conform to the behavioral needs of managers. Mintzberg observes that managers carry models and plans in their heads, favor current information over routine reports and prefer to develop their own information networks. Further, decision making is an iterative process in which answers to one question often lead to another question. A decision support system tailored to individual managerial needs that allows managers to extend their particular decision-making approach would appear to be of significant value.

A few decision support systems are in operation in the business sector as reported by Carlson. By and large these systems provide for a wide selection of spontaneous as well as scheduled report formats and graphic capabilities. They are interactive, allowing a decision maker to pose and repose questions on a real-time basis. The systems provide various capabilities (models and statistical techniques) for analyzing and evaluating data; they can access narrative and statistical sets of data that reside in a centralized data base so that the decision maker (user) has complete control over reports generated by the system.

These capabilities enable the manager to use discretion and judgment in combination with relevant data. The system displays pertinent data in a manner and format desired by the individual decision maker. Further questions can be answered quickly by additional data queries or by arranging the data by different classifications and categories. Graphical analysis can be used to clarify and emphasize comparative relationships and trends. Being able to observe these trends and relationships in a manner meaningful to the decision maker often stimulates further creative analysis and improved problem solving.

A conceptual structure of a library decision support system appears as Figure 2.6. In this scheme, the Decision Maker Subsystem is comprised of the decision maker, an interactive terminal and screen as well as a command language capability.

For a decision support system to be effective, the decision maker must be able to interact with all elements of the system. A command language is needed to allow the manager to access and query the system. A broad spectrum of software programs should be available to the decision maker to exploit the system's capabilities in support of the decision-making process.

The Decision Models Subsystem is comprised of data analysis programs for tabulating and presenting data in various modes and formats, standard modeling programs such as regression analysis, time series analysis, etc., as well as specially developed models to support decisions at various managerial levels. The purpose of the model generation and update is to keep the decision models current in the face of the changing environment. The Data Base Subsystem is comprised of data sources from transactions within the library and within the parent institution as well as from data sources external to the institution. The dynamic nature of the system and its use require the data to be continuously updated to reflect recent occurrences.

DESIGN CONSIDERATIONS

A highly structured decision situation can be programmed to such an extent that a decision support system can be devised which prescribes a specific course of action. Only in exceptional instances would the decision maker elect not to follow the prescription. On the other hand, less structured situations require an interactive relationship between a decision maker and his/her support system. In essence, the support system must contribute to a human-machine interaction in which the decision maker's capacity to comprehend, analyze, deduce and evaluate are amplified. However, the support system must not constrain the decision maker's freedom to investigate, question, probe and, ultimately, choose.

The first principle of decision support system design must be to maximize effectiveness at the level where the human-machine interface takes place. The decision maker requires timely access to appropriate data and to appropriate tools of data analysis. The goal is to produce more effective decisions and to promote exploration and managerial learning.

A second design guideline recognizes that the value of information is a relative quantity. Information provided by a decision support system has value only to the extent that it improves decision making. Thus, the value of the support system can be computed as the absolute worth of the decision (perhaps in budget dollars expended) times the potential for improvement. Both ingredients must be present to produce an overall significant benefit. Decision support system development projects must therefore be selected on a priority basis with the above considerations in mind.

Finally, the concept of decision support is not static. A successful system is one that is designed to be flexible and allow for evaluation under changing circumstances. New data sources, tools, problems or technology must not render a system obsolete, but rather, must provide it with an opportunity to contribute greater value. Also, when a new appointment

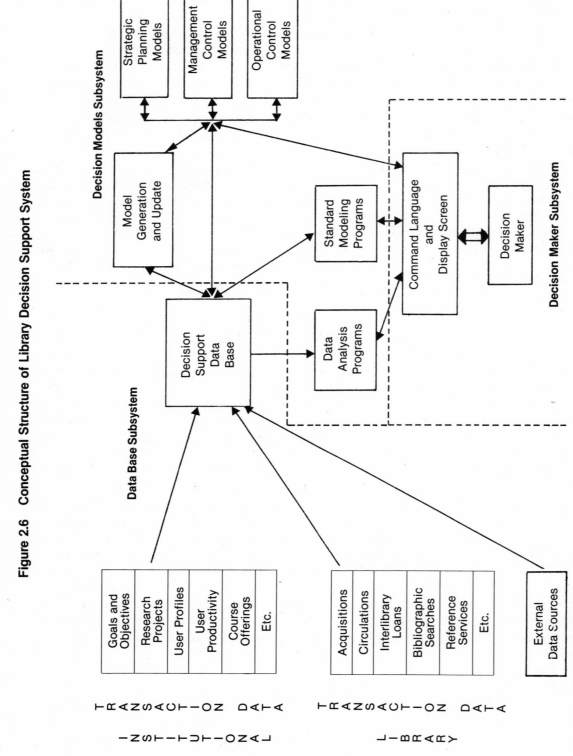

Figure 2.6   Conceptual Structure of Library Decision Support System

Source: Adapted with permission from "A Decision Support System for Banks," by Ralph Sprague and Hugh Watson, OMEGA, Vol. 4, No. 6, 1976, Pergamon Press, Ltd.

is made to a particular management position, the support system should be adaptable to the needs and style of the new occupant.

SUMMARY

The quality and effectiveness of decision making depends to a great degree on the availability of relevant information. In this information-rich environment in which most managers operate, the ability of persons to make good decisions is a function of how information is handled within the organization. Information is not a substitute for good decision making. The experience and judgment of decision makers remains a critical and vital factor in the process. For this reason the decision support system should be tailored to the unique needs of the decision maker and provide the capabilities to extend his/her decision-making abilities.

3

Planning, Decision Tasks and Information Needs

Planning is the process of identifying organizational goals and objectives, developing programs and services to accomplish these objectives and evaluating the success of those programs. The planning process acknowledges that organizations cannot do everything and that resources must be allocated on a priority basis to those activities that lead to the most effective accomplishment of goals and objectives. McClure (1978) suggests that the activity of planning provides a rational response to uncertainty and change; focuses attention on what is to be accomplished; is important as an aid in resource allocation by establishing priorities for funding; serves as a basis for determining individual, departmental, organizational or program accountability; facilitates control of organizational operations by collecting information to evaluate various programs or services; and orients the organization to a futuristic stance.

Sellers believes that the keystone in planning is careful analysis of the library's role to formulate a statement of mission. Based upon this, projects can be developed and a review process can be established to track success and failure. He stresses the need for consistent participation of all personnel in the planning process to insure its success.

Miller proposes a user-oriented planning tool whereby user preferences for current services and for suggested change in library information center operations are collected and analyzed to offer comparisons between different potential means for improving service.

A strategy presented by Webster calls for planning and effecting change in the management of academic libraries through the employment of the Library Management Review and Analysis Program (MRAP). Such MRAP studies involve a systematic investigation of the top management functions in an academic library using self-study and group process methods for planning, identifying problems and developing alternatives within a set of management topics. A review of a cross section of the MRAP studies reveals an emphasis on the individuality of each library with resulting differences in the identified strategies and directions developed.

As depicted in Figure 3.1, academic and special library directors have the responsibility of insuring that their library's overall objectives are developed. Further, they are ultimately responsible for seeing that the library's resources are effectively distributed to the programs which contribute most to the achievement of these objectives. Performance measures for evaluating the progress or success in attaining these objectives must also be specified. To insure a high degree of success in this planning process, library directors must actively seek advice and involvement of their staff and clientele.

Figure 3.1   The Planning Process

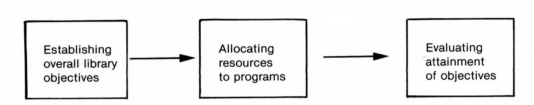

This chapter will stress the need for developing clearly defined overall objectives for the library; it will deal with the allocation of resources and overall performance measures viewed in terms of how these contribute to goals achievement; and finally, it will examine decision tasks and information needed for evaluation as they relate to functional area and organizational level.

OVERALL OBJECTIVES

The effectiveness of any system depends in part upon an explicit set of overall objectives describing what the system is attempting (or should be attempting) to achieve. This set of objectives should be comprehensive and as free from internal conflicts as possible. Conflicts, if they exist, should be resolved if the accomplishment of one objective will have a negative effect on the achievement of another. Equally important is that the set of objectives becomes an integral part of the decision-making process at all managerial levels. This requires that managers at all organizational levels become involved with the system's objectives and cultivate an awareness of how each decision affects these. Without a set of precise and consistent objectives to provide guidance and direction, managers cannot make decisions and develop plans which yield the greatest contribution to the system's performance. The effectiveness of a special or academic library is no exception to this rule.

As the concept of management during the past two decades has moved away from the management of activities and toward results-based management, increased emphasis and importance have been placed on the setting of goals and objectives. One result is that institutions have become interested in incorporating the concepts of goal-oriented management into the overall institutional management process. Harvey cites the following assumptions on which this management process is based:

- "The clearer the idea one has of what one is trying to accomplish, the greater the chances of accomplishment.

- "Progress can only be measured in terms of what one is trying to progress toward.

- "Clear objectives for each program, unit and individual within an institution provide the basis for establishing concise authority and accountability relationships."

Chait has drawn attention to the recent intensity of activity on the part of colleges and universities to define goals and publish statements of purpose. Trustees, college presidents and administrators are requiring their institutions to develop a mission statement specifying goals and objectives. Establishing such a stance for an academic library may be somewhat less demanding than for the total institution. However, unless care is exercised, the statement can be so general as to lose operational significance for the library staff and administration.

McClure (1978) has noted that mission statements for libraries usually include two types of organizational philosophies. One involves assumptions regarding the role of the library within its institutional environment, together with the identification of external factors such as technology and information production which are having an impact on that relationship. The other involves value judgments and expectations regarding the nature of the clients to be served and the types and extent of services which are to be provided.

A further guide to the formulation and application of goals and objectives in academic libraries is provided by the Office of University Library Management Studies, Association of Research Libraries (see Gardner and Webster). This work presents the general and operational issues associated with designing and implementing a goals and objectives program. It includes several examples of mission statements of university libraries as well as specific goal and program objective statements for various levels of organizational hierarchy within academic libraries.

Similarly, objectives for a special library should be clearly defined and should be consistent with the objectives of the institution which it supports. The objectives should define the specific functions and responsibilities which justify its continuing support and provide internal direction for library administration. In general, the objectives for most special libraries should be more precise than those for libraries serving the diffuse teaching and research activities prevalent in an academic setting. For examples of objectives for special libraries see Strable and Special Libraries Association.

RESOURCE ALLOCATION

The need for a systematic procedure for channeling available resources in a manner consistent with institutional goals and objectives has been cited in a number of studies (see, for example, Webster and Hamburg et al., 1976). Decisions must be made as to the distribution of funds and personnel among library units, such as company and departmental libraries, and among the various functions and service areas within individual libraries. A system or systems must also be devised for monitoring and controlling these resources.

Allocations to library units, programs and services should be made consistent with the library's goals and objectives and the expected performance or benefits to be gained.

In recent years, a number of resource allocation models have been proposed to help library management make better funding decisions. Rouse (1975) has developed a mathematically based procedure for the optimal allocation of resources among the many processes of a library system. This allocation is defined as one which considers the chance of success as well as the outcome of the decision. Hamburg et al. (1976) suggest developing cost/benefit ratios for each service, then concentrating resources on those services offering the greatest return. A model for book budgeting based upon rate of use of materials, how the use contributes to the institution's goals and the associated costs is proposed by Gold. Kohut and Walker have devised a model for making resource allocations on monograph and serial purchases, while McGrath (1969) offered an allocation model based upon factor analysis for allocating funds to different subject areas.

Goal programming models have been developed by McGeehan, and Gross and Talavage to deal with the problem of allocating scarce resources in an organization complicated by the presence of multiple, and often conflicting, managerial objectives. This is particularly applicable to academic and special libraries which are being pressed by both funders and users of their services to improve the effectiveness of their operations.

Summers describes the various methods which have been used to apply formulas and their associated disadvantages. The latter arise mainly from political factors which must be taken into account in the final decision making. Perhaps the most famous allocation formula is that of Clapp and Jordan, which unfortunately has the drawback of relying on the experience of librarians to determine the recommended resource levels for materials acquisition instead of being guided by independent institution-wide parameters. The lack of specific dependence of library allocations on independent parameters is illustrated by Baumol and Marcus who found little correlation between library resources for acquisition and student enrollment.

Formula methods of resource allocation may be useful in times of growth. However, in times of relative decline, the recipients may be inclined to favor more politically responsive allocative methods, especially if they believe they will achieve more favorable outcomes than from the former method.

Raffel (1974) has expanded on his earlier analysis of economic considerations in library decision making, which was based on studies at MIT. Because of the nature of the library's role, the more critical the decision, the more the thrust of the decision moves from the strictly economic to the political. He cites campus surveys of alternatives for library services that clearly indicate that subgroups of the university community either have different objectives in mind or view different alternative actions as being best for meeting common objectives. This means that the alternatives faced by library and university administrators involve major choices among various subgroups on campus.

Since there is often no economic way to resolve differences among alternatives which meet different objectives adhered to by different subgroups, a political solution is suggested. Raffel cites Easton's model and analysis as a basis for consideration of the political issues in such a situation. Easton defined politics as the authoritative allocation of values for a society, and cited universities as examples of private governments, as opposed to public governments where all citizens are members. The questions then arise: Can private governments be democratic? Who gets what, when and why?

Recognizing that the rational analysis of decisions and decision makers in libraries is a very complex and difficult subject, Raffel suggests that there are several areas that librarians should consider relative to their decision making:

- The definition of the relevant library system;

- The extent of the environmental constraints which limit or appear to limit the available choices;

- Which groups make demands and to what extent do such groups represent all potential users;

- What is the general climate of support for the library and what assumptions are made by users or administrators which limit the consideration of alternative policies;

- Who plays a role in decisions about the library;

- Who benefits from library services, who pays for the library and how well is each group served;

- What feedback is available to evaluate current allocations, and do non-users have an opportunity to provide feedback?

The point is made that economic analyses alone are insufficient to deal with all library decision making, and that political system analysis can help identify and clarify the broader environment in which library decisions are being made.

PERFORMANCE MEASUREMENT

Closely related to library objectives is the need for meaningful measures of performance to assess what the library is attempting to achieve and whether it is successful in achieving it. Without appropriate performance measures, it is difficult to determine how well the organization is progressing. These measures are needed to determine whether a particular decision or course of action should be pursued and whether funds are being allocated in the most effective manner.

Skeptics argue that library performance is too subjective, too complicated and too intangible to be measured. Increasingly, however, library managers are being required to demonstrate the positive role played by the library system in implementing the institution's overall goals and strategies. It should also be pointed out that decisions are being made by library managers keeping some form of criteria in mind. What is needed is to explicitly define and articulate these measures which are already being used in an implicit or informal sense.

Critical to any evaluation of a program is the availability of measures of performance by which the output of a system can be assessed according to some stated criterion. For service activities, three types of effectiveness measures have been cited by Elton and Vickery:

- Performance measures — the extent to which actual services to actual users are effective;
- Impact measures — the extent to which potential use is actualized;
- Availability measures — the extent to which potential services are actually provided.

Herner, in a basic paper covering system design and evaluation, notes that there has been a procession of evaluation methodologies available ranging from surveys to management studies, to user studies, to technically based performance measurements on specific operations. He advocates considering the total information operation as a system and considering a broader evaluation process which includes a combination of those earlier methodologies. Evaluation is a matter of quality control, and the important questions to be posed are therefore:

- What services should the system be performing?
- Is the system performing all the services it should be performing?
- Is the system performing any services it should not be performing?
- Is it performing the services as efficiently as possible?
- If not, what are the causes and what can be done to remedy the problem?

Some measures of effectiveness for such managerial decision making and planning for information processing and delivery activities appear to be emerging. Early measures dealt with level of effort or standards for library resources. Later studies focused on measuring user characteristics. Many other studies attempt to measure value by user satisfaction.

Musselman and Talavage advocate evaluation based upon three attributes of service itself:

- Quality from a user's viewpoint;
- Value to the organization;
- Effectiveness from a performance standpoint.

These attributes are further divided into such factors as accessibility, applicability, technical quality, timeliness, recall ratio and precision ratio. The two authors conclude that application of this evaluation methodology will allow information center managers to recognize when a system is not responding to the needs of those who use it and to direct improvements.

Starting from the premise that the library deals with information in the service of knowledge, Kantor (1976a) argues that one would really like to measure the contribution a given library makes to the transmission and growth of knowledge within a given time period. The direct measurement of knowledge is not possible, so related events which can be identified are measured. Kantor arrives at the concept of Contact Time per Potential User to measure the usefulness of a library transaction either within the library, or external to the library as occurs in a circulation transaction.

Hamburg et al. (1974) have analyzed the relationship of a library's goals and objectives to overall performance measures and warn that some university library objectives may be too general to yield suitable performance measurements. However, certain performance measures, such as the proportion of users satisfied, document retrieval time, document exposure counts, item-use-days and document exposure time can be used to relate back to library objectives.

Urquhart (1975) stresses the need for measures of performance based upon availability factors relating marginal increments in cost to marginal increments in service. Wills and Oldman present a concept of subjectively derived value; Weinberg formulates a concept for subjectively assessing the probable value of an information document; while Orr (1973) suggests a document delivery test as an overall measure of user satisfaction.

More recent studies have focused on a broader institutionally based criterion of information input as related to user output. For industrial or corporate libraries, Kates proposes as a measure the percentage of references used in papers published by company staff which were contributed or obtained by the information center. Rosenberg (1969) and White (1979b) suggest measures based on the benefit or contribution to project success supplied by the library in relationship to library costs as a way of evaluating industrial library performance. A series of field experiments to assist an information systems manager in assessing various programs for improving the overall system is suggested by Rubenstein and Birr. Finally, Allen (1977) identifies the "gatekeeper" function (that person who links his organization to the technological world at large) and suggests special support for enhancing this person's role as an information resource. These represent some of the few reported attempts to directly measure the productivity of information services.

DECISION TASKS AND INFORMATIONAL NEEDS

In addition to determining library objectives, resource allocation modes and overall measures of performance, library managers must make a number of decisions at both the strategic and management control levels. Each of these decisions would benefit from access to appropriate decision models and pertinent information. As a means for specifying relevant modeling aids and informational elements to be included in a decision support system, key decision tasks are identified and categorized by library functional areas and organizational level. A decision task is defined as the set of decisions which must be made with regard to a problem or opportunity which directly affects library performance.

Interviews with selected library managers showed substantial agreement in identifying the key decision tasks, although there was disagreement as to the ranking of importance or priority for each task. These differences of opinion reflect different phases of a library's evolution and differing environmental influence. For example, a library with adequate space for collection expansion will not rank the weeding decision task as high a priority as a library with space limitations. A library with severely constrained resources for collection development will rank the access to other collections decision task higher than a library with substantial resources for collection development. A listing of key decision tasks and selected performance measures associated with them is given in Table 3.1.

In addition to mapping out key decision tasks, a search was performed to identify the more significant literature pertaining to each of these tasks. This literature was reviewed and summarized for two important reasons.

1) To provide library managers with a brief overview of the types of decision models, formal as well as informal, proposed as aids in solving problems relating to each

Table 3.1   Decision Tasks

Key Functional Objective Area	Strategic Planning Decisions	Management Control Decisions	Performance or Effectiveness Measures
Collection Development	Determining collection development goals.	Allocation of funds to subject areas; Funds allocated for books, serials and reports; Types of books and serials to be acquired; Degree of duplication; Weeding policy and procedures; Current vs. retrospective acquisitions; Replacement of lost, damaged or worn documents; Selection process.	Percent held of sample bibliographies; Patron complaints; Number of reserves for books; Circulation/subject area/document; Circulation/user group; Citation distribution analysis; Selection cost/document; Minimum standards; Ratio of documents selected/documents published; Document retrieval time for local/interlibrary loan; Percent demands satisfied.
Technical Services	Level of cataloging; Timeliness and cost efficiency of document processing.	Acquisition process; Cataloging data source; Type of public bibliographic record; Maintenance of public bibliographic records; Physical preparation and maintenance of documents.	Request-receipt time; Receipt-shelf time; Cost/document processed; Entry points in catalog per document; Patron complaints; Public service staff complaints.
Reference and Bibliographic Service	Level, coverage and quality of reference assistance; Level, comprehensiveness and quality of document identification service.	Ready reference; Bibliographic search; Current awareness; Public relations.	Bibliographies prepared; Searches conducted; Search time; Percent relevant citations obtained; Patrons served; Cost per search; Cost per relevant citation; Sample recall ratio; Response time; Relevant bibliographies services/subject area; Number served by SDI; Requests per SDI. Reference questions received: Directional Informational Reference; Percent questions answered; Cost per question; Test score for sample questions; Percent time staff providing reference service; Percent telephone requests; Number patron orientation programs; Number patrons contacted; Number of class presentations; Complaints.

Table 3.1   Decision Tasks (cont'd.)

Key Functional Objective Area	Strategic Planning Decisions	Management Control Decisions	Performance or Effectiveness Measures
Collection Access	Ease of access to collection.	Hours of library service; Arrangement and location of collection; Level of collection security; Reshelving and shelfreading activities; Circulation control policy and procedures; Quantity and type of AV equipment; Reserve collection policies and procedures.	Reshelving time; Percent documents misshelved; Percent requests in remote storage; Storage cost/document; Percent documents lost; Half-life/periodical subject area; Percent documents in correct location; User access time; Document retrieval time; Percent demands satisfied; Number of patrons; Number of user hours; Percent collection in open stacks; Circulation/user group; Circulation cost/documents circulated; Circulation/document in open stacks; Circulation/document in closed stacks.
Access by Interlibrary Loan	Interlibrary loan cooperative arrangements.	Accessing documents held by other libraries; Supplying documents to other institutions.	Retrieval time; Percent documents obtained; Cost per document; Number of documents borrowed.
Physical Facilities	Quality and adequacy of user area and furnishings.	Allocation of area; Number and type of user furnishings.	Number of users; User hours; Seating/student; Staff area/staff member; Density of document storage.

decision task. Review of these decision models should be helpful to managers in developing further understanding and improved mental conceptualizations of decision problems.

2) To identify informational elements which have been proposed or have proven to be of value in each of the decision tasks. These informational elements serve to define the data to be collected and stored in the library's data base to be accessed by a decision support system.

Chapters 4 and 5 describe the key decision tasks and review the more significant decision models which have been proposed or are currently being used. As part of this review, performance measures and information elements potentially useful in the decision-making process relating to these key tasks are identified. Decision tasks associated with the collection (collection development and technical services) are addressed in Chapter 4 while decision tasks associated with user services (reference and bibliographic service, collection access, interlibrary loan and physical facilities) are discussed in Chapter 5.

4

The Collection

Collection development goals must be determined at the strategic planning level. As can be seen in Table 3.1, management control decisions focus on: allocating funds among subject areas; distributing funds among books, serials and reports; determining types of books, serials and reports to be acquired; deciding upon duplicate copy policy; adopting weeding policy and procedures; determining the degree of emphasis on current versus retrospective acquisitions; deciding a policy for replacement of lost, damaged or worn documents; and finally, specifying the selection process.

Strategic planning decisions for technical services relating to the collection focus on the level of cataloging to employ and the timeliness and cost efficiency of processing documents. At the management control level, decisions must be made relating to the acquisition process, cataloging data source, type of public bibliographic record, maintenance of the public bibliographic record, and physical preparation and maintenance of documents.

The literature reviews in this chapter should serve as a guide to readers who wish further analysis of the factors relating to a particular decision task (see Bibliography for citations).

COLLECTION DEVELOPMENT

Collection development activities involve the planned, systematic growth of a library collection through acquisition of bibliographic and informational resources in various media. The selection of these resources is consistent with a broad framework of objectives and/or limits established for the collection. Collection development efforts involve the formation and maintenance of library collections which support the objectives, programs, services and needs of both the library and the parent institution. These efforts require effective coordination of librarians and other institutional staff in the selection of materials to support the reference, instruction, learning and research needs of the institutional community.

Strategic Planning Decision

Determining Collection Development Goals

Subject boundaries, collection density and collection intensity goals for each subject area must be decided upon with respect to the immediate and long-range needs of the institution. Subject boundary parameters include such considerations as breadth of coverage, chronological period, language, etc. Collection intensity describes the level of current collecting activity, whereas collection density defines the scope of existing collections. The collection development goals for each subject area should reflect the character and direction of the institution's programs, the information needs and expectations of the library's clientele, general and specific information trends, economic conditions, cooperative arrangements and the existing state of the collection.

Guidelines have been promulgated by the American Library Association (1977) to assist librarians with the formulation of a collection development policy which will serve as a planning tool and communication device. The policy should clarify objectives, identify need areas, identify collection strengths and facilitate coordination of collection development and cooperative services. Elements which should be considered in formulating the policy statement include both institutional and subject-specific information. Library and institutional information elements might include:

1) Clientele to be served.
2) Kinds of programs or user needs supported (research, instructional, recreational, reference, etc.).
3) General subject boundaries of the collection.
4) General priorities or limitations governing subject area-specific parameters including:
   a) Breadth and depth of collection (collection density).
   b) Current level of collection activity (collection intensity).
   c) Desirable level of collection density and intensity (minimal, basic, study, research or comprehensive).
   d) Language, chronological periods and geographical areas collected or excluded.
   e) Forms of material collected or excluded.
   f) Library unit or sector with primary responsibility for the field.
5) Regional, national or local cooperative collection agreements which complement or otherwise affect the policy.

Documented Approaches to Collection Development

Magrill and East provide a comprehensive review of the trends and literature in collection development in large university libraries during the 1960s and 1970s. They observe that collection development policies are often produced in connection with other efforts or pressures — a collection evaluation project, a long-range planning operation, a new collection development department or officer, budgeting constraints or participation in a resource-sharing scheme. They conclude that the most significant trends emerging to cope with budgetary constraints are greater selectivity in new acquisitions, more emphasis on efficient procedures and increased reliance on other libraries. Hoffman believes that information should be gathered from five different sources in establishing collection development objectives. These sources include institutional objectives, program goals, use data, availability of material and staff research interests.

A self-study procedure for analyzing and improving research libraries' collection development practice has been developed and successfully employed as reported by Gardner (1979). This procedure is designed to assist the research library in evaluating its collection program with respect to environmental forces, university needs, library programs and policies, and the research collection. Environmental forces include price trends, publishing trends, new technology and shared resource arrangements. University needs are identified with respect to both current and future instructional and research programs as evidenced by student enrollments and faculty research interests. The collection itself is evaluated for its strengths, weaknesses, physical dimensions and major attributes that contribute to satisfying current needs as well as future requirements at both local program and national levels.

Bonn identifies five different methods for evaluating library collections: (1) compiling statistics on holdings, use and expenditures; (2) checking lists, catalogs and bibliographies; (3) obtaining opinions from regular users; (4) examining the collection directly; and (5) applying standards and testing the library's document delivery capability. Some of the suggested measures include volumes held (which correlates with measures of academic excellence) as reported by Jordan, volumes added, unfilled requests, interlibrary loans, subject balance (proportional analysis by subject area size, duplicates, dates and courses offered), circulation and expenditures.

A comprehensive review prepared by Lancaster (1977) details the quantitative, qualitative and use factor approaches to collection evaluation. Quantitative measurements suggested include absolute size, size of collection by various categories (subject material, date, type of material), growth rate, size as a ratio to other variables (population served, circulation, etc.) and expenditures on the collection (including per capita expenditures and proportion of budget spent on the collection). Qualitative evaluation approaches include "impressionistic" methods and evaluation against standard lists or holdings of other institutions. Use factors measure the amount of collection activity as reflected in statistics of circulation and in-library use.

Converse and Standers have computerized an academic collection development policy. A separate collection development profile is generated for each of 45 distinct department areas. Each of these profiles includes data on relevant subject areas defined by Library of Congress (LC) and Dewey Decimal (DD) classification numbers, level of collection development effort, forms of material, language restrictions, geographical restrictions, predicted life of material, current versus retrospective acquisitions, etc. Changes in collection status are easily made in this system without requiring a rewrite of the entire statement.

A project to design a broad management information system on collection development in a group of academic libraries is being conducted in the SUNY system by Evans (1978b). The system is being designed to relate collection development information to user needs for library materials supporting teaching and research programs. This system will provide improved information for planning, resource allocation, material selection and collection evaluation. The information requirements of collection development personnel and library managers identified in the study include:

- Information on publishing output and costs by subject area;
- Information on specific academic programs and their demands on the library collection;
- Information on current acquisition patterns;
- Information on collection use and predicted future use;
- Information on user satisfaction.

The Bell Laboratories Library Network, as reported by Spaulding and Stanton, has devised a similar system for selecting documents based on profiles of member libraries. In this system, selection profiles have been established for each library that defines by explicit classification number and verbal descriptor a degree of coverage or collection level for each subject of interest. The profiles are reviewed annually to insure compatibility of level assignments with respect to data on subject usage by technical departments and locations, program changes, expenditures by classification number, etc.

Management Control Decisions

Allocation of Funds to Subject Areas

Guidelines must be established which prescribe the amount of funding to allocate for purchase of materials in each subject area. Purchases must then be monitored to assure that actual expenditures meet the budgeted guidelines for each subject area. Factors to consider in allocating these funds should include collection development goals, patrons served by the collection, use made of the materials, material costs, cooperative arrangements and publication activity in each subject area.

Lately, there has been increased interest in developing models and guidelines for the efficient, equitable and justifiable allocation of materials budgets among library subject areas. Schad believes that book allocation models originated principally as a device for preventing powerful departments from monopolizing available funds. He stresses the importance of allocation models that respond to the needs and development goals of the collection.

McGrath (1969a) devised a book fund allocation formula using a factor analysis approach including different variables descriptive of the number and cost of books published, strength of existing collection, faculty and teaching load, credit hours taught, enrollment, circulation, references in theses, interlibrary loan and other miscellaneous measures for each subject area. An analysis of the variables resulted in the identification of three primary factors which were descriptive of (1) subjects of books and serials used or available; (2) the users; and (3) books and serials cited by graduate students in theses. An allocation model was then developed using these three factors to allocate funds among subject categories. Subject categories were defined according to LC and DD divisions and related to academic disciplines and departments. In a later study, McGrath (1975) proposed a book allocation formula based upon library circulation data and average book prices in each subject area. In effect, the model allocated more funds to those subject areas which experienced greater circulations, taking into account variations in book prices.

Dillehay proposes an objective approach to budget allocation, basing acquisitions in an industrial library on material costs, material published, material circulated and institutional research budgets by subject area. In addition, she advocates close cooperation between the library and research staff in making this allocation.

A book allocation formula based upon such factors as average book price, number of majors in a department and size of departmental collection has been suggested by Pierce (1978). He also considers a hard/soft characteristic which is defined as a measure of the degree of structure or acceptance of a theoretical construct within a particular discipline. Goyal (1973) uses a linear programming model for allocating funds based upon the importance of a discipline and the number of students enrolled in the department related to the discipline. Gold proposed a model for book budgeting based upon the rate of use of material, costs and explicit value judgments about how much such use contributes to the institution's goals.

Data on cost and circulation were collected and analyzed for 55 cost centers (primarily academic departments) and 26 LC classes at the University of Pittsburgh. This data, displayed in report form with some simple computations for means and standard deviations, provides valuable information for book purchasing decisions.

Funds Allocated for Books, Serials and Reports

A decision must be made to distribute funds between books, serials and reports for each subject area. The types of programs supported (academic, research, general reading, etc.) as well as the manner in which knowledge is disseminated in different fields must be considered. Recurring interlibrary loan costs provide some indication as to which needs might better be met with local materials. The commitment to serial collection continuity must also be weighed against the rapidly rising costs of serial subscriptions. These indicators must then be balanced against the need for easy accessibility and minimal library staff services (i.e., on the shelf vs. interlibrary loan, book format vs. machine retrievable information, etc.). Likewise, the cost for collecting and maintaining reports such as government documents, trade literature, technical reports, pamphlets, patents, etc., must be weighed with respect to institutional needs and other funding alternatives.

Spiraling price increases for serial subscriptions since the early 1970s, coupled with little or no increase in materials budgets, have resulted in a significant shift of funds from the book budget to the serials budget, according to Fry and White. This dramatic shift in expenditures has caused librarians to question whether the integrity and strength of the various book collections will be negatively affected. The initial response to this trend was to cancel duplicate serial subscriptions. The next phase was to search for valid decision rules and policies for serial selection and management.

Decision rules, of course, must be moderated to accommodate differences in the manner in which knowledge is transferred from one discipline to another and to reflect the goals of the collection development effort. For example, Baughman demonstrates that social science scholars rely on non-serial literature much more than do physical scientists. In an academic setting scholarly journals and periodicals are the primary materials used by faculty and graduate students, whereas books seem to be more important to the undergraduates. In an industrial library setting, reports take precedence over both books and serials. A decision rule should take these differences into account.

The use of citation data to aid in serial selection has been suggested by Scales, Line and Sandison, and Singleton. This approach of using an aggregate journal citation source as the sole criterion for selecting journals has been criticized by Koenig (1979). This method ignores differences in institutional programs and goals and is misleading without consideration of journal costs; it also neglects other important data such as availability of journals elsewhere, amount of use, and coverage by indexing and abstract services.

Kraft and Polacsek suggest ranking all journals according to the computation of a cost-benefit ratio. Journals with low ratios would be retained or added to the collection whereas journals with high cost-benefit ratios would be dropped or not acquired. The worth or benefit measure of a serial is determined by a number of specific factors within the general categories of usage, relevance and availability elsewhere. The usage measure is comprised of such components as circulation use, in-house use, volume of interlibrary loan traffic, number of times the serial is cited in an automatic retrieval search and the number of times the serial is cited in other publications. The relevance category considers such factors as number of volumes of the serial currently held, indexing and abstract coverage of the serial, whether the serial is included in a prestigious library collection, opinions of experts and reviewers, intellectual level, subject categories and the appropriateness of the serial for the anticipated user group. The last element, availability elsewhere, considers the convenience and cost of acquiring copies of the serial from other libraries. This is a negative factor taking into account the consequences of not buying the serial. All these factors are then combined into a measure of journal worth, which, when divided into the journal subscription cost, yields a cost-benefit ratio.

A study by Olafsen observed that the number of loans of articles from periodicals in medical libraries can be expressed as a simple function of the periodical's rank and age. A strategy for deciding the optimal volume of a library's periodical holdings is formulated based upon minimum total costs incurred for the use of periodical articles. Parameters are then provided for making decisions on buying versus borrowing and storing versus discarding.

Newman has considered the need to limit the size of the technical report collection, reduce costs and enhance user access to information. Policies were implemented to collect data on report usage for future acquisition and weeding decisions, to stop indexing reports received and to place greater reliance on accessing reports on an "as needed" basis from major distribution centers such as the Defense Documentation Center (DDC) and the National Technical Information Service (NTIS). This latter policy can be carried out with little loss in user access as a result of increased current awareness efforts (SDI), greater availability of external indexes and data bases for report identification, and shorter response time for receiving reports.

The specter of restricted or zero growth budgets for materials, along with the inflationary costs of materials, has fostered renewed interest in programs directed toward sharing resources. These prospects have been supported by DeGennaro (1975) and Bourne and Gregor (1975) along with the concept of a national periodical center as reported by the Council on Library Resources.

Types of Books and Serials to be Acquired

Acquisition of hardcover, softcover or microformat items differ in price and in the space required for their service and maintenance. A decision regarding types of material to acquire must consider such factors as degree of accessibility, expected utilization rates, retrieval facilities, storage space and the necessity for duplicates.

There is little question that libraries are purchasing microform copies of a title to satisfy space restrictions and to extend the useful life and adaptability of a library's physical facilities. The costs involved in converting current holdings to microform on an individual library basis are difficult to recover through space savings alone, according to Duncan and Parsons. Initial purchases of titles on microform, however, do represent savings in space costs as well as savings on the purchase price.

A number of libraries now prefer to discard their paper copies of journals at the end of the volume year rather than having them bound; instead, they purchase permanent microform shelf-copies of the journal from a micro publisher. This practice saves storage space, insures the availability of complete and unmutilated volumes of back issues and often costs no more than the expenses associated with binding and preparation (see Reed, 1976).

Heilprin has proposed the concept of a duplicating library which makes and distributes copies from a master copy held by that library. This procedure would insure that no locally held documents would be inaccessible because they were temporarily charged out on loan to another user. The added cost of providing this service would be defrayed in part by the elimination of labor-intensive circulation activities.

Major drawbacks to using microform copies include their difficulty to control and user resistance. Unless a master file of microform titles is maintained and controlled by library staff, microforms can be easily misfiled, lost or stolen. The additional costs of complete staff control of the microform collection must be weighed against collection integrity and patron accessibility.

User resistance to the use of microforms for reference activities does not appear to be significant, as reported by Greene (1975). However, user resistance to using microforms for study activities appears to be very high. In a study reported by Lewis, 85% of the users opposed a conversion from supplying reports in hard copy to supplying reports in microform. Many theories exist to explain this reluctance to use microforms, ranging from personal inconvenience to lack of flexibility in adapting to a new technology. Saffady (1978b) suggests that microform use will be more readily accepted if users gain or perceive to gain some measure of added value. An example of added value is making difficult-to-obtain documents more readily available. Automatic machine retrieval of information on microform via a computer terminal or a desk-top automated retrieval device is another example of value added, as documented by F.W. Lancaster (1978).

Degree of Duplication

Concentrated enrollments, intense research activity or high use statistics in a particular subject area, may well signal the need for duplication of locally held materials. Specific requests to provide books on reserve in support of a particular course assignment in an academic institution require additional duplication. These factors, as well as purchase costs, storage costs and weeding costs, all affect duplication levels.

A high degree of title duplication increases the availability of high use or popular titles. Expenditures for duplication, however, reduce the funding available for additional unique titles, thus reducing immediate accessibility to a wider range of holdings. This trade-off between expenditures for duplication versus expenditures for additional titles represents a dilemma which has been confronting librarians for years. Buckland (1975) developed a model to predict the use of a duplicate copy of an individual title. In his study, information on the number of requests, pattern of requests over time, ratio of borrowing to in-library use, loan period distribution, reservation practice, recall delays and number of copies purchased were inputted into a computer simulation model. The output of the model predicted the in-library requests satisfied, the percentage of requests satisfied immediately and the pattern of delays experienced following a reservation. Morse (1968) developed a queuing model providing similar information on duplicate copy use.

Indeed, most of the research in this area focuses on predicting the use of a duplicate copy of an individual title. An exception is a study performed by Bommer (1976) which provides guidelines for determining the proportion of the collection which should be duplicated, triplicated, etc. In this study, a queuing model predicts the number of uses experienced by multiple copies of titles when various proportions of the collection are duplicated, triplicated, etc. Data input for the model includes average request rate for the collection, distribution of request rate over the collection, the effect of title obsolescence on the request rate, mean loan period and the decision variable—proportion of collection to be duplicated, triplicated, etc.

Weeding Policy and Procedures

A policy is needed for identifying and retiring less used materials to less costly (and less accessible) storage areas as well as for permanently retiring materials from the collection. Considerations in formulating this strategy include the collection density goal of the subject area, storage costs and constraints, and use information.

A large volume of literature exists which deals with the collection-weeding problem. Interest in this problem was probably sparked by the rapid growth in library collections during the 1960s, coupled in the 1970s with the lack of funds to construct additional collection storage space. An annotated bibliography on weeding in academic and research libraries, covering a number of relevant publications, has been compiled by Rice.

Most weeding models are based upon the concepts of Bradford's Law of Scattering and document obsolescence (see Buckland, 1975, for a good overview). Bradford's Law of Scattering describes a diminishing returns phenomenon in which each additional item added to a collection satisfies a decreasing number of demands. Although this concept was originally developed for journal use, its applicability to the entire collection was recognized and popularized by Trueswell whose studies resulted in an 80-20 rule: that is, about 80% of the usage is experienced by about 20% of the holdings. The obsolescence factor refers to the decrease in the use rate as a document ages. This pattern of decreasing use with document age was recognized by Fussler and Simon in their study.

The primary characteristics for predicting future document use which are identified in various weeding studies include document language, publication date, amount of past use and last circulation date. No single criterion has emerged which is best suited for all subject areas and all types of materials. A number of studies have used one or more of these characteristics in developing a weeding policy for retiring documents permanently or to remote storage locations. A decision on the permanent retirement of a particular document often considers the continued availability of the document through a resource-sharing network. Other factors of concern include the costs associated with storage of materials either in a primary or remote location, and the costs associated with the weeding process, including deselection, transportation and record maintenance.

The advent and adoption of computerized circulation systems provides a wealth of data for dealing with the weeding problem. These data, coupled with the capability of computers to handle large programs and data efficiently, provide library administrators with the capability to experiment with different decision rules. For example, it would be relatively easy to determine the number of books that would be weeded if the criterion employed was to retire all books published prior to 1970 which have not circulated in the past five years.

Current vs. Retrospective Acquisitions

The degree of effort and resources devoted to filling gaps in the collection of each subject area must be determined. Retrospective acquisitions include the acquisition of entire sub-collections to meet a new or emerging research project or academic program, as well as individual purchases of important dated materials overlooked during previous selection processing. Citations for such retrospective purchases may come from interlibrary loan requests, published bibliographies and staff recommendations.

Studies on book use have demonstrated that most books are in greatest demand when they are new. Book use diminishes at various rates for different subject areas as the books age (see, for example, Bebout, Davis and Oehlerts). Wiberley has found that these differing obsolescence rates and the degree of reliance of a discipline on primary sources should be considered when calculating the benefits of acquiring retrospective material to fill in collection gaps. Other factors to take into account include the collection development goals and the cost of purchasing a document as compared with the cost and availability of obtaining the document through interlibrary loan. Interlibrary loan request data would be a primary determinant in identifying individual documents for retrospective collection.

The acquisition of back volumes for journals is discussed by Line and Sandison, who cite interlibrary loan data, citation analysis, cost of purchasing the volumes, cost of borrowing and degree of accessibility as important ingredients to be considered.

Replacement of Lost, Damaged or Worn Documents

Replacement of lost and mutilated material has reached significant proportions. Magrill and East report that two member libraries of the Association of Research Libraries (ARL) surveyed in the early 1970s found that replacement copies accounted for between 15% and 20% of new book purchases. Undoubtedly, as electronic security systems become more effective and more widely used, the number of books lost by theft will be reduced. Lost or mutilated books are normally from the more active section of the collection, since losses are most often recognized when a user requests a particular document.

Little literature seems to exist concerning decision strategies for replacing lost or mutilated documents. Undoubtedly, such factors as loss rate, age of book lost, perceived value of the book to the collection and user, cost and availability of replacement volumes, and accessibility of the title via interlibrary loan are important in developing such a decision strategy.

Decisions affecting the disposition of worn documents require similar evaluations. Worn documents can be rebound, replaced by the purchase of a new copy, microfilmed or discarded. The factors to consider in formulating a decision strategy include space availability, appropriate costs, predicted value of document to collection users and accessibility via interlibrary loan . A number of papers and conferences dealing with this issue (see, for example, Darling, 1977 and Brock) demonstrate interest in this area.

Selection Process

A decision must be made regarding the funds for and type of tools for selecting documents. Edelman (1979) suggests that book identification and selection take place in three stages. The first stage involves bibliographic tools such as national and trade bibliographies, publisher fliers and brochures, booksellers' lists, reviews in library and book industry trade press, and blanket orders. User requests, recommendations and reviews in professional academic journals are used in stage two, which also serves as a quality check on stage one. The third stage, often omitted because of funding and personnel constraints, is a retrospective review of the collection using subject bibliographies and bibliographic references.

A survey conducted by Futas reported that the major selection tools used by academic libraries in order of preference were as follows: *Choice, Library Journal, Publishers Weekly, Booklist, The New York Times Book Review* and various professional journals. No such list could be compiled for special libraries as a group because of their wide diversity. Baatz found that libraries are turning to approval plans and blanket orders as a means of coping with personnel shortages. He also reported that subject specialists often confer with institutional staff on selection in their areas of special interests and knowledge.

In a survey by McCullough, Posey and Pickett, 80% of responding academic libraries have or have had approval plans. Approval plans were cited as an economical and efficient acquisition procedure by libraries currently using them; problems with subject coverage, subject profiles, service problems, and discounts and pricing were mentioned most often as reasons for discontinuing the plans. Hulbert and Curry compared books selected via an approval plan with books selected by other means. They found that 57% of all books selected were provided by the approval plan and that only 11% of the approval plan books were rejected. The authors, library managers themselves, were able to substantially reduce the work required for book selection at their library by eliminating selection tools which identified few new unique titles.

"A Guide to Selection Tools" has been developed by the Collection Development Committee of the American Library Association, as reported by Sellen. The guidelines list requirements for selection tools and briefly describe and evaluate the more popular tools. Factors which should be considered in determining which selection tools to use include cost, coverage, timeliness and ease of use.

The procedures and philosophy employed in the selection process determine to a great extent the required staffing level. In addition, the type and mix of selection tools utilized, the degree of liaison activities with institutional staff and the volume of materials selected are all factors in determining the required staff size. The amount of effort and funds expended for selectivity in this process will naturally detract from the funds available for additional acquisitions of current materials.

Parker and Carpenter identified and ranked 20 separate activities performed by collection development staff. The ranking from most important to least important activities is listed below:

Priority

1	Liaison with institutional staff
2	Collection evaluation
3	Writing collection policies
4	Liaison with other libraries
5	Choosing materials
6	Coordination of selection
7	Liaison with cataloging and technical services
8	Gift and exchange
9	Deselection: cancellation and weeding
10	Collection maintenance
11	Monitoring of expenditures
12	Bibliographic searching
13	Policy preparation and implementation
14	Budget justification and allocation
15	Personnel
16	Design and monitoring of routines
17	Preparation of orders
18	File maintenance for selection
19	Transfers
20	Clerical support for administration

Finally, Evans (1970) found that librarians selected more useful titles than did faculty members, and faculty members selected more useful titles than did book jobbers. Although this would imply that the benefits of having librarians select titles are greater than having book jobbers perform the same task, one would have to look at the associated costs before determining the best strategy.

TECHNICAL SERVICES

Technical Services is that library function which procures, catalogs and maintains all incoming library materials for use. Procurement involves placing orders, monitoring orders, receiving documents, preliminary processing and maintaining fiscal records. Cataloging creates records for each item held by the library for access purposes and provides maintenance and upkeep for a permanent public record (or catalog). Maintenance means the physical preparation and preservation of the documents themselves.

Strategic Planning Decisions

Level of Cataloging

The quality of indexing and cataloging is a function of the level of accuracy, detail, cross-referencing and guidance provided the user in the publicly accessible catalog. These factors affect the use of the catalog(s) as well as the degree of success achieved in identifying and locating needed materials. The level of quality provided depends on such considerations as history and traditions of the library, the nature of the collection, the needs and sophistication of its users, specific cooperative library arrangements, types of cataloging data sources, closed and/or open stacks, degree of conformity or compliance with recognized national standards and restraints imposed by the need for cataloging economies.

Lucker cites such factors as the growth of knowledge and publishing output, stable or shrinking economic resources and new technologies in determining the degree of bibliographic control in a particular library or in groups of libraries. His article emphasizes that decisions about level of cataloging cannot be isolated from other library operations, such as acquisitions and reference, or from the national/international library world.

A summary of card catalog use studies by Lancaster (1977) indicates that most searches are for known items. Factors that increase success in known-item searches are: the amount and accuracy of information that the user brings; the search strategy (probably developed as a result of experience in using catalogs); the willingness to persevere; and the presence of multiple access points, redundancy and nonstandard bibliographic clues.

Users remember titles or key words in titles better than they remember authors, though they are more likely to use the author in their first search for a known item. Searching under author requires more card examinations than searching by title, especially if the searcher has inaccurate information. Searching for a known item under subject headings is even more inefficient, though usually successful if other methods fail. Subject searches often fail either because the searcher does not choose the heading chosen by the cataloger or because the searcher cannot determine the relevance of an item from the information given on the catalog card. Patrons seem to have little knowledge of the structure and contents of the catalog and, more often than not, begin a search with inaccurate or incomplete data.

Since catalog searches are successful in direct proportion to the amount of effort expended, catalogs should be designed to lessen the amount of time and effort it takes to find an item. For example, more cross-references and content notes or annotations would improve the success rate of subject searches. While Lancaster reviews what is known from catalog use studies, Weintraub concentrates on what is unknown, pointing out the lack of a theory of bibliographic control. Use studies have provided information about specific successes and failures of existing catalogs. However, little has been done to correlate the findings of various studies into an overall theory of catalog function in relation to user needs and habits, especially in the area of access to information by subject.

Marcus, Kugel and Benenfeld studied the indicativity of various types of catalog information. Indicativity is defined as a measure of how well the catalog information conveys the contents of the document it represents. Title, abstract, subject phrases and matching subject phrases were analyzed with the results indicating a positive correlation between the length of the catalog description and its indicativity.

Bates (1979a) reports on a study of the use of LC subject headings by undergraduate and graduate students. She found that subject expertise, even that of an undergraduate major, may actually interfere with effective use of the LC subject headings. Expert users typically felt that the headings were not specific enough. The need to limit file size and the labor-intensive nature of producing and maintaining a card catalog have affected the present method of subject access. Bates suggests that automation presents a radically different opportunity—that of using many access points for a particular item and deliberately introducing redundancy as an aid to all users, experts and non-experts alike.

Decisions about level of cataloging, in their simplest form, are decisions about the amount and kind of data to include in a bibliographic record. The conflict between adherence to network, national and/or international bibliographic standards and the creativity and flexibility that automation makes possible in response to local user needs is a constant factor in technical services decision making. Level of cataloging decisions have traditionally been made at the local library level. Byrum and Coe (1979) report considerable intentional local variation in research libraries from the standard *Anglo-American Cataloging Rules.* The variations are usually due to dissatisfaction with the rules and the desire to simplify the bibliographic record or adapt it to particular local needs. With the advent of the MARC format and the growth of networks, the full MARC record and Library of Congress cataloging policies have become a sort of national standard, seen as less expensive to use and beneficial for cooperation.

The U.S. Library of Congress, recognizing varying requirements among libraries, has proposed a National Level Bibliographic Record which "contains specifications for the data elements that should be included by an organization creating cataloging records in machine-readable form for its own use, which will also be acceptable for sharing with other organizations or for contributing to a national data base." In its proposal for minimal level cataloging for less important materials, the need for varying levels of bibliographic control is recognized.

Gorman believes that short machine-readable records, such as those comprising online circulation systems, are useful as retrieval mechanisms and provide a good basis for future, more elaborate online bibliographic systems. However, much of the existing work to make bibliographic data machine-readable was done without regard to future needs. The resulting nonstandard records cannot be used in newer systems without upgrading, an expensive and perhaps impossible undertaking.

Rosenthal reports how decisions about bibliographic control are being made at the University of California-Berkeley in planning for the transition from traditional card catalogs to new catalogs based on machine-readable data. The assumption is that machine-readable cataloging will be prepared according to national standards and provide at least the same access points as the card catalog. Martin (1979) recommends creating machine-readable records "according to a standard format (MARC) and standard content (AACR/LC)" in order to insure maximum future usefulness and flexibility.

Timeliness and Cost Efficiency of Document Processing

Minimizing the time between the decision to order an item and its appearance on the shelves yields direct benefits to the user by providing earlier availability of the material. However, the benefits of reduced processing time must be balanced against potentially increased processing costs and long-term service implications. Increased processing costs might result from higher staffing levels to expedite items through the process, or from the original cataloging of a higher proportion of items. In the long run, additional service costs might arise as a result of: excessive duplication or unavailability of documents due to inaccurate citations or improper verification; and deficiencies in descriptive cataloging which prove detrimental in reclassification projects or inputting records on computerized data bases.

A number of recent articles report on cost and time studies of OCLC-based cataloging. Ross reports on a detailed analysis of the cost of the transition from manual to automated cataloging, with a savings of approximately one dollar per title for books cataloged on the automated system. Reduction of professional staff in the catalog department accounted for the savings. Landram examines costs in comparing OCLC cataloging with a system based on ordering Library of Congress cards. The OCLC system was found to be slightly more expensive, but processing speed increased dramatically. The LC card ordering system allowed 80% of the books to be cataloged within five weeks, while 83% of the books were cataloged within one week using OCLC. Pierce and Taylor developed a model for comparing the costs of automated cataloging systems with manual systems. One-time costs, fixed recurring costs and use-sensitive costs are compared. Major savings are possible by substituting paraprofessional positions for professional ones in labor-intensive technical services operations.

Hamburg et al. (1976) identify data elements for determining the benefit-cost ratio for temporarily cataloging materials. Benefits are a measure of the estimated number of uses a document receives from the time of receipt until it is permanently cataloged, while costs consider the time and effort for temporarily cataloging items.

Brown and McHugh surveyed library costs in technical processing and interlibrary loan as part of the development of a bibliographic network. By means of a questionnaire and 12 case studies, they gathered detailed information on expenditures, staffing patterns and work output. One of the major findings of the survey was that cataloging cost per unit was higher in both large and small libraries than in medium-sized libraries.

Wessel proposed four techniques for evaluating effectiveness and efficiency: SCORE, SCOUT, CORE and GAME. SCORE analysis divides each activity into a sequence of events in which each is dependent on successful completion of the one immediately preceding it. SCOUT analysis determines whether a library is allocating its resources to best advantage in terms of service to users. CORE analysis identifies libraries that, within a particular group of institutions, deviate most from the norm in time or cost for a particular operation. Finally, GAME analysis is a technique that analyzes an operation systematically to identify unnecessary steps, to arrange steps in an optimum sequence, to standardize work methods and to develop standards for the time that should be spent on each step.

Fischer, Sisco and White describe the Los Angeles County Public Library System's experience with work measurement, using techniques developed in industrial engineering and adapted to the library workplace. At the end of the five-year study, the library established a permanent work measurement/systems team to provide management with information for evaluating procedures and justifying budgets—decisions which formerly had been supported largely by subjective criteria. Pizer and Cain suggested time-sampling techniques, in which staff were asked to record certain data each time a buzzer sounded at random intervals. These data on how staff time was spent can be used to measure different kinds of library operations for purposes of comparison or for self-assessment.

Brutcher, Gessford and Rixford apply principles of cost accounting to library operations with emphasis on acquisitions and cataloging. An attempt is made to recognize differences in difficulty among various units of output in the same task. Waldhart and Marcum state that in the present economic climate, libraries must increase productivity in order to sustain the momentum of growth of recent years. By using hypothetical library examples, the authors show how existing methods of productivity measurement might be adapted to measure such production-oriented library operations as cataloging.

Management Control Decisions

Acquisition Process

A key decision is to determine the amount and mix of resources (personnel and computer support) to allocate for the acquisition process. Closely related is a decision involving the degree of sophistication employed in the acquisition process to verify, order, monitor, receive and create fiscal records. A more sophisticated information system allows fewer errors and delays in the acquisition process and provides improved records for budget management purposes, but such a system requires more resources to operate and maintain. The resulting procurement time (time from initial request to receipt of book) is a function of both the resources employed and the level of sophistication of the acquisition procedures.

A decision must also be made as to whether preliminary information for establishing bibliographic control in the cataloging process is to be developed to shorten the cataloging process and to inform users of books on order. In manual acquisition systems this additional service of informing users of materials on order can be provided at the expense of time and resources in the procurement phase. However, the integration of automated acquisition designs with automated systems for cataloging can provide these benefits at little increase in cost.

Stephen Ford reviews all aspects of ordering and buying library materials and suggests that automation may offer solutions to growing problems of acquisitions file maintenance. Reid evaluated the effectiveness of OCLC, which began as a cataloging data base, in acquisitions verification. The OCLC data base was found to be the most productive of five commonly used verification tools, in the number of items found and in amount of search time. Stokley and Reid compare vendor performance for book orders and discuss variables which contribute to good dealer performance, including speed, ease of reading invoices, order status reports, discounts and convenient book return policy. Data in these studies were gathered by recording statistics and analyzing purchase orders.

A comprehensive bibliography of automated acquisition systems is provided by Heyman and Abbott. Kountz provides a survey form for determining the most appropriate service or system for acquisition needs. Three concepts identified as essential in implementing an automated acquisition system are the library-supplier contract, the supplier's inventory and subscribed-to publications. Bruer stresses the need for automated acquisition systems to interface with other library systems such as cataloging, circulation, etc., and to provide library staff and management with appropriate information. Such a system would reduce redundant keyboarding, allow library staff to query the system for status reports for an ordered document and provide management with budget control and acquisition performance information.

Cataloging Data Source

A major decision in the cataloging process is the selection of a cataloging data source or combination of data sources which will provide that level of cataloging which combines efficient bibliographic control and effective access to the local collection. The choice of cataloging data sources varies from original MARC tapes of LC classified documents to manual and online commercial vendor services, to automated, shared cataloging data base networks. Managers must weigh the quality of cataloging data source services provided against the costs of the system, including local costs to augment and support the system. Some of the factors in evaluating service include timeliness of updates, data reliability, degree of adherence to national standards, applicability and adaptability of the system to the local situation, volume of original cataloging required at the local level, degree of adaptability to new forms of catalog presentation, new means of accessing information and the ability to create new data bases to interact and support other activities of the library (interlibrary loan, circulation, acquisition, etc.). In addition to the cost of the service, the costs of the professional and clerical staff needed must also be considered.

A comparison of BALLOTS and OCLC by Levine and Logan gives library administrators factual information about these two major bibliographic utilities. Their data bases and services, products, bibliographic control and financial and administrative status are assessed. Meyer and Panetta compared OCLC services with those of Blackwell/North America, based on direct experience in the use of the two services. OCLC's larger data base was judged advantageous because it enables users to find cataloging information for a greater percentage of their titles. The Blackwell/North America data base, while much smaller than OCLC, is considerably cheaper to use and thus would appeal to many libraries.

Veaner (1977) describes the BALLOTS system as it is used at Stanford University. A primary design requirement was that the new system would have to provide no less service than the manual system it replaced. CRT screens and formats were designed for easy use by people familiar with traditional catalog card format. Prompting commands, commands based on natural language expressions (FIND, DISPLAY, etc.), mnemonic tags, online error detection and flexible Boolean search keys were all designed with the idea of using technology to make the system responsive to the variety of needs and habits of its users. Change was deliberately evolutionary, with all levels of staff involved in evaluation and planning.

Allison and Allan have gathered seven essays on various aspects of OCLC. The articles by Scott from the viewpoint of a library administrator, Gapen on workflow and productivity, Hogan on shared cataloging and Kamens on serials, show the range of problems that librarians should consider when contracting for OCLC services.

OCLC is usually thought of in connection with large academic or public libraries. Davis and Dingle-Cliff, however, report a 65% "find rate" for searching via OCLC in a small special library implying that even such libraries can benefit from network participation.

Horny describes the development of an automated cataloging data source at Northwestern University. The system was developed locally to support a full range of library operations including acquisitions, catalog creation, maintenance and circulation. A key element governing planning decisions was to make the data content and design of the system flexible enough to grow in response to future demands.

The articles discussed so far in this section emphasize comparisons and choices of data sources for current cataloging. Many libraries are considering, or are already engaged in, retrospective conversion of cataloging to machine-readable form. The same bibliographic systems used for current cataloging can be used for retrospective conversion projects, but the planning is somewhat different. Butler, Aveney and Scholz compare various types of conversion projects, discuss the steps necessary in converting existing bibliographic data to machine-readable form, and document the experiences of various types of libraries that have performed retrospective conversion by assorted methods.

Type of Public Bibliographic Record

Several kinds of catalogs may be created for public access to the collection: card, book, COM catalog or an automated online file. Access points in the catalog generally provide traditional author-title access and a varying degree of subject entry points, depending upon local policy. The degree of subject access accorded depends upon the assessed needs of the local clientele and the judgment of the local librarians as to the adequacy of subject heading systems (Library of Congress, Sears, etc.) in meeting these needs.

In general, the more access points in a catalog for a particular document, the greater the patron ease-of-access. While numerous entries per document are desirable from one point of view, this policy requires more staff time in creating and in revising the catalog either for new headings and terminology or for deselection. The size of the catalog is also a concern, whether stored in card, book or computer files. The traditional card catalog is more easily updated than the book catalog which must be reproduced or supplemented to add new items. On the other hand, if a book or COM catalog is produced from data held in an automated data source, it may be possible to add additional entry points at relatively little cost.

The online catalog appears to combine the best of both attributes. Costs, the adequacy of each form to the library and the user public, portability of the catalog and number of retrieval ports available to users are factors which must be considered. Choice of formats may depend on the catalog data source selected and on considerations related to expected maintenance problems.

Aveney and Ghikas report on patron comparisons of COM with book and card catalogs, as determined in interviews combining specific and open-ended questions. Comparisons were made on the basis of wait, difficulty, time and readability. The study concluded that COM is more acceptable to patrons than book or card catalogs; specialized equipment is not an obstacle to use; the most significant factor in patron satisfaction is minimum waiting time; there is no appreciable difference among types of users in reaction to the COM catalog; and staff training, proper installation and information about the new catalog are important factors in increasing patron acceptance. The study also confirmed the theory that COM catalogs will increase patron use of the catalog. In addition, an activity index was developed and tested as a means of determining the number of microform viewers required for a particular location.

Patron response to a COM catalog at the University of Oregon is reported by Dwyer.

The catalog consists of a basic (frozen) catalog plus supplements. Statistical methods were used to test five hypotheses about user behavior in relation to the catalog. The author concludes that "given the principles of least effort and the principle of information processing parsimony, it is unrealistic to expect readers to employ such complex devices to full advantage." The COM catalog was established primarily because of cost considerations, but has distinct disadvantages, including its multipart nature and its legibility qualities which inhibit patron acceptance.

Blackburn reports light use of COM catalog supplements, a discovery that led to consideration of other means of updating the basic catalog. Ninety percent of the users do not go beyond the basic data found in the indexes to the catalog, with use of the full bibliographic record confined mostly to the library staff. Readers made better use of a combined COM catalog than they did of separate card catalogs before the introduction of COM. This suggests that users only want to look in one place for catalog information.

Cox and Juergens report on a catalog test designed to compare the acceptability of catalog microfiche and microfilm. Results showed that a majority of users preferred microfilm. Strong preference for film over fiche was correlated to frequency of library use, age of user, education level of users, previous use of microforms and type of catalog search.

There seems to be little reported regarding public use and acceptance of online catalog records. This lack of reporting is undoubtedly a result of little user experience with these types of systems. At this time online catalog systems are considerably more costly than other types of systems and consequently are not widely used. Online searching of bibliographic data bases will be addressed in the next chapter.

Maintenance of Public Bibliographic Records

The amount of local resources allocated for catalog maintenance, as opposed to catalog growth through new accessions, must be determined. Records must be withdrawn upon deselection or modified when materials change location (e.g., open to closed stacks, main to branch library, etc.). Continuously changing access terminology requires an overall decision as to the degree to which records indexed under older terms will be replaced and relocated under newer terms. Additional resources are required if a periodic inventory is undertaken and to update cross-references which need continual attention and revision. The costs of these services must be balanced against the needs of the users and possible compromise solutions must be considered.

Cataloging copy from an outside source must be integrated into an existing catalog and, as cataloging rules and subject headings evolve, decisions must be made as to the degree of maintenance necessary. While the use of computer terminals and an online data base for searching and card production simplifies and speeds up the clerical routines of cataloging, the intellectual operations of maintaining the catalog and integrating new catalog records remain the same. Dowell analyzes in detail the decisions required in catalog maintenance, outlining the pros and cons of changing the new cataloging, changing the existing catalog, using cross-references or performing no maintenance at all. Problems in the use of shared cataloging in OCLC are discussed by Ryans who studied 700 OCLC member input records. Sixty percent of these were correct according to OCLC standards and could be used without editing. The majority of errors occurred in the collation and the subject headings.

Physical Preparation and Maintenance of Documents

The initial preparation of volumes for shelf use requires labeling and associated processes for identifying, locating and circulating the physical volume. By and large, this is a labor-intensive task which can be ameliorated by the use of equipment or machines which speed the process. For example, a linkage to automatic labeling processors connected to the creation of the catalog record would simplify some of the associated chores and prevent errors between record and material. A decision must be made with regard to the mix of personnel and automated resources required to accomplish this task, considering processing delay times and associated costs.

A policy for maintaining the collection with respect to document deterioration prevention, repairing and rebinding documents and preserving document content via conversion to microform also requires a set of decisions. The critical parameters involved in these decisions include cost, longevity of the document, projected use rate, storage restrictions and the alternative availability of equivalent documents through cooperative arrangements. Decisions in this area should relate closely to the weeding policy and procedures in collection development.

Physical preparation of library materials is one of the easiest aspects of technical services to analyze from the point of view of cost and efficiency. Some relevant studies have been reviewed in the section on Timeliness and Cost Efficiency of Document Processing earlier in this chapter.

Decisions about maintenance focus on which library materials to preserve and how to preserve them. Darling (1976b) advocates that each library establish preservation goals in harmony with the institution's overall objectives. Deciding which materials to preserve becomes a collection development decision. All of the books acquired by a library may not need to remain in the collection forever and not all damaged materials can or should be saved. As items wear out or are lost, the library must decide whether to replace, reproduce (in microform or by photocopying), restore or discard them. Darling proposes a test: "It will cost x dollars to bind, repair, restore, or replace this item. If we didn't already have it, would we spend that much today to acquire it?"

To answer this question, a number of related questions on the specific needs of each library must be considered. Is the collection made up of one-of-a-kind research materials or is it primarily made up of mass market items designed to support a changing curriculum or to provide recreational reading? Is up-to-date information the primary concern of the library's clientele? Is a particular subject area or type of material collected in depth? Are the library's holdings in that area unique? Is the lost or worn item easy to replace? Is an exact replacement necessary or would a later edition or another book on the same subject be preferable? Is the item readily available through interlibrary loan or is it so frequently used that such limited access would be inadequate? Should the item be given to another library where there is a stronger interest in and better facilities for preservation?

Darling (1976b) advocates that libraries learn to discard in order to concentrate on saving what is worth saving. Once the difficult decisions are made about what to preserve, the library can go on to the relatively straightforward tasks of developing staff preservation skills and setting up procedures for in-house preservation or sending materials to outside experts as required.

5

User Services

User services encompass the set of library functions that directly serve the institution's community. They include reference and bibliographic service, collection access, interlibrary loan and physical facilities provided to users. This chapter analyzes decision tasks for these user services at both the strategic planning and management control levels. As in Chapter 4, relevant literature is summarized for readers who wish to develop a deeper understanding in a particular area. Full citations are provided in the Bibliography.

REFERENCE AND BIBLIOGRAPHIC SERVICE

Reference and bibliographic service covers the assistance provided users in clarifying information needs and in the identification and location of resources which satisfy these needs. Reference and bibliographic service is often conceptually divided into direct and indirect service. Direct service activities include staff assistance to users in answering questions of a factual type, in guiding users in the use of library resources, performing literature searches, developing and conducting current awareness services and presenting formalized instruction in library use skills. Indirect service includes providing users with reference tools including reference materials, indexes and abstract services, specialized files and bibliographies, library user's handbooks and guides, and displays and newsletters for the promotion of learning and the library.

In this section, strategic planning decision tasks relating to reference assistance and bibliographic service are discussed. At the management control level, decision tasks for ready reference, bibliographic search, current awareness (SDI) and public relations are addressed.

Strategic Planning Decisions

Level, Coverage and Quality of Reference Assistance

The array of reference assistance services offered and the level of services afforded to patrons must be determined. Such direct services might include personal assistance for locating brief factual data in general resources; specialized and in-depth assistance to individuals in the use of library resources to meet particular needs; and formal lectures and courses in library-use skills. Indirect services in this area include the provision of commercially acquired reference tools; internally prepared general and specific reference aids; handbooks, guides and programmed learning devices for assistance in the use of the library; and promotion of learning and the library through displays and public relations efforts.

The degree of emphasis placed on each of these services and the relative emphasis placed on direct and indirect services should be articulated. In general, increased emphasis on indirect services usually results in greater patron independence in the use of the library, but can create increased requests for direct service of a more sophisticated and specialized nature.

A survey of the literature reveals that most attempts to evaluate reference service do not measure the quality of services performed but represent mere aggregates of activities with little understanding of their effect upon library users. Rettig chides the profession for defining reference service as "what goes on in the reference room." He attempts to move away from empirically built paradigms and define reference activity in a model borrowed from communication theory. In this he follows Vavrek who centers reference service theory on interpersonal communication.

These efforts respond to a growing attitude in the profession that the "reference interview" is crucial in determining patron need and matching it with appropriate instruction or with one or more information sources. Skill in "negotiation" and "dialoging" become attributes as important to providing service as actual knowledge of sources. The significance of the reference interview underlines deficiencies in attempts to evaluate reference service wholly in terms of measuring the volume of questions and/or evaluation of responses to those questions, important as they are in guiding the administrator. The categorizations employed to measure information desk or telephone service usually provide a classification for in-depth counseling on the selection of resources or access tools. These aspects of reference assistance are open-ended and may require great differences in time expended and expertise required from query to query. The possibility that the library patron may in many cases actually discover or define his/her information need during the course of the reference interview represents a challenging aspect to measure in quantitative terms.

Little has been done to assess the contribution of indirect services in providing information to users. The selection of materials and creation of local finding lists, special guides or catalogs require considerable effort and expense. However, it is difficult to measure the extent to which they assist the user in procuring information.

Many ready-reference questions can be increasingly answered using online services. These reference data bases either contain the specific information or identify the source for finding the information. The degree of commitment to this type of service must also be determined.

The contemporary emphasis on user instruction as a legitimate function of reference services is motivated by a recognition, well documented by Perkins, that even the basic tools for library use are little known or understood by users. A number of techniques including lectures, self-paced workbooks and computer-assisted instruction packages have been developed in the hope of increasing library use and lessening the burden of the simple, repetitive inquiries that form a large part of a reference librarian's day-to-day work load.

Lindgren acknowledges the need to base user instruction on such abilities but thinks undue concentration on the mere mechanics of library use inhibits imaginative exploitation of library resources and prevents adequate attention being given to the problem. The role of heuristic instruction in the creative use of information sources and libraries is obscured in user instruction by overemphasis on those specific library skills in which it is easiest to test progress. Library managers who base staff work loads only on those aspects of reference service for which measurable data can be or have been accumulated run the risk of making allocation decisions which actually may exclude certain high-quality kinds of reference service.

Allocation of direct and indirect assistance in providing reference services should be made with regard to both the institutional programs and the level of user sophistication. In summary, the strategic decisions to be addressed in the reference area focus on the level of emphasis or priority to be placed on providing:

- Reference resource tools and materials (acquired and developed by reference staff);

- Quantity and quality of reference staff who aid patrons in shaping and responding to in-depth questions as well as answering factual queries;

- Formal and informal instructional programs to increase patron knowledge and self-sufficiency in more fully utilizing library resources.

Level, Comprehensiveness and Quality of Document Identification Service

Support of document identification or literature search efforts designed to find bibliographic material on a particular subject can be provided by one or more of the following: manual search performed by patron or staff using index and abstract services; computerized searches accessing information stored in one or more machine-readable data bases; subscription to a commercial or locally developed selected dissemination of information service (SDI). A balancing decision must be made as to the degree of commitment and resources supporting each of these modes for different user groups. The type of programs supported and different levels of user sophistication will determine the degree of access by each user group. The level of direct assistance offered for each of these activities must be made with respect to budgetary and cost-recovery considerations.

The emergence of computer-based information bibliographic service adds a dramatic new dimension to the library's capacity for meeting information needs. Rarely before, except in certain specialized libraries, have reference staffs been able to provide such comprehensive service. Online bibliographic information service not only provides access to a broad range of information sources but also provides the most up-to-date access. In most institutions supported by special libraries, timely information is recognized as a valuable resource. Kornfeld reports that online systems are valued for increasing staff productivity while reducing labor-intensive costs associated with searches formerly performed manually.

Unlike industrial libraries, academic libraries usually must consider computer-based searching as a value added. Use of these data services may allow the cancellation of some subscriptions to abstract and indexing services, especially in large systems having duplicate copies in several locations. However, Saffady (1979) feels that different levels of need will not permit total reliance on computerized access and will therefore result in too few reductions to offset all costs for electronic access. Since academic libraries are not likely to off-set data base searching costs either by large-scale reductions in printed abstract and index matter or by reducing library labor costs, Saffady concludes that justification must be seen as an "added value" service. He offers five possible advantages: (1) greater indexing depth (2) free text searching (3) unique data bases available only online (4) improved timeliness and (5) greater flexibility (of output and in location of terminals).

Another option available to libraries with data base search capabilities is the provision of SDI. This personalized form of current awareness service, pioneered by Luhn, combines individual interest profiles with periodic searches of appropriate machine-readable data bases. On most SDI systems, patrons are provided with periodic bibliographic information in their fields of interest as data bases are updated or added. Once a user's profile is specified, the profile is entered, citations are retrieved and a listing is provided to the user. This type of service can usually be justified in business and industrial settings in which ongoing research projects are used to pay for the service. In the academic setting, this service can usually only be justified as a value added commodity, except by faculty who can charge the related costs to an ongoing research grant.

Finally, the emphasis to be placed on providing abstract and index material must be determined. Some users find online bibliographic services inadequate for meeting search needs and still rely heavily on manual methods. In the academic setting the cost of providing all students with online bibliographic service is still prohibitive. In these cases abstracts and indexes are still a necessary part of literature searching efforts.

Management Control Decisions

Ready Reference

A major proportion of direct service offered by academic and special libraries involves answering questions of a factual nature and assisting users in finding resource materials. The effectiveness of reference activity in providing this service depends upon the quality of the reference tools available and the ability of the staff to use these tools. The quality of this service can be evaluated in terms of how completely, accurately and efficiently all user demands are satisfied. Lancaster (1977) suggests that the following data should be collected in evaluating ready reference service:

- The total number of questions received (during a specified period);

- The proportion of these questions the staff makes some attempt to answer;

- The proportion of the "attempted" questions for which the staff provides answers;

- The proportion of the "answered" questions that are answered completely and correctly;

- The average time it takes to answer a user's question.

Librarians have long been aware of differences in reference queries that are not usually reflected in gross statistics. Researchers have attempted to categorize the types of queries involved in reference assistance in order to differentiate the time, cost and expertise needed for response. Rothstein suggested a schema containing four types of questions: directional (locational); ready reference (simple answer, facts, etc.); search (involving more than one source of information); and reader's advisory (assistance in the choice of sources). St. Clair and Aluri used a variation of this plan, identifying directional, instructional, reference and extended reference activities. A different approach was used by Spicer, with recorded statistics divided into categories dependent upon the time necessary for a response. This shifts the classification of questions from the perceived user's need to measurement of staff activity necessary to provide the answer.

Quantitative measurement of question answering activity is only the first stage in the ultimate goal of evaluation of effectiveness. Statistics kept by types of questions, as identified by librarians, do not necessarily measure the satisfaction of users. Rothstein reports that librarians consistently judged themselves to have a high rate of success in answering reference questions, ranging from an 88% to a 99% success rate. This satisfying picture was somewhat tarnished in studies reported by Crowley and Childers of reference services in New Jersey libraries using unannounced telephone queries to libraries over a number of days, asking identical questions at each library. In one study success in answering queries, for all libraries, was only 54.2%. The study further indicated that libraries were particularly deficient in providing current information.

In a similar study a scale of "correctness" in judging responses was introduced, yielding a 54.7% success rate on all questions posed with 63.8% on all questions attempted. A correlation was noted between the number of questions answered and the number of professional staff, as well as the size of the collection, but none between success and per capita expenditure. A study by King and Berry in a university library tends to support the proposition that library effectiveness in answering reference-type questions is less than was earlier supposed.

Common to those studies which break down the reference process into analyzable components is an attempt to classify the activity into units more amenable to accurate recording. Such classifications yield a basic measurement of activity which has implications for the type of staff employed. Especially important to ascertain is the level of difficulty of the questions posed and the ability of the combined efforts of staff and resources to satisfy a given type of information need. The studies (no matter how many categories employed) show an obvious division of data into two segments—questions which are answered simply (ranging from 40% to 70% in various reports) and those requiring more thought, training or knowledge for an adequate response. This elementary separation of questions into two types is now reflected in the new national reporting system instituted by the National Center for Education Statistics, as reported by Emerson. Included in the Center's LIBGIS (Library General Information Survey) format are categories for reporting "Reference Transactions" and "Directional Transactions."

Whether such a simple categorization will satisfy the library profession remains to be seen. The subject has generated a lively debate concerning the use of nonprofessionals at reference and information desks to handle the less exacting transactions. Enthusiastic endorsements for the use of less highly trained staff are cautioned against by Falk. Central to the issue is whether the reference question, as placed, is indicative of the patron's real information need. Halldorsson and Murfin found that professional librarians perform distinctly better than nonprofessionals when confronted with a series of "indirect" and "faulty information" questions. The professionals' ability to draw out the real information need from the indirect questions, and to identify "faulty information" as the culprit in frustrating an information search, attests to the importance of the reference interview in reference work. It also suggests why communication processes have become central in discussions of reference service.

Hoover divides online reference services into reference data bases and source data bases. Reference data bases contain secondary information that identifies primary information sources. Examples include bibliographic references of citations and directory references to people, organizations, contracts, research projects, etc. Source data bases contain complete information (primary data) for meeting a user's need. Examples of this type of data base include numeric data such as census and economic data; full-text data such as patents, court decisions, a journal article, etc.; and dictionary data such as definitions, chemical properties, etc.

Many of the measures for evaluating traditional ready-reference service would seem applicable for measuring online service as well. Blair, for example, suggests measuring volume and type of use, user satisfaction and searcher efficiency in evaluating online service effectiveness.

Bibliographic Search

Allocation of resources for personal assistance, computerized bibliographic data bases, indexes and abstract services for document identification activities must be determined. In making this decision, the breadth and depth of coverage of machine-readable data bases, indexes and abstract services, and degree of direct personal service offered in the literature-searching process must be specified. Consideration should be given to the degree of substitution of computerized searches for manual searches using indexes and abstract services. Levels of access for different user groups and a fee structure must also be established. Some of the factors to be considered in assessing different search capabilities include subject area, the response time of the search, the relative costs, and the number, currency and relevancy of the citations recovered.

Most studies evaluating the effectiveness of printed abstracts and indexes for performing literature searches have employed criteria of coverage and ease-of-use. Bourne (1969b) reports on studies of index coverage using citations derived from major review articles in the field. The proportion of citations listed in a particular index provides a rating for coverage. The ease-of-use component consists of a number of factors including time to perform a search and the success in identifying relevant citations. The success of a search depends in large part upon the organization and structure of the particular index as well as how closely a user's search strategy matches the format of the index. The number of subject entry points and cross-listings in an index has a significant effect on the success of a search.

Lancaster (1977) lists the following elements as critical factors in a user-performed search:

- User's ability to express needs verbally;
- Degree to which index vocabulary matches user's vocabulary;
- User's ability to search systematically;
- Assistance and guidance provided by an index itself.

He further suggests three different measures for assessing ease of use: recall, precision and unit searching time. Recall is defined as the proportion of known items retrieved by a search. For example, if it is known that a particular index contains 100 relevant items on a particular topic and if 80 of these items are identified via subject entry search of the index, then the recall percentage is 80%. Precision is defined as the proportion of relevant items identified of all items identified in a search. For example, if a subject entry search yielded 100 potentially relevant items of which 70 were later found in fact to be relevant to the topic, the precision percentage would be 70%. Unit searching time is defined as the total time required to perform a search divided by the total number of relevant citations identified in the search.

Subjective studies have been performed to assess the user's preference for and satisfaction in using certain types of indexes. In comparing the usefulness of *Analytical Abstracts* and *Chemical Abstracts* for analytical chemists, Drage found that *Analytical Abstracts* was preferred for current awareness purposes because of its specialized emphasis, the availability of the index and the quality of the abstracts. This coincides with Allen (1977) who identified information channel accessibility and ease of use as significant factors in determining whether an information channel will be accessed again.

Computerized access to major data bases has enhanced the ability of most special and some academic libraries to meet the information needs of their clients by providing rapid access to specific data and by enabling searches to be individually tailored to users' needs. Data base searching can be used for identifying and verifying known items, for quick reference and for comprehensive literature searching. Output can vary from simple bibliographic citations, to abstracts to full text. Subject coverage and access have expanded as the number of files has increased. Jacob, Dodson and Finnegan report that increased use and confidence in online data bases are leading to decreased acquisitions of hard-copy indexes and catalogs in special libraries.

Many of the measures used to evaluate bibliographic searching activities such as recall, precision and unit searching time apply to both online and manual searching methods. Similarly such measures as coverage, access points and currency can also be used to evaluate online services.

When costs for a particular patron's time are considered, Lantz has shown that computerized searching compares favorably with manual techniques in academic institutions, despite large differentials in salaries between the various patrons—faculty, teaching assistants and graduate students. Rarely, however, would a library administrator be able to use research time saved, scattered as it would be throughout various departments, faculty and students, as justification for adding the service into the library budget. Rationales for implementing computerized searching systems in academe, therefore, are usually advanced without benefit of cost comparison with manual searching performed by the user. The cost savings for using online bibliographic searching systems is relatively easy to justify in special libraries where research staff time savings can be documented.

By whatever means libraries justify or recover costs, it is becoming clear that the introduction of online search services significantly affects library use patterns and budget considerations in other areas of the library. Martin (1977) reports dramatic increases in interlibrary loans in special libraries where computerized searching services are available. Wanger et al. note that 28% of the library managers surveyed in their study reported changes in acquisition policies in response to needs identified in searches.

It is not surprising, perhaps, that the new powers of document identification available through computerized searching result in document delivery problems. Efforts to satisfy the rising expectations of users may be ameliorated by enrichment of data base content beyond that of simple title and bibliographic citation. The availability of abstracts along with the citation allows discrimination in selecting the most relevant documents. The ultimate in data enhancement is the availability of full-text online searching. These options may diminish overloads in document delivery and interlibrary loan systems, although the patron will usually need a printout in hard copy or on microform. Several vendors presently offer document delivery and automatic ordering of documents. The possibilities available depend upon the data bases chosen. Whenever the selection of data bases places a particular library in this position, the library must decide whether to buy document packages, purchase on demand for certain users, or pass purchase and handling costs along to the user.

The introduction of search services will affect staffing considerations in reference service. Wanger et al. found the median time to complete an online search to be between 40 and 50 minutes. Two-thirds of that time was spent in pre-search negotiations and post-search tasks. At present, because of the complexities and lack of standardization, efficient searching requires a trained person interacting between the various data bases and the user, a task which demands training, skills and work patterns different from those employed in traditional reference services. Saffady (1979) predicts the development of tutorial and directive computer programs which will eventually facilitate searching various data systems by untrained persons, but until that time the need for the information specialist as intermediary will continue.

Current Awareness (SDI)

A decision must be made regarding the level and fee structure for and types of SDI or current awareness services. The service can range from a publication of selected recent library acquisitions for one or more groups of people to a listing of new citations tailored to the specific interest profile of a particular individual. In general, the value of an SDI service is directly proportional to the effort spent in developing an individual's interest profile; in monitoring pertinent literature; and in selecting relevant citations. The sophistication of SDI systems is affected by the quality and quantity of direct professional assistance committed and the available access tools.

Libraries that have introduced data base searching capabilities can usually provide this service as a spin-off from the searching system. While most researchers can attest to the value or benefits of a current awareness service, it is difficult to assess the cost savings associated with such a service. In most cases SDI service is viewed as a "value added" commodity for increasing a researcher's productivity.

An important element in an effective system is the careful construction and refining of the interest profile. In this regard, the user's purpose for the search is most significant. A large amount of false drop (irrelevant citation) may be tolerable in one-time retrospective searches but in an SDI, continuing confrontation of subscribers with irrelevant material will have a dampening effect. Some users, however, may be using an SDI system to sample areas in subject territory peripheral to their main research thrusts. Thus, the profile interview is crucial in articulating such differences in need. Saracevic (1971) concluded that the user's freedom to modify and tailor a profile to meet his/her own individual needs was a major factor in system performance. Periodic follow-ups should be made with each subscriber for possible profile modification.

The library will have to decide which members of the organization will qualify for the service, if there are to be charges passed on to the user and/or what portions are to be assumed by library and department. Packer and Soergel have found evidence to indicate that SDI is more useful to scholars in disciplines with high scatter of information. Provisions of SDI service should also be considered for institutional "gatekeepers" who serve as information resources to research colleagues. This may be a factor for a library able to offer only selective services to its constituency. Whatever the limitations imposed, the combination of electronic retrospective literature searching and SDI services enables libraries to offer information products on a scale undreamed of heretofore.

Public Relations

Library publications, exhibits and events are all designed to inform the population being served as well as stimulate interest in using the library. Examples of the goals of this program are: to demonstrate the relationship of the library to institutional programs; to provide information about library services and resources; and to interpret the relationship of library programs and the library profession to the clientele. This program also represents one of the few avenues open for the library to convert non-users to users. While the primary purpose of this type of promotion may be directed toward the population to be served, its effect on the budgeting process should not be overlooked. Waldron points out that every unit in an institution is in competition with every other unit for funds, space and personnel. Public relations is therefore a must for special libraries, for unless people know what the library is accomplishing no one will come to its aid during budget discussions. Allocation of resources to this area should consider the appropriate benefits as well as the costs.

Bernays stresses the need to establish goals, develop strategies and determine the resources necessary to accomplish the goals in public relations efforts. Oboler identifies target groups and organizations within the academic and corporate communities with which the library should communicate, including the administration, regular patrons, non-users, campus and company newspaper, etc. He suggests displays on themes featuring celebrations, topics of general interest, specific library services, etc., as all being most effective forms of public relations. Strauss, Shreve and Brown identify four specific "publics" for industrial libraries: library clientele; company management; library staff; and professional colleagues. They emphasize the need to analyze each public in terms of why each should be reached, what facets should be emphasized and the mode of communication to be used.

COLLECTION ACCESS

Access to the local collection can be conveniently viewed in terms of physical and accessibility (e.g., use policies, document location, document availability, etc.) and intellectual accessibility (e.g., subject headings for document in catalog, ease of catalog use, etc.). Whereas intellectual accessibility has been addressed in the functional areas of technical and bibliographic services, the function of physical accessibility is discussed in this section. Decision tasks covered in this functional area include ease of access to the collection at the strategic planning level and hours of library service, arrangement and location of the collection, level of collection security, reshelving and shelf reading, circulation control policies and procedures, type and quantity of AV equipment and reserve collection policies at the management control level.

Strategic Planning Decision

Ease of Access to Collection

The ease of access to documents in the local collection is governed by a number of implicit and explicit factors associated with a series of interrelated management decisions. User group privileges and hours of library operation directly affect document availability to different patrons, as well as directly affecting operating costs. The location, arrangement and density of the collection have both a positive and a negative effect on access. On one hand, a well-weeded collection situated in a central location and arranged to allow for browsing is ideal for the majority of users. Unfortunately, a limited number of individual patrons require access to less-used documents which have been retired to a closed stack compact storage location. The alternative of providing equal open access to all documents is expensive and often results in an overall lesser degree of accessibility because of the sheer size of the collection.

Another factor to consider is whether books are located in departmental or branch libraries or in one central collection. Location of the collection in departmental or branch libraries in close proximity to clients' work space increases ease of access for a majority of users but again is usually a more costly alternative in terms of duplication of materials and staff services. Further, in a university setting employing a departmental library organization, some students and faculty experience frustration when they have to use a number of departmental libraries in meeting information needs.

The degree of control of the collection also has both a direct and an inverse effect on ease of access. The greater the degree of circulation and physical control in terms of number of books allowed to circulate per patron, the length of the loan period, the degree of security, etc., the less accessible the collection will be to the individual patron. Correspondingly, the greater the degree of control, the greater the degree of accessibility to patrons as a group, since an individual document is more likely to be available for use within the library when needed. An ease-of-access policy statement should articulate the philosophy regarding such factors as user group privileges, availability of the documents to individuals and groups and promptness of access with regard to the economic realities and constraints.

Orr (1970) suggests that scientists, in selecting a channel to meet an information need, weigh the relative likelihood of success in acquiring the desired information against the relative cost. The scientist's cost is a weighted composite of a number of variables, including his own time, the physical-psychological effort required and any expenditures of manpower and funds.

Others have suggested that, rather than estimating the likelihood of success, scientists weigh the perceived benefit of an information search against the perceived cost. Allen and Gertsberger, in a study of research and development (R&D) personnel behavior in selecting information channels, asked engineers to rank information channels according to technical quality and content (benefit) and to rank these same information channels according to accessibility (cost). They concluded that these R&D personnel act in a manner not intended to maximize benefits but rather to minimize cost. Rosenberg (1966a) reached similar conclusions in a study of professional level government and industry R&D personnel. In his study, information channels were suggested more on the basis of "ease of use" than on the basis of "amount of information" expected. In a later study, Allen (1977) found that R&D personnel faced with a subsequent problem would tend to use those information channels with which they were more familiar.

In the university setting, Dougherty and Blomquist suggest that faculty rank ease of accessibility higher than the comprehensiveness of the collection, while Soper found a high correlation between document accessibility and the likelihood that it would be cited for faculty writing scholarly articles in science, the social sciences and humanities.

The implications of these findings are that ease of access is of paramount importance in an individual's choice of information sources or his choice as to whether to use the library at all. Further, if a user experiences relative ease of access in using a particular information service, that individual is likely to use that service again in meeting a subsequent information need.

Measures of document availability—one component of ease of access—have been proposed and employed in a number of studies. Urquhart and Schofield employed the concept of a success rate in a study at four universities in the United Kingdom. Patrons who could not find a book held by the library were asked to place a pink slip, listing the author and title, on the shelf in the place where they looked for the book. These slips were then analyzed to determine the reasons for failure and, when compared to circulations, a success rate or proportion of demands satisfied could be computed. The reasons most often cited for failing to find a desired book were that it was out on loan or being used in the library. Other reasons of lesser importance were that the item was lost, at the binders, misshelved, or that the patron was looking in the wrong place. The success rate of finding a desired item held by the library in this study ranged from 75% to 87% for various user groups (faculty, graduate and undergraduate students).

Kantor (1976a) uses a branching diagram approach to demonstrate rate of success in obtaining a document. Reasons for a patron's inability to obtain a desired item were classified into the following categories: not acquired by the library; circulating; being used in the library or being reshelved; library error; and user error. Probabilities for each of these areas were then combined to obtain an overall chance of success in finding a desired item. Whitlatch and Kieffer carry this analysis further, analyzing user success in identifying and locating the citation in the catalog and in actually finding the document on the shelf. They found an average initial user success rate of 77% in the card catalog and a subsequent 76% success rate in the library bookshelves, giving an overall success rate of 59%.

In an effort to measure both document availability and access time, Orr et al. (1968)

proposed a Document Delivery Test. In this test a sample of 300 citations was randomly selected from recent articles relevant to the user population. Each citation was first checked in the library catalog to determine whether or not the item was held by the library. A measure of the "coverage," i.e., the proportion of the items actually held, of the collection was then computed. The sample was then checked against actual holdings to determine the status of each item. The various status categories included: item available on open shelves, item in remote storage, item out on loan, item lost, item not held by library, etc. Standard times were established and agreed upon for accessing an item for each category. These standard times reflected, for example, the time needed to recall a book out on loan and the time needed to acquire through interlibrary loan a book lost or not held by the library. The number of items in each status category were then weighted by the appropriate standard times and a mean document delivery time computed for the 300 citations.

The use of a standardized list to determine a success or availability rate has come under sharp criticism, according to Schofield, Cooper and Waters. Critics argue that a list of selected citations does not necessarily reflect the needs and demands of the library's user population. The list approach also does not allow for the possible "clumping" of demand for particular items, and does not measure the availability of items at the times when they are actually wanted by a user.

Management Control Decisions

Hours of Library Service

A decision must be made as to the hours the library will be open and the range of services offered to users during different times of library operation. In making these decisions, the marginal cost of extended hours and service must be weighed against increased use by patrons and the perceived benefits of this use.

Little literature exists to help library administrators in dealing with the issue of hours of library service. The only article of substance is a report on a survey of librarian attitudes and practices for coping with extended hours, conducted by Wells. The survey concentrated mainly on staffing schedules and librarian attitudes for working evenings and weekends. The public services offered at night and on weekends for the surveyed libraries ranged from full services to virtually none. Many librarians reported their frustration at being caught between the ideal of wanting to provide full services during every hour of operation and the practicality of providing limited services, considering the unattractive staffing hours and financial limitations. No insights are provided as to the benefits of extended hours to the users.

The important question which needs answering is whether demand for services (other than study space) is really created by extending hours or if users would change their pattern of behavior to conform to the library's schedule. Closely related to this is a determination of the impact on user perceptions of the library when limited or lower quality public service is offered during the extended hours.

Arrangement and Location of Collection

Determining the manner in which the collection is to be arranged and located depends upon an analysis of several factors. Arranging and locating documents by department or subject consideration generally increases the overall ease of access but at the same time increases operating personnel costs and encourages inefficient use of interdisciplinary materials. In general, ease of access is increased by physically locating the collection closer to the primary user groups and by offering a collection and service tailored to the particular user group's interests and needs. Ease of access to interdisciplinary material located in another part of the collection is diminished, however, unless this material is duplicated in both parts of the collection. Generally, material arranged by subject area increases direct user access, whereas material arranged by size or type of document (hard copy, microform, etc.) is more storage-efficient and easier to control.

The location of and access to less-used material in remote, usually closed stack storage facilities must also be determined. This decision ties in closely with the weeding policy and procedures covered in the collection development function. Cost of storing documents in both open and closed stack locations must be weighed against document utilization considerations.

Lancaster (1977) cites two major factors of physical accessibility affecting library use: (1) the location of the library itself; and (2) the arrangement of its collections. Little attention appears to have been given to the location and organization (central library, departmental libraries, etc.) of libraries in an academic setting. Coughlin et al. identified a high inverse correlation between public library use and patron distance from the library while Slater reports that the exact location of an industrial library influences use. One would expect that a distance or time factor separating a user from the library is an important determinant of the user's perception of the library's accessibility.

Decentralized library systems using a departmental library structure normally minimize the distance or time factor of accessibility. The added costs incurred for staffing departmental libraries, for purchasing duplicate copies of titles, and the frustration experienced by faculty and students involved in interdisciplinary programs in locating documents has moved many academic libraries to the use of a more centralized system. Davenport assesses the impact of centralizing a library system on the degree of user crossover, usage patterns, retrieval times and need for assistance.

Much has been written regarding the housing of less-used portions of the collection in remote or compact storage. Ellsworth (1969) reviews the three reasons most often mentioned for storing little-used books elsewhere: (1) to save money, (2) to save space and (3) to improve access to the books. He disagrees with the money-saving criterion, claiming that the cost of identifying less-used items, physically transporting them to a remote storage location and updating the appropriate records exceeds the savings realized by freeing up shelf space in the main collection. The advent of computerized record systems and computerized circulation systems considerably reduces the cost of some of these activities. A number of studies deal with strategies for deselecting items. Most of these studies, referred to in the section on weeding, use a criterion based upon circulation use, last circulation date, language and publication date.

There is little question that the removal of less-used items to remote storage locations can present problems. Whether this action improves access to the overall collection is not as clear. In a recent study Shill reports that direct access (open stacks) contributed to an increase in library use and a decrease in circulation. This implies that users make relevant decisions at the shelf rather than borrowing a large number of books from a closed stack arrangement in hopes of finding something useful. Goldhor has shown that making groups of books more accessible has resulted in a measurable increase in the use of these items. Greene (1977) found that although browsing was responsible for 31% of the books borrowed, only 18% of all the books borrowed via browsing were rated as essential. References identified from catalogs, colleagues and other publications all ranked ahead of references identified by browsing in terms of a "value-to-user" criterion. Further research is required to ascertain whether a core collection of most frequently used books supplemented by a collection of lesser-used books in a remote storage location increases the ease of access to *all* books.

The recent development of document delivery systems, as reported by Dougherty, may de-emphasize the importance of collection location and arrangement. These systems for delivering requested materials have been evaluated positively by the users. The system frees users from spending time on trips to the library, locating materials, filling out call slips and carrying journals to be photocopied. Finally, the prospect of electronic transmission of information directly from the library or data source to the user may make the collection location and arrangement issue passé.

Level of Collection Security

In general, the greater the degree of collection security, the fewer the documents which are stolen or mutilated. The level of collection security can range from checkout guards to electronic detection devices, to monitoring personnel and equipment, to closed stack systems. Bahr (1981) suggests a number of factors which should be considered in devising a theft-prevention system including the annual rate of pilferage, the materials most susceptible to theft, how much theft is costing the library, the effectiveness of a security system, its costs and the degree to which the system affects patron ease-of-access. She cites three methods for assessing book loss: the book census (gross count of volumes held compared to records); the book inventory (an attempt to locate each individual book recorded as being held by the library); and sampling. The sampling method is viewed as a relatively efficient, inexpensive and quick method to determine the level of book loss compared with the census and inventory methods.

A study by Bommer and Ford using the sampling method outlines a cost-benefit approach for determining the worth of an electronic security system (ESS). The rate of book loss by theft and the predicted rate of book loss with an ESS are estimated. The value of this difference when compared with the cost of installing and operating an ESS provides a cost-benefit ratio for determining the value of an ESS. In a follow-up study, after an ESS system was installed, Michalko and Heidtmann determined that each dollar spent for an ESS was saving $1.73 through a reduced loss rate. These figures do not reflect the increased benefits of greater book availability imparted to users when this system is in operation. Operation of an ESS does not appear to significantly affect user ease of access.

In libraries without ESS systems, checkout guards are usually stationed at exits to inspect outgoing material. There appears to be little research as to the effectiveness of such a process with respect to costs. Libraries assume that having door guards check patrons as they leave is an excellent psychological deterrent and eliminates removal of books from the library by sheer error. Gordon suggests that closed stacks be given more serious consideration. The savings in books lost by theft and storage space would have to be weighed against the increased retrieval costs and the loss of browsing privileges by the users. Other alternatives such as roving monitors and closed-circuit TV might be considered as a deterrent to document mutilation.

Reshelving and Shelfreading Activities

Prompt reshelving of documents used in the library or returning from circulation increases the availability of documents and associated access to the user. Availability and access are also enhanced by staff shelfreading tasks designed to confirm that documents are in their proper location. In determining the appropriate staffing level for these activities, library managers must compare the cost of reducing reshelving time and misplaced documents with the benefits associated with increased user access.

A large number of requests for books may not be met because the item is waiting to be reshelved after returning from circulation or after being used in the library. The longer the reshelving time, the greater the failure rate in obtaining a desired item. Although there is never a great number of items waiting to be reshelved, these items, by virtue of a recent use, belong to the class of more actively sought-after items. The net effect of extending the reshelving time is to increase the observed loan periods for documents since these documents are usually unavailable when in the reshelving process. The effect of an increase in loan period can be predicted by queuing and simulation models of the type discussed by Buckland. The trade-off between increased availability caused by reduced reshelving time and increased staff cost to perform the reshelving must be assessed. A study by Benford et al. reported a reduction in reshelving time from four days to one day and a decrease in reshelving cost as a result of streamlining the reshelving process.

Cooper and Wolthausen found about 5% of the books at the University of California Berkeley campus to be misshelved. About two thirds of these misplaced books were misplaced on the shelves where they belonged. The above authors have proposed a model for dealing with the misshelving process. Data used in this model for determining an optimum shelfreading interval include the lost circulation rate for misshelved books, the frequency with which shelves are read, the error rate of the reshelver and the number of books in a section.

Circulation Control Policy and Procedures

Managers must make a number of decisions affecting patron ease of access to the collection. The length of the loan period and the number of books allowed to circulate per patron are two of the more important decisions in this area. In general, a longer loan period and an allowance for a large number of books to be borrowed per patron enhances the access for the individual user. This policy, however, reduces the number of books available for other users, decreasing their access. Since the books which do circulate are usually the most sought-after books, access by other patrons is reduced in a disproportionate fashion.

Decisions regulating the time for checking in and reshelving returned books can further affect the availability of books to the users. Other decision factors involve the degree to which an automated and/or computerized circulation system might be employed. In this case, the benefits of reduced processing time and greater reporting capabilities need to be weighed against the costs. Penalties for overdue books and procedures for requesting documents out on loan must be determined. Finally, circulation policies regarding the periodical collection need to be established.

Buckland investigated the influence that varying loan periods and duplication policies had on book availability at the University of Lancaster in England. In analyzing the loan period as a potentially important decision variable, he reports a marked pattern in which users returned books when they were due regardless of the length of the official loan period, the status of the borrower or the subject matter of the books borrowed. He also found little relationship between length of the official loan period and frequency of renewals. These results are supported by Shaw who reports that, on the average, a book will be used for 10 hours whatever the official loan period.

Before the study was undertaken, the University of Lancaster had a 60% satisfaction rate (proportion of user requests which could immediately be satisfied); moreover, approximately 45% of the most used and most recommended titles (about 9% of the collection) were not available, using a semester-long official loan period. Calculations on level of satisfaction were made using a simulation model employing data documenting demand for various portions of the collection, amount of in-library use, probability that a reader will place a reserve on a particular item, number of duplicate copies and varying length of loan periods. The resulting strategy was to introduce a one-week loan period for the 9% of the collection most in demand. Employing this strategy increased the user satisfaction rate to 86% and lowered the percent of most-demanded titles out at any one time to 8%. The revised loan period policy also had the effect of increasing circulation per capita by a dramatic 60%. This finding suggests that demand for library services increases as the level of service improves. Yagello and Guthrie found similar results and reported a 21% increase in usage when the loan period on high-demand items was reduced.

Morse (1968) has developed analytical models for book use as a function of loan period and duplication based on queuing theory. These models predict the expected fraction of time titles are off the shelf and the expected number of unsatisfied requests, given past circulation rates, number of copies, use time and loan period. The effects of changing the loan period for different classes of books can be estimated in terms of user satisfaction.

Saracevic, Shaw and Kantor have documented a study which analyzes the reasons why many libraries experience low user satisfaction rates. They identify and collect data on a number of elements in four major categories:

1) Requests for books not acquired by the library

2) Requests for books circulating
   a) on loan;
   b) used in library;
   c) being misshelved.

3) Library malfunctions
   a) missing and known by library;
   b) missing and not known by library;
   c) misshelved;
   d) book being repaired.

4) User errors
   a) incorrect call number;
   b) book properly shelved but not found;
   c) book located elsewhere.

Using this approach Murfin, in a study on periodical use, reports that 55% of the requests were satisfied, with 15% not retrieved due to user error, and 30% not retrieved due to library problems.

In a similar study involving the library's ability to supply serial volumes, Piternick analyzed reasons why users failed to find a particular journal. The reasons for failure included:

- Journal not held;
- Current issue not yet received;
- Volume requested in bindery;
- Volume being used in the library;
- Volume out on loan.

Many libraries are now developing in-house computerized circulation systems or are purchasing commercial ones. Bahr (1979) provides a good review and evaluation of these systems. Veaner (1970) cites three major reasons why library functions might be automated:

- To do something less expensive, more accurately or more rapidly;

- To do something which can no longer be done effectively in a manual system because of increased complexity and volume of transactions;

- To provide some additional function which cannot be performed in a manual system.

Using cost as a sole criterion, Mosley demonstrates that automated circulation systems are in fact more costly. However, he cites improved service to library users and benefits provided to library managers as justification for installing a system. Lipinski and Almony discuss the potential reports that can be generated from data collected by an automated circulation system. Some of these reports include:

- Charges by subject area;
- Charges by borrower category;
- Books placed on hold;
- Overdue items;
- Use history for individual items;
- Logging searches and explanation for why item not found;
- Delays in obtaining materials;
- Loan period;
- Items charged for in-library use.

Reports of this type can provide valuable information in making decisions on loan periods, books to duplicate, books to weed, collection development, etc., to increase library performance and user satisfaction. Johns and Peischl caution that data provided by such a system alone are of limited value in making collection development decisions. They cite the importance of other information, including academic programs, enrollment trends, new courses, research interests, level of collection, collection limitations, etc., along with circulation data, in making collection development decisions.

Quantity and Type of AV Equipment

The number and variety of microform readers, tape recorders, movie projectors, slide projectors, record players and other equipment necessary for patron use of special document formats must be determined. The number of documents requiring a particular type of equipment, the projected acquisition rate of these documents and the demand rate for these documents are important variables in this analysis.

A number of publications discuss the trends in selection and use of AV materials (see, for example, Cabeceiras and Bahr [1978]). Few guidelines, however, have been offered with regard to the resources to be allocated in this area. Dranov (1976) points out that economic considerations are forcing libraries to purchase a greater percentage of microform materials. This trend would imply increased expenditures for microform equipment. The question remains—how much support equipment is really needed?

Force and Force developed a computer simulation model to help library administrators answer this question. The model uses patron arrival rates and service times to provide information on patron waiting time and equipment utilization for various numbers of units provided. Similar results could be obtained using queuing models. The major informational elements governing the demand for various types of AV equipment would seem to include the quantity, type and popularity of AV materials held by the library and procured via interlibrary loan, the user population requesting AV materials and the patron service time when using AV materials. Gardner and Rowe report that 52% of the users of a technical library have microform reading equipment in their offices. If this trend continues, it should temper the demand for additional in-library microform equipment.

Reserve Collection Policies and Procedures

Policies for acquiring documents to place on reserve in support of specified course assignments in university libraries must be determined. The number of copies of a document placed on reserve is a function of course enrollments and the nature of the assignment (background reading, required reading, etc.). In addition, the number of copies available in the local collection, the cost of purchasing additional copies, as well as future projected uses, should also be considered. Associated decisions involve the access period for reserve books, as well as whether reserve documents should be allowed to be removed from the library.

In evaluating reserve systems, Downs stated that the most common abuses were placing too many books on reserve, keeping books on reserve that are infrequently called for and seldom revising reserve lists. He called for increased cooperation between faculty and library staff members in improving the quality of reserve service and reducing unnecessary costs. Stevens suggests a number of alternatives to counter criticisms of reserve service:

1) Identification of a broader range of materials that might be appropriate for a specific course and that might lessen competition (reducing theft and mutilation) for materials;

2) The placing of fewer items on reserve for shorter periods of time;

3) Closer follow-up on student use of material;

4) Wider use of permanent noncirculating basic collections;

5) Development of reserve collection circulation policies which permit more flexibility in length of loan period;

6) Wider use of on-demand publication programs for materials.

Some methods have been developed to determine the number of copies and the loan period for items placed on reserve. A model developed by Bommer (1971) employing regression analysis and queuing analysis techniques can be used for determining the number of multiple copies to acquire for a particular title. In this model, demand rate for a title is predicted as a function of the number of students enrolled in the course for which the title is on reserve. This demand rate, along with average use periods for the item and the decision variable—the number of copies on reserve—can then be used to predict the probability of a user having to wait for a copy and the mean waiting time. More precise predictions of demand could be obtained if faculty were required to indicate the type of use to be made of the item, e.g., background reference, required reading, one section in a book, etc.

Another model using simulation techniques has been developed by Baumler and Baumler. In their model, data on demand rate, reading assignment length and number of copies on reserve are used to predict the percent of requests met immediately. The model was also programmed to determine user satisfaction as a function of different policies limiting the time for which a reserve book may be held. A computerized system for technical processing of reserve material is reported by Rao and Jones. The system is intended to generate reserve statistics, identify reserve books with faculty placing books on reserve, provide multiple access points to the reserve catalog and increase the efficiency of the reserve catalog process.

In the past, multiple copies of journal articles or chapters in books could be provided economically via photocopying. The 1976 copyright law would appear to sharply curtail this activity.

ACCESS BY INTERLIBRARY LOAN

Interlibrary loan service supplements a library's resources by making available, for the use of an individual patron, materials from other libraries. Fees may or may not be involved in the transaction. Originally an informal courtesy service to meet the special needs of faculty and scholars, interlibrary loan has recently developed into a major physical access service for a broader range of library users. For all types of libraries, interlibrary loan has served to relieve the pressure of meeting all the needs of patrons through local collections.

Cooperative arrangements have grown out of the need for more efficient and less costly interlibrary loan service and for a more equitable distribution of lending burdens. Two or more libraries may cooperate with each other by initiating reciprocal library use and borrowing privileges. A number of libraries in the same geographical area or with a similar subject interest may join together to form a consortium which has some degree of formal administration and procedures. Many of these organizations coordinate publication of directories and union catalogs. They may serve as interlibrary loan clearinghouses to establish hierarchies for location and borrowing of materials, and to reimburse libraries for lending costs. Multilibrary networks coordinate the central development of cooperative programs and services and generate standard network procedures and protocols. The expanded use of TWX, computers and telecommunications has speeded and enhanced the growth of such library networks.

Strategic Planning Decision

Interlibrary Loan Cooperative Arrangements

The degree of emphasis placed on accessing documents held by other libraries depends on the needs of the user population as defined by academic and research programs and the resources available in the local collection. The success of an interlibrary loan activity can be measured in terms of the percentage of requests satisfied, the time taken to satisfy these requests and the associated costs. Performance of interlibrary loan networks in terms of probability of success and retrieval time needed to satisfy requests is enhanced when identification, location and availability information can be easily accessed. Existing computer technologies such as shared cataloging networks and automated circulation systems can be useful in rapidly obtaining this availability information. Desired documents can be verified, located, availability status ascertained and requested, all in the same process.

Entrance into a cooperative arrangement usually requires reciprocal services. The increased burden placed on the local collection by requests from other libraries must be ascertained. Increasingly, fees are being assessed for interlibrary loan requests. The fee structure, along with local processing costs, should be considered in collection development decisions. The ease of access to other libraries, demands placed on the local collection, cost of membership and fees charged and received for interlibrary loan requests will all have to be weighed when deciding upon the types of cooperative arrangements to enter.

As the volume of information continues to increase, libraries and information services will be forced to place greater reliance on "access modes" and less reliance on "local holdings." This shift from holdings to access via shared resources is becoming an increasingly important element in library functioning.

Markuson has identified three distinct levels of sharing arrangements with respect to progressive administrative authority and control:

- Library cooperation: activity between two or more libraries to facilitate, promote and enhance library operations, the use of resources or service to users.

- Library consortia: a specialized type of cooperative activity restricted to limited geographical area, number of libraries, type of library or subject interest and having some degree of formalized administration and procedures.

- Library network: a specialized type of library operation for centralized development of cooperative programs and services, including the use of computers and telecommunication, and requiring the establishment of a central office and a staff to accomplish network programs rather than merely coordinate them.

Kent identified three types of cooperative or network organization: star, hierarchical and distributed. In the star arrangement, one member holds virtually all resources with other members accessing these resources. In the hierarchical arrangement, members refer requests to the next greater resource center until they are satisfied. The distributed arrangement is comprised of members with equal but different resources, with each member able to access another directly. DeGennaro (1975) suggests that the star form of arrangement is preferable to hierarchical arrangements. He cites that most interlibrary loan requests are for recent English serials which could most easily be satisfied from a centralized and specialized facility, leaving the research libraries available to handle the few exotic and obscure retrospective materials requested.

Advances in computer and communication technology appear to have an impact on interlibrary loan activity. Martin (1981) reports a significant increase in loan requests as a result of implementing computer-based literature searches. Kilgour reports that an online union catalog (OCLC) significantly accelerates interlibrary lending among member libraries. The OCLC interlibrary loan subsystem provides users with immediate access to the OCLC union catalog and the loan file. This system should result in reduced document delivery time and reduced processing costs, as well as access to a nationwide bibliographic data base. Document delivery times may be reduced even further in the future, using facsimile transmissions and developments in computers and telecommunications.

Management Control Decisions

Accessing Documents Held by Other Libraries

To facilitate the speed with which other libraries fill requests, the requesting library should verify all requests, supply complete and proper bibliographic information and process the requests according to standard format. Verification and location can be facilitated by accessing bibliographic tools, union lists and networking systems. The more accurately a request is verified and routed, the easier it will be for the lender to locate the material. Requests, once received, need to be controlled and monitored. Efficient and effective accomplishment of this process will make other libraries more willing to lend materials at a future date.

The amount of staff time and resources provided for document identification, verification and location are prime decision variables. Other factors which should be considered include: access to union lists and computer networks for locating documents, membership in cooperative networks, staff availability for processing requests and retrieval time by mail service or electronic transmissions, with associated costs.

The performance of an interlibrary loan activity can be measured by three criteria as summarized by Lancaster (1977): (1) the proportion of requests satisfied, (2) the time required to satisfy requests and (3) the cost for satisfying requests. Evaluation of the effectiveness of the document delivery capabilities of any loan network or cooperative agreement must consider these factors.

Document delivery capabilities can generally be measured by using some type of citation pool or by surveying actual patron interlibrary loan requests. The question of bias may be raised if a citation pool is not representative of actual user needs. Using actual patron requests as an indicator of document delivery capabilities assumes, however, that user requests fully reflect user needs. It does not consider requests not made because users are unaware of interlibrary loan, lack confidence that it can meet requests in time or any other reason.

Thomson suggests that the success rate for obtaining requested material is a function of:

1) Size of the libraries involved;
2) Distance between libraries;
3) Characteristics of materials requested, including date and form of publication;
4) Care used in verifying the citation;
5) Availability of union lists in the region.

Added to this list would be factors considering the accessibility of strong resource libraries in the immediate network and previous success with a particular library or channel.

The timeliness or delay factor of document delivery as a function of the value to the user is explored by Reisman et al. who constructed utility curves relating value to the user and access time of materials using the Delphi technique. In a similar study, Stuart concluded that the delay factor was less important than believed by many librarians and inconvenience to the user was minimal.

Williams et al. conducted a comprehensive study comparing the costs of owning versus borrowing serial publications. The economic conclusions of owning versus borrowing are tempered somewhat by the enactment of the 1976 copyright law, which restricts the number of photocopies that can be made of periodicals not owned by the library.

Rouse and Rouse (1979) discuss a design for an online system to provide information on interlibrary loan performance with respect to probabilities of success, delivery times and costs. The system utilizes a data base orientation for efficient data storage and retrieval. Various types of reports can then be generated online to support various decisions in this area. Information provided by this system, for example, assists library managers in making decisions and establishing policy regarding the routing of interlibrary loan requests to alternative resource libraries, and weighing the trade-offs between delivery times, probability of success and costs.

Supplying Documents to Other Libraries

The manager must determine the effort needed to fulfill interlibrary loan requests by other libraries. Membership in a cooperative network, loan service provided by other libraries, the number of requests received and the reliance on shared resources to meet local needs are factors in this decision. Document delivery capabilities for supplying material to other libraries depend upon the accuracy of request citations, availability of documents in the local collection, effectiveness of recall procedures and the volume of requests received. Policies must be formulated covering requests by non-network libraries and the manner in which documents will be provided (hard copy, electronically, microform, etc.). The level of service provided in processing requests and supplying documents as well as the fee to be charged other libraries for satisfying a request must also be determined. The actual cost of providing a document and the fee structure of other members of the co-operative system are critical factors in determining the fee.

Trudell and Wolper report on the results of a study of interlibrary loan traffic in the New England region. Information was gathered on the patterns of lending by different types of libraries, the flow of interlibrary loan among libraries, use of OCLC data base for verification, age of materials requested, fill rates and delivery times. These data confirm that large libraries lend more than they borrow. The survey was part of a project to develop a strategy for leveling out the load within an interlibrary loan system. A June 1978 article by the same authors describes a proposed model to be used to design and evaluate strategies that would equalize the lending load for all libraries in the system.

Spencer developed a unit cost system for assessing the expenses associated with the tasks involved in filling an interlibrary loan request; questions which need to be resolved include:

- How should costs for requests which cannot be filled be assessed?
- How much, if any, of the acquisition cost of the requested document should be included in the cost?

In a subsequent study, Carr et al. report on characteristics, costs and use activity in an interlibrary loan network.

PHYSICAL FACILITIES

Physical facilities consist of the space for the collection, user services and library operations, as well as necessary furnishings. This section considers decision tasks relating to the quality and adequacy of user area and furnishings at the strategic level, and allocation of area and user furnishings at the management control level.

Strategic Planning Decision

Quality and Adequacy of User Area and Furnishings

The library manager must determine whether the physical facilities of the library are adequate in both size and structural setup to meet current and future needs for storing the collection and providing for its use, while also allowing sufficient space in which the flow of day-to-day library transactions can take place. Future needs should consider projected size and mix of user populations, institutional program directions, trends in library technology, and trends in the form and publication rate of library materials.

In determining the optimum design and use of physical facilities, such factors as attractiveness, environmental climate and the efficient and effective use of space should be taken into account. A decision must also be made as to the quantity and style of user furnishings desired.

Ellsworth (1973) cites a number of forces which affect the nature of library services and must be considered in planning physical facilities. Some of the forces include:

- Growth in numbers of carriers of information a library must acquire;
- Developments in new communication technology;
- Changes in the composition of the campus and in enrollment patterns;
- Degree of emphasis on independent study;
- New interdisciplinary types of teaching and research programs;
- Developments in automation and computer support technology for performing operations and providing expanded service.

Orne cites the proliferation in types of carriers of information—audio and visual, data banks, reports, manuscripts, microforms, etc.—as another significant force in planning for physical facilities. He believes library design will change to provide for greater user space than materials space. The trend to adopt the concept of access rather than ownership is cited by Mason (1976) as a significant factor in planning library physical facilities. Ellsworth (1968) chronicles the errors in building fixed-function libraries and advocates the use of modular design in which most floor space can be used interchangeably to support different activities. This structure provides the flexibility and adaptability to cope with changing and uncertain future trends.

Metcalf and Mount provide very detailed, step-by-step procedures for planning academic and special library buildings, respectively. Program formats for assessing requirements for user seating, collection accommodation, public catalog, service desks, staff facilities, and other space needs are included, as are spatial arrangements of user services and library operations.

A number of articles discuss centralized versus decentralized or departmental library arrangements. Raffel and Shishko (1972) provide a model for comparing the benefits of increased use and reduced user access time by locating libraries near classrooms, offices and dormitories, versus the increased costs of such a decentralized arrangement. Data necessary for such an analysis include user locations, user needs by subject area, user population group and economic cost information. Allen's (1977) finding that accessibility, or ease with which an information channel can be contacted, is the primary motivation for reusing such a facility would seem to favor the development of decentralized or departmental libraries. Ellsworth (1968) argues that centralization of service is preferred, because decentralization results in fragmentation of unity of knowledge, isolation from other users, lower quality of professional staff coverage and increased costs.

Management Control Decisions

Allocation of Area

The manner in which the building area is allocated for storing the collection, for providing user study area, for providing space for library operations and commons area (meeting rooms, lounge areas, etc.) must be determined. In making this allocation, consideration should be given to the size of the collection, user population and needs, as well as library staffing level and needs. Decisions as to temperature, humidity and lighting should weigh the costs of achieving an optimum document preservation environment, which also considers user comfort, against the benefits achieved by maintenance of such climatic factors.

Metcalf discusses space requirement formulas for collection storage, service points, staff needs, reader needs and other needs. A number of different formulas are provided for collection storage depending upon such factors as open or closed stacks, compact storage, height of shelves, leaving space for growth, aisle widths, etc. Booth analyzes the effectiveness of a variety of different configurations of library stacks. Other considerations for collection storage space must include reference collection, current periodicals, newspapers, reserve-room book collection, public documents, map collection and other special collections.

User area requirements include the manner in which collections are arranged, e.g., current periodical reading area, reference reading area, etc. Factors in determining the user space required include: the number of volumes in a particular collection; the number of library patrons in various departments or programs; the reliance of the community on the library; and the availability of alternative study space. In addition, Metcalf presents formulas for staff area needs for public service staff, processing staff, administrative staff, maintenance staff and others.

Farber believes that advances in technology leading to more rapid interlibrary loan systems, compact storage techniques, more sophisticated weeding procedures and micrographics will help library managers cope with document storage space problems. Ellsworth (1975) reports that implementation of a national periodicals center, regional cooperative book storage programs, increased reliance on and use of interlibrary loan via OCLC-type systems and substitution of microforms for bound volumes will all reduce space requirements. He adds, however, that increased use of microforms, although it reduces document storage space, may require more library space to accommodate microform readers.

Ellsworth (1975) also predicts a shift in staffing space requirements. The use of computerized networks for centralized processing and serials record work will decrease the number of staff and staff space needed in the technical processing area. However, the number of reference librarians and their space requirements will have to increase to deal with the increasing sophistication and complexity of information access. Central library administrative staffs will expand to deal with the increased sophistication of management techniques in program budgeting, data processing, research and development, and employee relations.

Number and Type of User Furnishings

A decision must be made as to the number and type of study spaces to be provided. Desks and chairs, tables and chairs, carrels and lounge chairs represent the major items of user furnishings. In making this decision, consideration should be given to the current and future student enrollment and mix as well as use patterns of the library.

No definite formula seems to exist for providing seating for academic or special libraries. For academic libraries, recommendations for providing seating for between 25% to 90% of the undergraduates at any one time have been proposed, as cited by Ellsworth (1968). The ideal number of seats depends upon a number of factors including patron population and composition, availability of alternative work spaces, degree of emphasis on using library resources, peak demand periods, number of volumes in a particular collection, etc. Since seating and seating space are not inexpensive factors of library operation, one should probably plan to meet some percentage of the peak demand periods. Queuing models can be helpful in determining required capacity. The number of arrivals and departures as well as the time spent in the library are critical factors in these models. Cook explored different seating arrangements for increasing seating capacity, while Raffel and Shishko (1969) propose a model for determining a mix between different types of library seating.

Merchant discusses the need for specialized seating with electronic communication connections to AV equipment, computer terminals and the like. Again, queuing models and reliable predictions of future requirements in this area should be helpful in planning for these special seating requirements. As the amount of material on microform held by a library increases and as the use of computerized catalogs increases, these specialized seating requirements will increase.

6

A Data Base Approach to Decision Support

The customary procedure to follow in designing a decision support system (DSS) is to plan the user/data base interaction, i.e., the report formats and inquiry dialogue required by the manager. Then the designer "backs into" the design of necessary software, file structures and data capture procedures. This approach is not followed here for two reasons. First, the objective of this study is not to produce a system for a specific institution. Academic and research libraries differ widely with respect to problems, priorities and economic constraints; there exists no "typical" library for which one can tailor a system design. Second, the file structure which is to be proposed is new to the field of library management. The potential for decision support which is implicit in this file structure must be fully understood before attempting to identify specific retrieval objectives. Many forms of support are possible which, heretofore, have not been anticipated by library managers.

Designers of DSS have come to realize that most of the important decisions are unstructured. Structured decisions are recurring decisions with well-defined solution techniques and information requirements. To support unstructured decisions, the information system must be flexible, broad in scope and capable of relating data in a variety of ways. As time passes priorities will shift, planning objectives and performance standards will change and managerial styles will vary. The DSS must be capable of evolving in response to these changing needs.

The general nature of this discussion requires taking the broadest possible view of decision support. Then, recognizing that a complete implementation of all possibilities would not be feasible or necessary, various ways are suggested to identify a feasible subset consisting of those support measures dictated by needs and constraints. The data base approach allows one to do this. Within a general data base framework a specific, limited implementation is possible, as is the ability of a system to evolve with changing and growing needs.

To maintain a general decision support system capable of evolution, the underlying data base must be a model of all relevant features of the institution being managed and its environment. Components of this model include all relevant entities which exist, permanently or temporarily, and all relevant events which take place at various points in time.

For example, an entity might be a document or a set of documents, faculty member, employee, student, course, project or department. An event could be a circulation transaction, acquisition of a book, an interlibrary loan request, a student enrolling in a course or a researcher assigned to a project. The scope and detail with which events and entities are described is a design decision based on need and feasibility. Often it is sufficient to describe aggregations of entities of a certain type or of events over a period of time. Entities and events are described by their attributes—measurable values of relevant characteristics. Again, the choice of which attributes are worth recording is a design decision.

In addition to entities, events and their attributes, it is important to describe the relationship between entities and events. Relatedness is often overlooked when designing files and reports to support a specific decision. A general approach to designing a data base must include a capability to relate data in a flexible fashion. For example, the attributes of circulation transactions may be recorded in one file, while the attributes of the user community are recorded in another file. At some time a problem may arise which requires an analysis of the attributes of users having initiated circulations of a journal or of books in a specific Library of Congress (LC) category. At another time an analysis of the attributes of circulation transactions initiated by a specific subset of users may be required. Given the availability of data in the two files, programs could be written to produce either report. However, the cost of programming and the delay in waiting for a report often makes such an analysis impractical. A direct means of relating data of different types is necessary if the information system is to support *ad hoc* management requests.

A further illustration should demonstrate the variety of unanticipated ways in which data might have to be rearranged to address a specific problem. Suppose a periodic control report on interlibrary loan requests identifies an abnormally large number of requests for books in a specific LC category. A number of reports might be necessary to identify the cause of the problem. A profile showing the number of holdings in each LC category might identify inadequate coverage in the category of interest. A profile of acquisitions over the past few years by LC category might indicate that portions of the collection have become out of date. If neither of the above is true, then it is possible that poor selections of new titles are being made within that LC category. More detailed profiles of holdings, acquisitions, circulation and interlibrary loan requests within that LC category may be required. By identifying the various users in this LC category, the librarian can analyze their attributes and transaction patterns to see what specific demands are being met and not met. Key users can be identified and contacted. Depending on whether the demand pattern is judged to be transient or to represent a continuing shift in interest, a new acquisitions policy might be formulated.

No single, concise report could have provided the clues necessary to pinpoint the source of the above problem. Furthermore, the need for the various reports was generated only after the problem was recognized. Providing all of these data in periodic formal reports would quickly bury the library in computer output. Yet such data are regularly collected by libraries, especially those with automated circulation systems. Much of the cost of data capture and storage is already incurred. What is lacking is a flexible system for retrieving the appropriate data in a useful format at the time it is needed.

This chapter will attempt to establish a useful conceptual model upon which a library DSS can be based. We will then present a detailed, comprehensive specification of the relevant entities, events, attributes and relationships necessary to form a practical application of these concepts. Of course, the scope of this general data base will be far greater than any library would want to implement. Much of the data will produce redundant information. Some data are more useful than others, and some data are more costly to capture than others. Practical considerations in implementing a subset of the data base in specific environments is discussed in later chapters.

CONCEPTUAL DATA BASE MODEL

Certain conceptual components of the library system can be identified and related to form a "functional data base model." A major thrust of this discussion is to identify valid operational parameters which are descriptive of the activity of these functional components. What follows in this section is a discussion of these components and an explanation of their role in the functional data base model (refer to Figure 6.1 as terms are defined).

Productivity of Users of an Academic/Research Library

Productivity of users is measured in the organizational context as the effective contribution a user makes to the solution of a research problem or the accomplishment of an educational mission, as manifested by tangible achievements such as:

- Intellectual products such as course offerings, project activities, lectures, devices, materials, processes, patents, procedures, term papers and theses;

- Informational by-products such as published works, technical reports, patents, research and project proposals, formal presentations and demonstrations;

- Marks of recognition such as honorary designations, professional awards, promotions, monetary rewards, supervisor or peer evaluations, student evaluations and citations by colleagues.

Depending upon the context, a user may be an individual student or faculty member, employee, class, group, task force, program or a community of users with related interests. Since users often engage in a number of concurrent research or educational activities, it is helpful to initially separate each user's needs into sets or "problem spaces." The concept of a problem space is borrowed from Newell and Simon, who use it in a model of human problem-solving. As we use the term, a problem space is the way in which a researcher, teacher or student conceptualizes a problem or task in order to work on it. A problem space might be derived from a specific project, course or institutional unit specializing in a particular activity; a user associated with such an entity would adopt a portion of the entity's attributes as a problem space.

Information relevant to a problem space resides in one or more internal or external "information bases," a term used to represent any repository of text-format information within or outside of the institution. The user's personal holdings—books, periodicals or other sources of data previously acquired—form one of these information bases. Personal information bases include published versions of documents such as books, monographs, technical reports and journals (either in paper or microform), as well as duplications of

Figure 6.1   Model of Functional Components of an Academic/Research Library

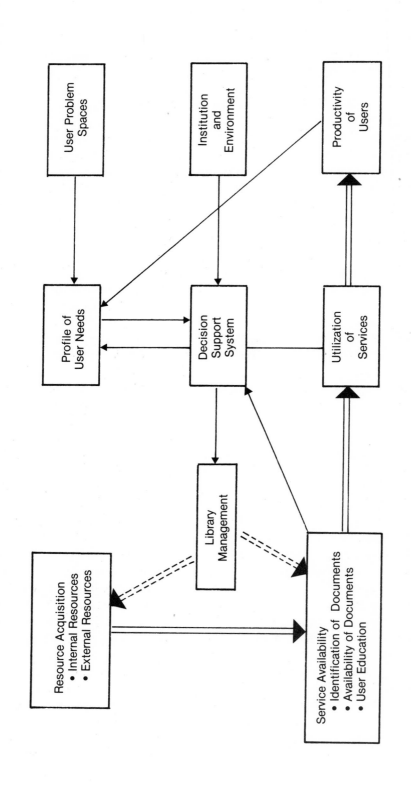

such documents which are products of previous retrieval transactions and which constitute a continuing use of information. Other information bases that might contain relevant information are at the primary library of the institution employed by the user, at other libraries that the user may contact directly or at libraries whose holdings are available indirectly through interlibrary loans.

In order to identify information relevant to a problem space within these information bases, the problem space must first be characterized in terms of a profile of user needs. This profile must then be mapped or translated according to the keys or descriptors commonly used by libraries or retrieval services to classify bibliographic material. In a method suggested by Swift et al. and Leggate et al., each user is characterized by a profile of his/her information needs mapped into "information descriptors," which are classification terms used to structure the manner in which information is acquired, stored and retrieved. These descriptors may be ranked within the profile by importance or organized into a hierarchical structure.

Over time, a user will complete research or teaching tasks, take on new tasks and make progress on continuing tasks. Therefore, the user's profile of needs changes with time and constitutes a dynamic component in the functional model. Taking the user's set of problem spaces as input to the library system and user productivity as the ultimate objective, some of the intervening attributes of the system will now be examined.

Utilization of Services

Utilization of services occurs when a user actually receives information from the system as evidenced by retrieval transactions. However, utilization is only an intervening step and not the ultimate productive act. An analogy can be drawn with management information systems theory where data are said to become information only when they are useful in a decision-making context. Likewise, unless user productivity is included, we are only studying a document transfer system, not an information transfer system. Measures of utilization of information services will require that a link be specified between utilization and productive activities.

Availability of Data

Availability is an attribute of an identified subset of the total holdings of information bases accessible by the user. To be available, a document must reside in one or more of the information bases and sufficiently match the user's information needs profile. Availability can be more precisely characterized by the following subconcepts:

1) *Completeness:* the proportion of all potentially identifiable documents which have actually been identified. This is seldom, if ever, known in relation to all possible documents, but it is a useful relative concept for comparing the completeness of specific data bases.

2) *Relevance:* the degree to which identified documents are, in fact, useful contributions to a problem space.

3) *Proximity:* the "nearness" of documents to the user, most usefully measured in units of time. Two types of time may be distinguished:

a) *access time,* during which the user is actively engaged in retrieval effort, and
b) *wait time,* during which a copy of the document is being transported to the user.

4) *Cost:* what it costs the user to acquire access. This can present a barrier to access since, in an economic context, the value of a document may not exceed the cost, or the user may have a limited budget to allocate for information retrieval.

5) *Psychological factors:* what causes users to be reluctant to use new technology or media. Training or learning barriers may exist, or differing user perceptions of availability may exist even though all physical factors are equal (see Gertsberger and Allen, Rosenberg (1966b), and Zipf). Library management may choose to conduct user education activities designed to encourage new utilization patterns.

Management is responsible for acquiring resources and providing services in response to user needs within the context of institutional objectives and subject to institutional constraints. Trends and shifts in the aggregate profile of the user community, as well as environmental inputs, form the nucleus of the DSS and give direction to resource allocation decisions concerning acquisitions and services.

Incorporating Functional Components into a Decision Support System

Maximization of availability is probably not the ultimate goal of most library managers. The degree to which the available resources are used and the ultimate contribution of a library to user productivity should also be monitored and reported. The relationships between availability, utilization and productivity have been the subject of some primary research, the results of which can be usefully applied in many settings. A DSS requires that ongoing feedback on utilization and productivity must be provided to the library manager for evaluating the potential impact of actions taken to improve the user community's exposure to available information and to improve user productivity. Thus, the key task of our work has been to demonstrate that practical and valid measures of these concepts may be implemented on an operational basis in an academic/research library. As demonstrated in Figure 6.1, the following necessary information flows are required by the DSS:

- resource availability
- resource utilization
- user productivity
- user problem spaces
- institutional and environmental impacts.

The last element of information flow requires some elaboration.

Library management will always be called upon to interpret institutional objectives and environmental opportunities in executing their planning and control activities. Formal, quantitative indicators of these factors are difficult to develop, and our approach only suggests that information assessments be explicitly recognized through assigning priorities which will put the aggregate institutional needs profile into a specific perspective. Some important institutional classifications of needs under which priorities may be assigned are:

- by project or general class of research activity;
- by undergraduate education/graduate education/research;
- by school, department or other institutional unit.

The degree of institutional emphasis among these categories can be assessed subjectively and expressed quantitatively by electronically adjusting or rearranging the aggregate profiles developed from individual users so as to emphasize one or another classification.

In summary, the explicit structuring of a library to meet institutional objectives requires a DSS comprised of a number of unique features to be developed and implemented. In particular, an active effort to obtain and periodically update individual and aggregate user need profiles is essential. The concepts and relationships employed in this conceptual schema have been demonstrated as useful in experimental settings. However, their articulation and structure in an operational setting, where factors such as system cost and user inconvenience are important, has not progressed to the point where implementation is straightforward. The following sections will discuss an operational approach intended to facilitate an implementation of the preceding concepts.

OPERATIONAL DATA BASE MODEL

With a conceptual framework established, the principal objective can be addressed: How can the DSS concepts be measured in a valid and economic fashion? This section will deal with the problem from a very broad perspective that will include all approaches which were thought to be feasible at the outset. The primary constraint placed on the measurement problem was that the methods must be capable of implementation on a continuing basis. This eliminated many valid approaches previously employed in research studies on a one-time basis.

Reliance on methods that involved extensive and costly capture of data not normally generated in the daily operation of an institution or its library was unacceptable. This was certainly the case with data capture requiring extensive user involvement or substantial clerical effort by library personnel. Furthermore, the differences that exist between academic/research libraries in the amount of available resources and technology which might be applied to developing a DSS must be recognized. Finally, at least some of the suggestions should be applicable in small libraries using limited computer technology.

CLASSIFICATION OF SUBJECT MATTER

Initially, we must deal with a crucial issue, the solution to which will form the foundation of the DSS. A user's activity or interest can be conceptualized as a profile, that is, as an expression of relative strength or emphasis across a set of categories or classes of subject matter. Similarly, circulation and available bibliographic resources can also be expressed as a profile of relative emphasis or strength across subject matter categories. In order to relate, compare or assess user activity, circulation and resources for management problem-solving, the set of subject matter categories must be identical in all profiles or at least capable of juxtaposition—i.e., the different sets can be mapped onto each other. There exists no such single, universal, generally accepted subject matter classification. A number of approaches are possible, none of which are ideal.

Classification via Bibliographic Data Base Profiles

Research interests of users are probably most validly expressed in the type of syntax used by bibliographic data bases. Many researchers employ these services and have profiles on file with their library. Many industrial firms and universities provide a selective dissemination service to their research and development personnel and faculty.

A dissemination system used at IBM was studied for possible applicability in a DSS setting. However, the management of the many technical libraries maintained by IBM appeared to be independent of the dissemination system. There appeared to be no formal attempt to report data from personnel profiles to library managers and no indication that this was a resource in making decisions concerning collection management. The profiles themselves were quite complex with no obvious means available to summarize or aggregate the data for an entire set of users.

The IBM experience points to the major drawbacks of bibliographic data base profiles in general. There appears to be no common thesaurus of terms applicable across a wide range of subject matter. Aggregations based on the relative occurrence of specific terms would also be misleading, since they appear within a logical, Boolean syntax within each profile. Furthermore, only a minority of the typical research community subscribes to such a service. Direct use of such profile information by library management seems doubtful unless some additional mapping of the profile onto a less robust set of terms is performed.

Publishers of abstracts in various fields usually employ a broad classification of their fields of interest, such as is done by the Association of Computing Machinery and the International Federation of Operations Research Societies. The NASA SCAN service also employs a limited thesaurus without Boolean constructs. However useful such profile sources might be, there still exists no single, universal set of categories for an entire academic/research community. Ultimately, some practical means of aggregating these diverse sources might emerge. Presently they are useful only if their terms can be mapped onto a more comprehensive set.

Perhaps the greatest difficulty with independently developed thesauri of subject matter terms is that the body of literature which is made available and circulated is only classified in these terms by the diverse means employed within various commercial services. These various thesauri are neither comprehensive in their coverage of the literature nor compatible with one another. Additionally, they are under constant revision since the state of the art in bibliographic searching is not fully developed.

None of the existing bibliographic search or abstracting service thesauri can be recommended as the common denominator for establishing profiles in a library DSS at this time. It would appear that what remains is either the Library of Congress (LC) or Dewey systems. Of these, the LC system is used in the vast majority of academic and research libraries. Employing the LC system, however, is not without its drawbacks.

Classification via the LC System

The principal advantage of the LC system is that the bibliographic material being managed is already classified within this system. Libraries have taken advantage of cataloging services such as OCLC to increase the productivity of their cataloging activities. To suggest to a library that it introduce additional cataloging tasks to classify its acquisitions according to another method of organization is simply not acceptable. Furthermore, OCLC provides a means of constructing a computer file of current acquisitions and existing holdings based on the LC system. The only practical means of creating a file based on another classification is to create a systematic mapping of terms. The reclassification could then be automated.

If mapping between systems of classification is to be undertaken, there are a number of important points to be considered. First, the DSS must not pose an excessive clerical burden on library resources; that is, the additional data capture activities required by the DSS must represent a small percentage of existing clerical activity. The acquisition of profiles of user activity and problem spaces would seem to pose the greatest additional burden. It would make sense to automate the mapping of these profiles onto the LC classification rather than take on the far greater task of mapping the collection and circulation statistics onto an independent system of classification employed for user profiles.

A second consideration is that the LC classification constitutes the natural language with which librarians work. The collection is already categorized in this mode and all activities relating to its management are organized accordingly. Management information must be expressed and organized in the natural language of the manager. To do otherwise would reduce the value of the information.

A final consideration is more technical but nonetheless important. A mapping from LC to any other system of classification would not necessarily be on a one-to-one basis and could result in simply renaming categories. For example, a book on the electrical properties of materials could be classified within many areas of physics and electrical engineering. If this book circulates, is it counted once or as many times as it appears in various categories of the user-oriented system? How will the manager interpret statistics based on multiple counts of circulations? For some problems, such a representation would be useful; for others it is not. This mapping could take place at the time the manager requests information if the data base is organized in LC terms. The reverse mapping is not possible, however, and true circulation counts by LC class would not be recoverable. It would appear, then, that the organization of the data base should be LC-oriented. Processing costs of data capture transactions and data base updates would be minimized. Mapping onto other systems of classification could then be effected at run time when reports requiring alternative categorizations are requested.

The HEGIS System

Having made the decision to employ the LC classification, some valuable existing research has proven useful. Of particular importance is the work of Evans (1978b) and Evans et al., in which a comprehensive mapping of the LC categorization onto the HEGIS

(Higher Education Generalized Information System) classification for academic programs is developed (see Appendix 1). The HEGIS system classifies academic programs and is used in New York State as a framework for reporting statistical and financial information by the Department of Higher Education (see Allman, Wing and McLaughlin). The mapping method developed by Evans indicates how library holdings and acquisitions contribute to the support of academic programs. The mapping is many-to-many; that is, one LC category may apply to several programs and one program is usually supported by many LC categories.

Many of the activities associated with a university and its members are conveniently classified by the HEGIS code. Events and entities such as faculty affiliation, departments, courses, student enrollment and research grants are easily categorized in the HEGIS code. In turn, the attributes of these events and entities can now be related to library activities and resources. However, the HEGIS code is much less specific than the LC categories we chose to employ. For this reason, some university activities may be best classified directly into the LC code or into independent classifications such as the NASA SCAN codes. Nonetheless, the mapping into the HEGIS classification is always available for reporting purposes. This is vital since the HEGIS code is made up of terms which are part of the natural language of university administrators and is generally accepted among faculty, administrators and legislators.

Data Base Interaction of Classification Systems

A code, similar to the HEGIS, could be developed for any industrial or research institution. Such a code would reflect the detailed content of continuing activities, issues and concerns of the institution and its industry. As the relative emphasis of the institution shifts over time, so should the emphasis of library management. Such a code could be assembled from several of the existing classifications of the type mentioned above.

Figure 6.2 shows the portion of the data base schema representing the classification system and its interaction with the rest of the data base. Each node represents a computer file containing occurrences of records. Each record occurrence corresponds to an actual entity and contains values of the attributes of those entities. In this case, some of the entities are logical, for example, the set of LC categories and the set of HEGIS categories. A detailed description of the entity attributes appears in the data base dictionary in Appendix 2. For industrial or research institutions, the HEGIS classification would be replaced by a unique subject matter code for the institution.

The arrows in the schema represent relationships between files. For example, the arrow from DEPARTMENT to USER indicates that for every department record there exists one or more faculty records associated with (or "owned" by) the department. In place of DEPARTMENT, one may substitute or add other USER affiliations such as project or program. This is usually a one-to-many relationship. To represent a many-to-many relationship, such as between LC-SERIAL and HEGIS, we require an intervening file, LC-HEGIS. This intervening file is essentially a matrix with each record representing one cell of the matrix. The files LC-DIV and HEGIS-DIV are simply broader aggregates of the LC-SERIAL and HEGIS codes and serve to illustrate that various levels of aggregation are possible to describe both subject matter and institutional activities. Note that users are directly classified by the HEGIS (or equivalent) code independently of department affilia-

Figure 6.2 Classification Portion of Data Base Schema

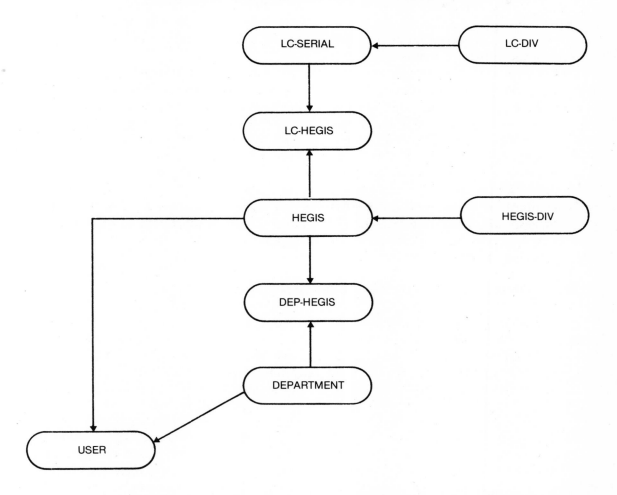

tion. Such a classification may be based on education, training or previous experience not wholly reflected by the attributes of the currently assigned department.

Adoption of the LC system of classification also provided an opportunity to employ a mapping technique developed by McGrath (1969b and 1975). This technique employs the skills of a catalog librarian to classify university courses within the LC system, a methodology used in field research with considerable success. Furthermore, the concept was extended to the classification of research interests, dissertation topics and the NASA SCAN categories. These applications will be described later in the section on profiling of user problem spaces and productivity. The method can also be applied to mapping an institutional equivalent to the HEGIS code onto the LC classification.

UTILIZATION PROFILES

Although a library provides a wide variety of user services, the data base development phase of this work limited the scope of the term utilization to document delivery. Document delivery services include circulation of the local collection, interlibrary transactions, photocopying (excluding self-service facilities) and in-library use. The approach to gathering information about other services would be analogous to the methods explored in the case of document delivery, but might differ among libraries, depending on how the library defines the scope of its activities.

The LC system provides a natural classification for utilization transactions and can be easily mapped onto the HEGIS or equivalent classifications to observe the use of materials provided to support various institutional programs. Other links must also be established in the data capture procedure. For each transaction (event) which occurs, with respect to any of the services listed above, the data capture procedure must record user data (identification number), document data (LC code) and reference data (date, time and usage location). Additional data concerning users, LC category, location, etc., are assumed to be on file in the data base and may be linked to the transaction during processing. There are obvious relationships of interest to observe among employees, faculty, students, departments, etc., with respect to utilization behavior. For example, type of utilization, LC category, and trends over time may all be possible dimensions for observing patterns of use. A complete discussion of report structures and dimensions is presented in Chapter 8.

Minimizing Data Base Retrieval Costs for the DSS

Minimizing the cost of data capture is critical to the success of the DSS. In the case of utilization, the increasing use of automated circulation systems can be of great help. In fact, a wide array of statistical reports is usually available from these systems but librarians have not yet been able to exploit their value fully. This experience is similar to what has occurred in business data processing systems over the past 20 years. The principal business application of computers has been in routine transactions processing with management reports being a tangential by-product. Such management reports have always been subject to the constraints of timing, format and available data which are imposed by the requirements of transactions processing. Files of stored data were always organized to optimally meet the needs of transactions processing. Only in the last 10 years have there been any significant implementations of systems designed specifically for management support.

A DSS still relies primarily on data originating through transactions processing. The full cost of data capture, processing, storage and retrieval can seldom be justified solely by the benefits derived by management through decision support. Though some primary data collection can be justified, the vast bulk of data is available only as a by-product of the institution's normal transactions processing and operations. Despite this economic barrier, recent developments in storage and retrieval techniques have made these data available in ways which can be tailored to meet management needs.

Software developments in the areas of generalized data storage and generalized reporting and inquiry have made it possible to provide flexible, timely and inexpensive servicing of management requests for support information. This software was first available only on large computers but now is appearing even in microprocessor-based systems. Thus, the major economic and technical barriers to developing a library DSS lie in the data capture procedures and facilities.

As noted above, an automated circulation system can provide much of the data required for the DSS. At the time of a circulation transaction a record is created containing data about the user, the document and the date, time and location of the transaction. Ideally these data are recorded without manual key entry. Machine-readable labels should be available on the document and on the user's identification card.

If an automated circulation system is in use, much of the capture cost of utilization data is already being absorbed by the institution. Other means are available to capture data without resorting to automated circulation, but if that is the case, the costs incurred must be attributed to the cost of the DSS. Some of these alternatives will be discussed in Chapter 9, which deals with implementation problems.

An automated circulation system may not be capable of handling all the transactions identified under utilization. In addition to the circulation stations, there must be input terminals for both interlibrary loans and photocopying as well as a portable device for scanning items to be reshelved after in-library use.

The schema for the utilization portion of the data base is shown in Figure 6.3. The four utilization files are CIRCULATE, INTERLIBRARY, PHOTOCOPY and INLIB-USE. All except INLIBUSE are linked to the USER file. To save storage space, a separate utilization record need not be maintained for each transaction, though this would be the theoretically straightforward way to record transactions. Each of the four utilization record types contains a transaction count for a given LC class or serial and a given publication date over a period of time, say, one year. Within some of these records, the count could be broken down by weeks though this is probably not essential. Thus, the data base update procedure only needs to take place periodically according to management reporting

Figure 6.3   Utilization and Availability Portion of Data Base Schema

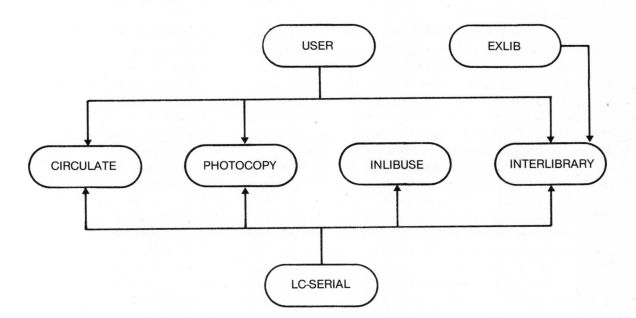

needs. Transaction records are accumulated and then processed in a batch run to update the utilization records. Details of the file contents are described in the data base dictionary in Appendix 2. Note that LC-SERIAL contains a separate record for each volume of a given periodical as well as all of the LC categories.

At this point files have been identified to store data about users, user affiliation and utilization, and these files have been linked to both the LC and HEGIS systems of classification. The variety of ways in which one can cross-tabulate attributes of these entities and events is discussed in Chapter 8.

AVAILABILITY PROFILES

The existing status of available resources is an essential factor in library decision making, and some method of measuring this factor exists in any library. There may, however, be some barriers to the flexibility and timeliness with which these data may be used for decision making. At a minimum, the library should know the distribution of its monograph collection in terms of the LC classifications at a useful level of detail. This is usually known even in manual systems. Keeping track of LC class distribution, while additionally recording the age distribution by publication date within LC classes, would burden a manual system, but it is certainly feasible. Manual tracking of trends in holdings, acquisitions and weeding are also feasible but again, burdensome. However, displaying these data in a variety of formats and levels of aggregation and relating them to utilization and productivity in meaningful ways would severely overtax a manual system.

As discussed earlier, technological support for producing a computer-readable record of a monograph collection exists through cataloging services. However, the lack of such a file does not prevent the library from keeping track of availability. The number and age distribution of holdings may be based on LC classes only and updated to reflect acquisitions and weeding. Thus, both utilization and availability could be reported only by LC class and not to the document level. Most reporting requirements would not be affected by this restriction.

As in the case of utilization, the specific methods employed are largely dependent on the state of existing technology in the library. A machine-readable file of monograph holdings may already exist in the library as a result of using computer-aided cataloging and perhaps by maintaining an online catalog instead of a card file. If this is the case, then little additional cost burden is placed on the DSS. However, justifying the acquisition of a machine-readable file of monograph holdings strictly for use by the DSS would be difficult. On the other hand, a computer file of serial holdings by volume is not a significant burden on the DSS budget and should be maintained.

Another significant dimension of availability is the interlibrary loan system. An important responsibility of the library is to identify external sources for serials and monographs. Knowing where to find documents, how much they will cost and how fast they can be delivered are critical components of operational information. Data can be accumulated from interlibrary loan transactions to provide this information. Figure 6.3 shows how this is accomplished. Each INTERLIBRARY record is linked to a record describing the source library, EXLIB, for assisting loans or copy deliveries. Each of these INTERLIBRARY records contains the number of documents requested, number received and average delay time in days. Note that this schema implies that LC-SERIAL contains not only local library serial holdings but also serials previously requested through the loan system. Monograph loans are also recorded in INTERLIBRARY by LC class, publication date and source library. The concept of availability, then, extends beyond the library's holdings and this is reflected in the data base.

PRODUCTIVITY PROFILES

In all of the profile categories discussed above, the attributes to be measured and the means of measurement are very well defined. Many opportunities also exist to accomplish tangential data capture through clerical activities already taking place in the library. Further, the events and entities being recorded all reside within the library itself. However, the conceptual entities and events associated with institutional productivity lie outside the library, and additional effort is required by the library to capture data in those areas. To complicate matters, there are no widely accepted or proven ways to measure attributes of productive events or even agreement as to what the relevant productive events are.

Because of the unique problems associated with the productivity dimension of the DSS design, the authors conducted field tests of a variety of approaches in an academic setting. Of special concern was the value of information produced by the measurement alternatives as well as their cost and technical feasibility. A number of alternatives which initially appeared to have potential were selected. An evaluation of these approaches appears in Chapter 7.

Productivity as It Relates to Library Decision Making

Before discussing the alternatives which were evaluated, one must define the meaning of "productivity" in the context of library decision making. This view might be quite different from the perspective one might take in judging the merit and value of the efforts of researchers, faculty and students for other purposes. Use of the term productivity refers to the amounts and kinds of teaching or research activity which are taking place in the institution and not to the ultimate value that society might place on those activities. The library should acquire the data necessary to assist in planning for and responding to existing and potential demands for its services. Resources should be allocated according to the amounts and kinds of activities taking place and according to the way in which these activities are distributed across departments, programs, projects, fields of study and, ultimately, across the LC classification of bibliographic material.

Any attempt to modulate the activity distribution with built-in value judgments for the purpose of allocating resources is considered to be outside the terms of reference of the library DSS. Certainly, it is true that historical activity data will not reflect the impact of new programs, projects, priorities and institutional directions. Such factors, as well as historical trends, should be taken into account when forecasting future activity profiles. Aside from such forecasting activities, any attempt to modulate the activity data should be at the explicit discretion of the planners and not implicitly built into the DSS.

Classification of Courses

In a university setting, all educational and research activity is, directly or indirectly, focused on faculty activities. In the case of research libraries, the focus is on the researchers themselves, either directly or through project leaders or technological gatekeepers. Thus, the data capture system can be conveniently focused on this relatively small group of library clients. The research and learning activities of students can always be linked to and characterized by courses, projects, theses and dissertations supervised by faculty. The quantity and type of teaching activity taking place may be kept in a file associated with the courses offered at the institution and their enrollment. Courses may be linked to departments offering the courses and faculty assigned to teach them.

These data are readily available, often on university computer files, through the registration process each semester. Thus, implicit characterization of the subject matter in each course is available from the attributes of the related departments and faculty. However, an explicit characterization of the courses requires a special effort and should also be undertaken. On the other hand, the research projects conducted by faculty or assigned to employees of research and development institutions can only be explicitly characterized by the attributes of the projects themselves. The explicit classification of courses and research projects is considered below.

Three possible sources of course classification were identified within the context of the LC system of categorization. The first method was suggested by McGrath (1969b and 1975) and involves employing a catalog librarian to classify the course title and description in the same fashion as bibliographic material. With this method there is a high initial cost when the course file is first created. Revisions to course offerings every one or two years will probably result in less than 10% of the records requiring update. A second source of data about course classification comes from the textbooks required for the courses. Records from the campus bookstore may be used for this purpose. The skills of a catalog librarian would not be required for this approach since the books will already have an LC code. However, there would be considerable clerical effort associated with obtaining the codes and producing a complete file update each semester. Further, many courses have no text, and many that do will not be accurately described by the text classification itself. The next chapter explores the relative cost-effectiveness of these approaches.

A final source of classification data is the reserve list for courses. Since library material placed on reserve is already coded, this source is the easiest of all to employ for data capture. Though only a limited number of all the courses have reserve placements, the data that are available could provide a significant profile for those courses making a direct and large demand for library support. The data base schema for teaching activities is shown in Figure 6.4. All of the coding possibilities described above are included, though it is unlikely that any actual implementation would include them all.

Classification of Research Activities

With respect to research activities, there are a number of tangible indicators which could serve as sources of data capture. Lists of researcher publications and technical reports are accumulated and reported by the institution. Libraries often attempt to accumulate copies of such documents for their files. Other possible sources are research grants applied for and received, project descriptions, bibliographic searches, theses and dissertations supervised, faculty and emloyee annual reports and direct survey instruments. All of these sources require primary data capture and, therefore, their cost-benefit in the DSS must be carefully evaluated.

Figure 6.4   Productivity Portion of Data Base Schema

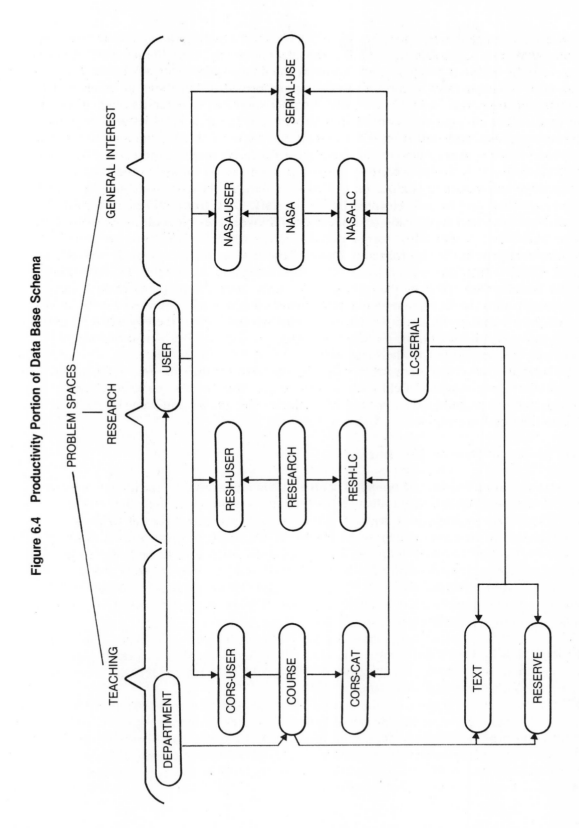

Direct surveys requiring researcher input are the most costly data capture devices. Attaining a high response rate also requires considerable attention by library staff. Results then have to be coded and key-entered. Much of the data required to track research activities could be obtained from researcher annual reports provided that these are available for inspection and transcription by library staff. Another source of research data would be the institution's office charged with coordinating project and research activities and/or publication records. Data gathered from these sources may be more timely than annual reports.

Whatever the source of activity data, the most expensive aspect of research data capture is the coding of activities according to the LC classification or some other system which may be automatically mapped onto the LC system. In the case of annual reports, this coding would have to be performed by library staff. Data from publications, project or research activity and supervision of student or employee research could be self-coded by users at some point in time when formal documents describing such work are prepared. A classification system in the natural terminology of the field of study is strongly recommended. Thus, by marking a checklist of applicable categories, the coding can be accomplished with minimum effort by the most knowledgeable party. A mapping of such categories directly onto the LC system could subsequently be done by computer. Furthermore, the checklist for coding the activity could be a mark-sensitive form, thereby eliminating the need for key-entry. Bibliographic searches and other research services performed by the library could also be subject to the same coding.

To simulate the type of data which might be obtained through the research sources described above, the academic field trial included acquisition of data concerning publications, research grants and student supervised projects. The quality and value of such data as well as their cost are explored in Chapter 7.

Further Sources of Data on User Interest

There are also a number of potential sources of data concerning user interest which are not directly associated with productive teaching and research activities. Some of these include the dissertation topic and degree field of the user, personal serial subscriptions and selective dissemination services such as the NASA SCAN. Each of these sources was explored in the field trial as well. Requests for monographs and serials to be added to the collection are also a potential source of data concerning current user interests and have the advantage of being voluntarily submitted and pre-coded. However, it is frequently difficult to associate these requests with a specific user, since they are often submitted to the library through a departmental representative.

The schema for research activities and general interest are shown in Figure 6.4. The file SERIAL-USE results from a survey of users who asked for serials frequently used in addition to those under personal subscription. The NASA SCAN was taken to be representative of any such selective dissemination service.

The next chapter will focus on the potential contribution of each of the above approaches for assessing user productivity and general interest. Development of availability and utilization profiles seemed to be straightforward, and therefore no primary research was necessary. Based on the results of the field trials, the data base schema developed above was refined and reduced in scope. The resultant data base design is presented in Chapter 9.

7

Developing User Profiles in a University Setting

This chapter describes a number of field trials conducted for the purpose of identifying feasible ways to implement the decision support data base in a university setting. The focus is on developing profiles of faculty productivity as manifested by their research and teaching activity, patterns of library resource utilization and expressions of interest in specific subject areas. The profiles should reflect the amount of activity as well as its distribution in terms of LC categories. The amount of activity will serve as a weighting factor in forming aggregates of faculty profiles. The profile of faculty productivity can be viewed as an operational construct reflecting user needs.

None of the field trials purport to use a representative sample of faculty which cuts across disciplines or institutions. In all instances an attempt has been made to merely identify efficient and valid data capture procedures. It must be recognized that patterns of activity in certain specialized fields may vary from those observed in these trials. Extensions of these techniques should be applicable, however, to all fields and Chapter 9 discusses their implementation. In addition, much of the experience gained in the field trials is directly transferable to the special library setting.

A total of 41 faculty members from three departments at Clarkson College participated in the trials. These departments included Economics and Finance, Electrical Engineering and Computer Science, and Physics. The data capture trials spanned one semester, though historical data were employed where necessary. The trials focused on the effort and cost required to capture data as well as the validity and potential value of the data in contributing to our understanding of institutional activities. In the sections that follow, these trials are described in detail.

UTILIZATION PROFILES

Two components of utilization were incorporated into the trials: circulation and interlibrary loan. Utilization was not explored for the purpose of discovering efficient data capture procedures, for, as is the case with availability, the technology and procedures are fairly well known. Rather, the primary concern was how utilization profiles compared to those obtained from sources outside the library. The value of data from additional sources has to be viewed as a marginal increment to that already available. It was suspected that many of the sources of activity data which were to be studied contained redundant information, both between themselves and with existing sources. Further analysis required some firsthand observation of potential redundancy.

Clarkson College's library did not have an automated circulation system. Thus, during the period of the study, circulation desk personnel manually recorded the transactions of participating faculty. Table 7.1 shows the data items collected for each transaction. For circulation and interlibrary loan transactions, a summary record can be accumulated as indicated in Table 7.2. The volume of circulation and interlibrary loan transactions prohibits long-term storage of individual records. Cumulative totals by month or year are probably sufficient for any realistic management reporting needs.

Table 7.1   Data Items Collected for Utilization Transactions

Circulation

1. User name[1]
2. Serial title (if applicable)
3. Complete LC call number[2]
4. Publication year
5. Transaction date

Interlibrary Loan

1. User name[1]
2. Serial title (if applicable)
3. Complete LC call number[2]
4. Publication year
5. Date of request
6. Date received
7. Source library
8. Number of pages (if photocopy)
9. Cost

[1] ID numbers assigned later.
[2] Only characters preceding the decimal point were entered into the data base.

This study assumed that no file of individual monographs was available at the library in machine-readable form. Therefore, circulation figures for monographs are associated only with their LC category just as is the case for monographs requested via interlibrary loans. This approach also demonstrates that a comprehensive monograph file is not a prerequisite to constructing a useful management data base.

Table 7.3 shows a typical profile for an individual faculty member, showing both circulation and interlibrary loan activity broken down by broad LC categories. This table

**Table 7.2   Initial Description of Summary Records Kept in Data Base
for Utilization Transactions**

Circulation	Format[1]
1. ID number of user[2]	xxxxx
2. LC code or serial code	AA 9999-9999[3]
3. Publication year	99
4. Transaction year	99
5. Accumulated number of transactions	9999

Interlibrary Loan	
1. ID number of user[2]	xxxxx
2. LC code or serial code	AA 9999[3]
3. Publication year	99
4. Year of request	99
5. Source library code	xxx
6. Accumulated number of requests	999
7. Accumulated number of pages (photocopy)	9999
8. Accumulated cost	999.99
9. Accumulated wait time in days	9999
10. Accumulated number of unsuccessful requests	99

[1] A = alphabetic; 9 = numeric; x = alphanumeric.

[2] Faculty are identified uniquely; students are grouped by rank and department with an ID number assigned to each rank/department group.

[3] Only that portion of the LC code appearing before the decimal is recorded from transactions. An LC category is thus the alphabetic division plus the four-digit (maximum) range number. Serials may be coded either by their existing LC code or by a more specific code unique to the serial and assigned by the library.

shows actual data from the study but does not constitute a suggested format for a management report. (This statement equally applies to all data reported in this chapter.) Formatting of management reports is discussed in Chapter 8. Table 7.4 shows aggregate activity of all faculty within a single department, while Table 7.5 depicts an aggregate profile of the three participating departments.

Circulation and interlibrary loan statistics together can given acquisition planners a significant picture of trends in demand across the range of LC categories. Coupled with availability statistics, the complete picture can indicate which areas are under- or over-serviced. Trends in use, especially with respect to interlibrary loans, can suggest new areas of emphasis. The level of service being delivered in interlibrary loans can indicate whether new acquisitions or more formal interlibrary arrangements are necessary.

Photocopying and in-library use of documents were not studied in the field trials. Photocopying (excluding self-service stations) can be recorded with the same procedures used in circulation. In-library use (including self-service photocopying) must be recorded during reshelving, and thus cannot be attributed to specific users. Taken altogether, these above sources provide a complete picture of document use throughout the library.

Interlibrary loan transactions occur infrequently enough to consider using key-entry devices for recording transactions on computer media (diskette or tape cassette). Key-entry might be too slow, however, for other transactions, where scanning devices for reading document labels and user identification cards might be advisable. This does not necessarily imply an automated circulation system. A wide array of applicable hardware exists and is in use in industrial settings for production and inventory control. Moreover, many existing automated circulation systems could be adapted to the full range of data capture discussed above. The economic requirements of various components of the decision support system will be considered in Chapter 9, given a variety of circumstances as to different technology existing in the library.

Table 7.3   Utilization Profile for a Single Faculty Member

| LC-Div[1] | Circulations | | Interlibrary Loans | | Combined Total | |
	Number	% of Total	Number	% of Total	Combined Number	Combined % of Total
H	2	6.5%	1	6.7%	3	6.5%
HB	2	6.5	3	20.0	5	10.9
HC	1	3.2	0	—	1	2.2
HD	8	25.8	2	13.3	10	21.7
HE	6	19.4	5	33.3	11	23.9
KF	3	9.7	0	—	3	6.5
QA	5	16.1	0	—	5	10.9
TA	0	—	1	6.7	1	2.2
TD	4	12.9	1	6.7	5	10.9
TF	0	—	1	6.7	1	2.2
TL	0	—	1	6.7	1	2.2
Total	31	100.0%	15	100.0%	46	100.0%

[1] See Appendix 1 for explanation of LC divisions.
Note: Discrepancies in percentage totals are due to rounding.

Table 7.4   Utilization Profile for the Electrical Engineering and Computer Science Department

| LC-Div[1] | Circulations | | Interlibrary Loans | | Combined Total | |
	Number	% of Total	Number	% of Total	Combined Number	Combined % of Total
Q	5	2.4%	3	3.5%	8	2.7%
QA	77	37.0	13	15.3	90	30.7
QC	15	7.2	5	5.9	20	6.8
QD	1	0.5			1	0.3
QH	1	0.5	1	1.2	2	0.7
T	5	2.4	1	1.2	6	2.0
TA	8	3.8	5	5.9	13	4.4
TJ	24	11.5	7	8.2	31	10.6
TK	71	34.1	48	56.5	119	40.6
TP	1	0.5	2	2.4	3	1.0
Total	208	100.0%	85	100.0%	293	100.0%

[1]See Appendix 1 for explanation of LC divisions.
Note: Discrepancies in percentage totals are due to rounding.

Table 7.5 Combined Utilization Profile for Three Participating Departments

LC-Div[1]	Circulations		Interlibrary Loans		Combined Total	Combined
	Number	% of Total	Number	% of Total	Number	% of Total
H	5	1.0%	1	0.6%	6	0.9%
HA	8	1.6			8	1.2
HB	26	5.2	6	3.9	32	4.9
HC	16	3.2	3	1.9	19	2.9
HD	19	3.8	5	3.2	24	3.7
HE	8	1.6	7	4.5	15	2.3
HF	3	0.6	9	5.8	12	1.8
HG	29	5.8	7	4.5	36	5.5
HJ	6	1.2			6	0.9
KF	3	0.6	1	0.6	4	0.6
Q	16	3.2	4	2.6	20	3.1
QA	101	20.2	16	10.3	117	17.9
QB	1	0.2			1	0.2
QC	97	19.4	10	6.5	107	16.4
QD	18	3.6	2	1.3	20	3.1
QE	7	1.4			7	1.1
QH	1	0.2	2	1.3	3	0.5
RA			1	0.6	1	0.2
T	5	1.0	1	0.6	6	0.9
TA	16	3.2	6	3.9	22	3.4
TD	6	1.2	2	1.3	8	1.2
TF			1	0.6	1	0.2
TJ	24	4.8	8	5.2	32	4.9
TK	74	14.8	51	32.9	125	19.1
TL			1	0.6	1	0.2
TN	6	1.2	8	5.2	14	2.1
TP	3	0.6	3	1.9	6	0.9
TS	1	0.2			1	0.2
Total	499	100.0%	155	100.0%	654	100.0%

[1] See Appendix 1 for explanation of LC divisions.
Note: Discrepancies in percentage totals are due to rounding.

PRODUCTIVITY PROFILES—TEACHING

Virtually all of the productive activity at a university is centered on the faculty, both in research and instruction. This project uses this insight to focus the data capture investigation on faculty activities and interests. However, since this inquiry emphasizes feasible continuing procedures, this precludes such direct techniques as questionnaires. The intention is to identify convenient continuing sources of data so as to minimize input participation of users and clerical work of library staff.

A readily available data source for teaching activity is the teaching schedule prepared by each department. Forwarding copies of these schedules to the library represents little additional effort. An alternative and even more centralized source is the registration office where such a schedule is likely to be available in computer-readable form. Enrollment statistics should also accompany this data to provide a quantitative measure of activity associated with each course.

Classification by Course Description

Beyond the acquisition of teaching activity data remains the problem of classifying these activities on the LC scale. Chapter 6 identified and described three sources with potential for practical implementation. These included the plans suggested by McGrath (1969 and 1975) for cataloging course titles and descriptions, textbook listings available from the campus bookstore and lists of documents placed on reserve for each course.

Among the three classification alternatives there is likely to be considerable redundancy. The amount and timing of costs associated with the three procedures will also differ. (As regards timing of costs, some procedures may have high initial costs and low maintenance while for others the opposite holds true.) Let us first look at our field trial results regarding the quality of classification data generated by the three data sources and then deal with implementation requirements.

The most direct and valid means of coding courses is to catalog course descriptions. A catalog librarian, who will automatically keep in mind the bibliographic implications of this classification, is in the best position to perform this task properly. One could argue that more material is required to produce an adequate classification, such as a course syllabus, reading lists and perhaps an interview with the instructor. Such attempts to improve the accuracy of classification must be judged on a marginal benefit/cost basis. Course descriptions are concise and readily available. Collecting further material such as course syllabi and reading lists represents a considerable addition to data capture cost. Also, the additional data must be reviewed, thus increasing the time required for cataloging. To what extent such efforts would result in better classifications is open to question.

There is no absolute standard of "goodness" to apply to cataloging. An experiment could be arranged in which courses were cataloged by different individuals with different amounts of available course data. Accounting for differences among catalogers, the resulting classifications would be subjective in nature. Such an experiment was not conducted in this project, but it might be worth investigating. It should be kept in mind, however, that the ultimate measure of benefit is the improved value of classifications in contributing to better decisions. Precision and detail become less important when course profiles are aggregated by subject matter or department.

To what extent might a planning decision be affected by the improved precision of classification? There are many uncertainties and qualitative judgments which influence all decisions and more precise profiles cannot contribute to reducing other sources of uncertainty. Moreover, no management decision is made with perfect information. In any decision situation, a balance must be struck between the cost of improving the quality and quantity of information and the benefit of improved decisions. "Perfect" information is seldom justified under this criterion. Thus, the assumption is made that cataloging of courses based solely on course descriptions will produce sufficiently valid classifications with relatively low expenditure. Should this prove unsatisfactory in practice then, and only then, should more costly refinements be contemplated.

The focus in the field trials was, in fact, directed at finding even cruder and less costly means of classifying courses than by direct cataloging. The ultimate cost of implementing a decision support system poses a formidable barrier. Therefore, it is important to discover means of providing adequate information at minimal cost.

Classification by Text/Reserve Lists

Using textbook classifications (available from the campus bookstore) to characterize courses avoids the need for cataloging. However, a significant data capture effort remains, in that each semester the LC classification of all texts on the bookstore list must be retrieved and key-entered. This constitutes at least an annual effort for most courses, since textbooks change frequently. On the other hand, cataloging does not require update except where existing courses have been changed or new courses are added. Furthermore, the textbook codes will never be as precise as a cataloger's description. Often, textbooks fall into a general subject classification, whereas the course description may divulge more detail concerning specific areas of coverage.

To supplement textbook coding, an additional, handy source of course data is the reserve list for those courses making use of this service. The LC classification of such materials is easily recorded and is thus an inexpensive data source. Other library services such as distribution of audiovisual materials, technologically assisted instruction and bibliographic searches conducted to fulfill course requirements may be coded with relative ease. None of these additional sources is comprehensive but their aggregate profile may be sufficient.

Comparing Methods of Classifying Teaching Activity

Course cataloging was performed in two departments: Physics and Economics/Finance. Courses in these two departments were also classified according to textbooks employed in the current academic year as well as materials placed on reserve. Each of these two alternatives appears to be feasible as a means of classifying teaching activity by LC categories.

As a means of assessing validity, a comparison of the resultant LC profiles generated by the two methods (cataloging by course description vs. by text/reserve) on a course-by-course basis was made. For each course, the percentage of matches that existed between LC categories generated by the two methods was computed. The results are shown in Table 7.6. Note that the number of categories generated by the cataloger is virtually always greater than the number generated by texts and reserve readings. Moreover, the text categories were almost always a subset of the catalogers' categories. This was expected, since the cataloger was attempting not only to capture the basic theme of a course but also all of the subconcepts mentioned in the course description.

An unfortunate result of the text/reserve method is that the LC categories for most college texts tend to be very general and do not reflect the full impact of courses in areas of related reading. This is demonstrated in Table 7.7 with a list of some typical descriptions of the LC categories garnered using both approaches. Note the higher degree of specificity generated by cataloging in comparison to the text/reserve categories.

The impact of these two approaches on management reporting is demonstrated in

Table 7.6   Comparison of Course Classification by Cataloging vs. Text/Reserve Lists

Course No.	Number of Students Enrolled	(A)[1] Number of LC Categories Cataloged	% of A in B	(B)[2] Number of LC Categories Cataloged	% of B in A
Economics					
150	210	4	25%	1	100%
151	214	5	20	1	100
201	10	6	16.7	1	100
350	395	4	25	1	100
351	216	5	20	1	100
353	11	4	25	1	100
355		4	—	0	—
356		2	—	0	—
357		4	—	0	—
358	41	3	33.3	1	100
360	56	2	100	3	66.7
364		2	—	0	—
365		3	—	0	—
366		1	—	0	—
367	18	3	33.3	1	100
369		3	—	0	—
370		4	—	0	—
374	15	6	16.7	1	100
380		2	—	0	—
463	31	0	—	1	—
468	25	3	0[3]	2	0[3]
470		2	—	0	—
471		7	—	0	—
487		7	—	0	—
592	6	6	16.7	1	100
650		2	—	0	—
660		2	—	0	—
665		2	—	0	—
687		7	—	0	—
692		1	—	0	—
Finance					
361	194	3	33.3	1	100
462		1	—	0	—
464	26	3	33.3	1	100
470		1	—	0	—
486		1	—	0	—
487		1	—	0	—
567		3	—	0	—
667	42	2	0[3]	1	0[3]
687		1	—	0	—
Physics					
101	700	5	20	1	100
102	603	4	25	1	100
107	65	3	33.3	1	100
111		5	—	0	—
112		4	—	0	—
113		2	—	0	—
114		2	—	0	—
203	178	4	25	1	100
204	184	6	0[3]	1	0[3]

Table 7.6   (Continued)

Course No.	Number of Students Enrolled	(A)[1] Number of LC Categories Cataloged	% of A in B	(B)[2] Number of LC Categories Cataloged	% of B in A
207		2	—	0	—
209		4	—	0	—
213		4	—	0	—
214		2	—	0	—
255	17	2	50[4]	2	50[4]
321		3	—	0	—
322		1	—	0	—
323		3	—	0	—
325		4	—	0	—
327		2	—	0	—
328		2	—	0	—
331	11	4	25	1	100
341		2	—	0	—
342		1	—	0	—
366		1	—	0	—
426		2	—	0	—
430		1	—	0	—
432		4	—	0	—
433		6	—	0	—
434		5	—	0	—
435		2	—	0	—
436		2	—	0	—
437		2	—	0	—
438		2	—	0	—
439		4	—	0	—
442		3	—	0	—
443		2	—	0	—
445		1	—	0	—
446		1	—	0	—
447	17	2	50	1	100
449		3	—	0	—
451		3	—	0	—
453		3	—	0	—
455		2	—	0	—
457	10	1	100	1	100
460		4	—	0	—
470		2	—	0	—
480		1	—	0	—
561		1	—	0	—
563		6	—	0	—
564		6	—	0	—
570		3	—	0	—
591		2	—	0	—
592		2	—	0	—
671		3	—	0	—

[1] (A) = Cataloged by course description.

[2] (B) = Cataloged via text/reserve lists.

[3] A and B generated non-overlapping categories.

[4] Only one of the two categories generated from A and B overlapped.

Table 7.7   Detailed Results of Typical Course Classification by Cataloging vs. Text/Reserve Methods

	LC Descriptions	
Course No./Title	**By Cataloging**	**By Text/Reserve**
EC150 Economic Principles & Problems I	Economics (general) Price theory Profit, macroeconomics Industries	Economics (general)
EC151 Economic Principles & Problems II	Economics (general) Price theory Labor economics Commerce Money	Economics (general)
EC367 U.S. & Canada in the International Economy	Commerce Tariff policy International finance, foreign exchange	Commerce
EC468 Credit, Money and the Economy	Banking Credit Stocks, investments	Interest Personal finance
FN361 Corporation Finance	Corporate finance Business administration Corporations, trusts, cartels	Corporate finance
PH101 Fundamentals of Physics I	Physics (general) Descriptive & experimental mechanics Theories of gravitation Elementary particle physics Mathematics	Physics (general)
PH203 Fundamentals of Physics III	Physics (general) Acoustics, sound Statistical physics Mathematics	Physics (general)
PH447 Nuclear Physics	Nuclear physics (general) Radiation physics	Nuclear physics (general)

Figure 7.1. By aggregating LC categories into the two-character alphabetic codes and using course enrollments as a weighting factor, there emerge two very different views of the bibliographic support required for the teaching programs in the two departments. The text/reserve approach severely understates teaching support required in the HD, HF, QA and TK categories. The TK category is particularly interesting. Though most text material in physics falls in the QC range, much of the subject matter in physics is contained in the TK range of the engineering holdings. The reverse is likely to be true for engineering.

    One benefit of the text/reserve approach is that only those courses actually taught in a

Figure 7.1   Comparison of Enrollment Profiles Generated by Cataloging vs. by Text/Reserve Methods (for Physics and Economics Courses)

% of Enrollees
Assigned to Category

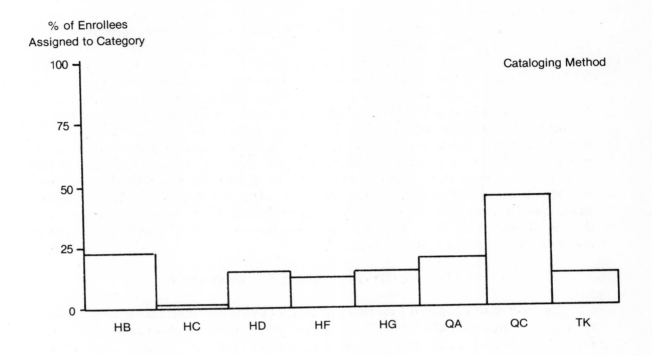

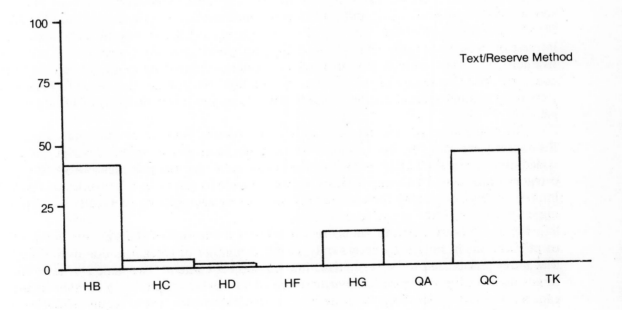

Capital letters denote LC divisions—see Appendix 1 for explanations of codes.

given year need to be processed. (Table 7.6 shows this to be about 50%.) Much cataloging effort went into specialized and graduate courses which are infrequently offered. The importance of this factor depends on the department and university. Over a number of years one would expect both distributions in Table 7.6 to be full. However, it is doubtful that the variety of categories appearing in the text/reserve list would change much. New texts tend to fall into the same bibliographic categories as do their predecessors.

In conclusion, the cataloging approach provides a more representative picture of the bibliographic spectrum of course offerings at an institution. The cost of the initial cataloging effort may be spread over several years with courses being cataloged as they are offered. Some cataloging will be required every year as new courses are introduced. The validity of the classifications can be verified by consultation with faculty where this is deemed necessary. Generally, the clerical effort of cataloging courses is comparable to that of retrieving the LC classification of textbooks. Once the bulk of existing courses has been cataloged, the annual maintenance of the cataloging effort is far less costly than the text/reserve approach. Furthermore, courses tend to be structured the same at different universities; therefore, much of the course cataloging performed at one university could be directly adopted at another. Thus, one must conclude that from the standpoints of validity and cost, the cataloging approach is superior.

PRODUCTIVITY PROFILES—RESEARCH

The field trials employed four basic procedures to identify both the type and amount of research activity for all LC subject categories. The methods of data capture included: (1) a survey of each faculty member's research activities, including research grants proposed and approved, student projects supervised, dissertation topics of faculty, non-funded research and consulting activities; (2) publications authored by faculty; (3) serials subscribed to or frequently used; and (4) categories indicated as interest areas in the NASA SCAN dissemination service. The use of serials and the NASA SCAN indicated areas of interest or problem spaces, while the other sources gave quantitative measures of productive activity. Serials subscribed to or used and faculty-authored publications were naturally coded by the LC category of the serial or monograph. No attempt was made to code subjects of individual journal articles, since this would be too costly in terms of library staff activity.

The research survey was intended only as a reference base for establishing validity. Responses were coded by our cataloger in much the same way as course descriptions were coded above. For the NASA SCAN service use, a cataloger mapped each NASA SCAN category onto related LC ranges. Thus, it was possible to assemble LC profiles of research interest or level of activity for each faculty member or aggregations of faculty by employing one or more of the above four sources.

Figures 7.2–7.5 illustrate the profiles developed from each of the sources. The profile of publications in Figure 7.2 shows only a limited number of categories due to the fact that many serials tend to be very broad in their subject content. The same is true of the serials-used profile in Figure 7.4. Furthermore, fields such as engineering contain significant numbers of publications in conference proceedings which would require specific coding efforts, and which could not be classified by the methods used here.

Figure 7.2   Profile of All Faculty by Publications Authored

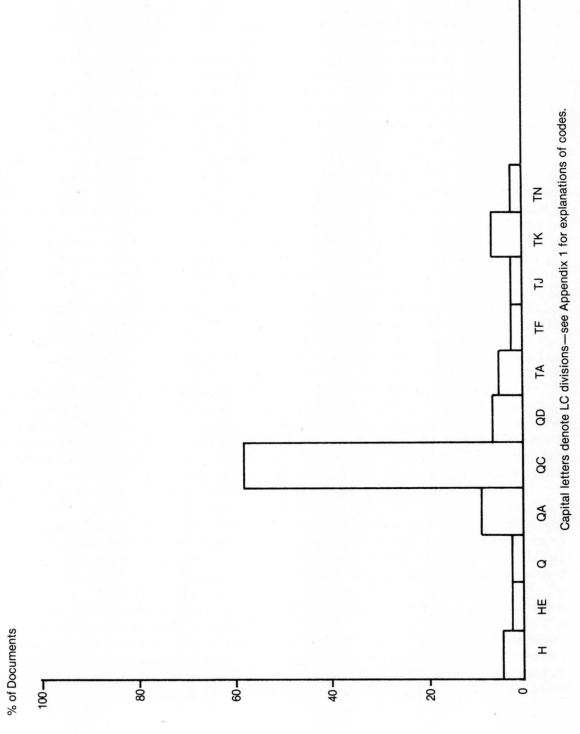

% of Documents

Capital letters denote LC divisions—see Appendix 1 for explanations of codes.

The research survey profile in Figure 7.3 shows a rich spectrum which cuts across virtually all applicable LC categories and forms a more reliable basis for identifying bibliographic requirements to support research. Detailed inspection of survey results showed that research grants, non-funded research projects and faculty dissertation topics provided the majority of the non-redundant data for this profile. Student research, usually funded by grants, was found to be tied to these efforts virtually without exception. The research survey was also advantageous because it reflected current work, as opposed to publications, which often lag far behind current research interests.

Serial use is reflected in the profile in Figure 7.4. As in the case of publications, the breadth of LC categories is limited. Furthermore, the serials indicated often did not differentiate well among various faculty specialties. All faculty, in some departments, subscribe to the same journals. This was particularly evident in Economics/Finance. Physics and Electrical Engineering departments subscribe to journals that are published in a number of separate series by field, which is helpful but still very general. Observation of serial use requires a direct survey of faculty. If one must resort to surveys, an instrument employing categories such as found in the NASA SCAN would provide a more specific classification of interest while minimizing data capture cost.

Finally, the NASA SCAN profile in Figure 7.5 shows the interest of faculty subscribing to this dissemination service by choice. Though a few Economics/Finance department faculty participated, the subject matter is primarily applicable to the Physics and Electrical Engineering faculty. Similar classifications exist or could be developed for all academic fields. The chore of mapping such a user-oriented system onto the LC classification is not an onerous task. A cataloger accomplished a mapping for the NASA SCAN in less than two days. Comparing the NASA SCAN profile to the research survey profile (see Figure 7.3) shows comparable coverage of areas (ignoring the economics codes which are not covered by the NASA SCAN).

A number of inferences, which will have impact on decision support system design, can be drawn from the above observations. For the purpose of establishing profiles of research interest, without quantitative indicators of productivity, the use of an established system of classification such as the NASA SCAN can give results which are comparable to a custom-coded, open-ended questionnaire. Precoding the user-related classification eliminates the need for continuous cataloging of data.

Data capture can be performed indirectly in most instances. In our case many faculty voluntarily subscribed to the NASA SCAN dissemination service. Additionally, one could require that grant proposals, student theses and dissertations, and faculty-authored publications also be coded using the same system of classification by means of a standard checklist-type form. Such documents could be read by mark-sensitive readers for computer processing, thus eliminating any manual coding by library staff.

Though interest profiles may be established using all of the above sources, a quantitative measure of productivity can only be obtained from documents arising from productive activities, i.e., grant proposals, dissertations, publications or other formal research activities normally reported to the institution. The productive events could then be accumulated and used as weighting factors in developing individual and aggregate profiles. For example, an indication of interest from any source can be given a base weight of 1 in an individual profile. A publication, grant proposal, etc., would give an additional weight of 1 for those

Figure 7.3   Profile of All Faculty by Research Survey

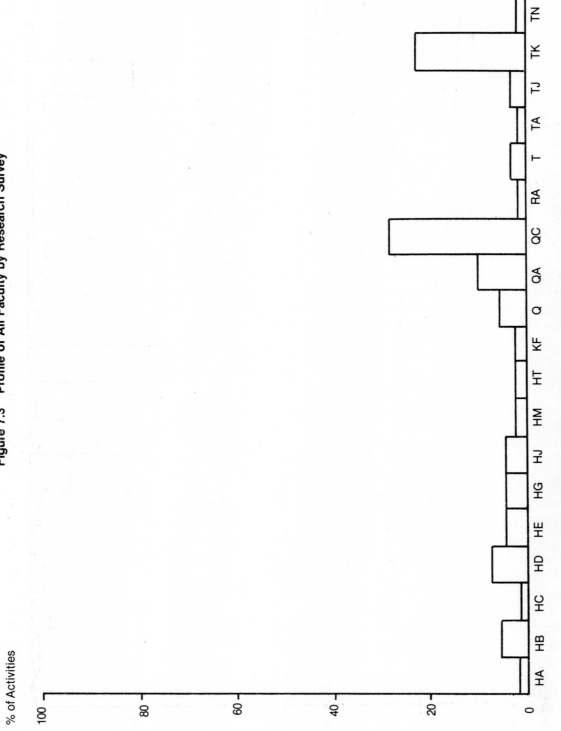

Capital letters denote LC divisions—see Appendix 1 for explanations of codes.

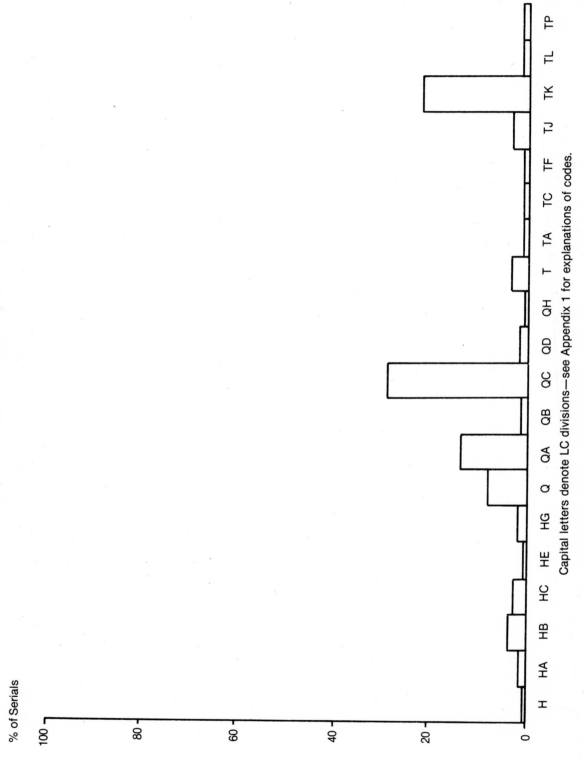

Figure 7.4   Profile of All Faculty by Serials Used

Figure 7.5   Profile of All Faculty by NASA SCAN Survey

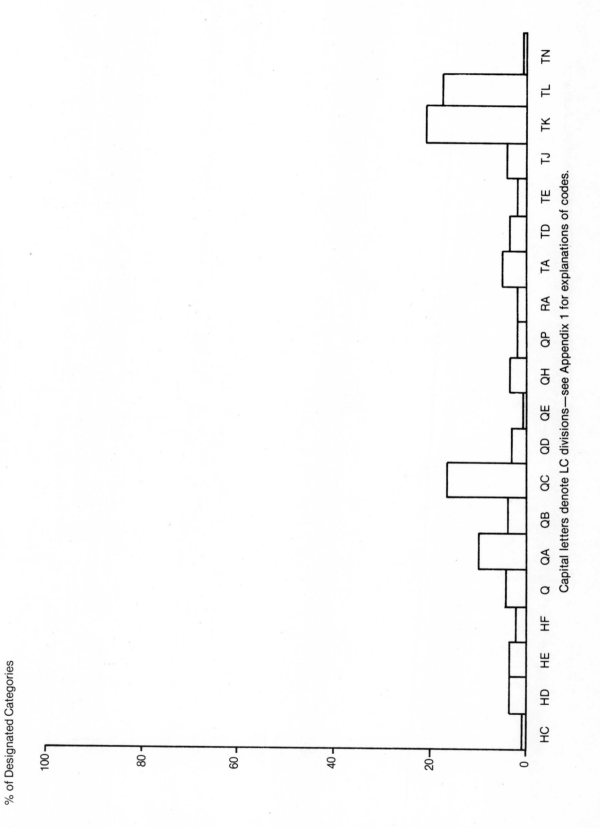

Capital letters denote LC divisions—see Appendix 1 for explanations of codes.

Figure 7.6   Profile of All Faculty by Combined Score from Research Projects and Publications Authored

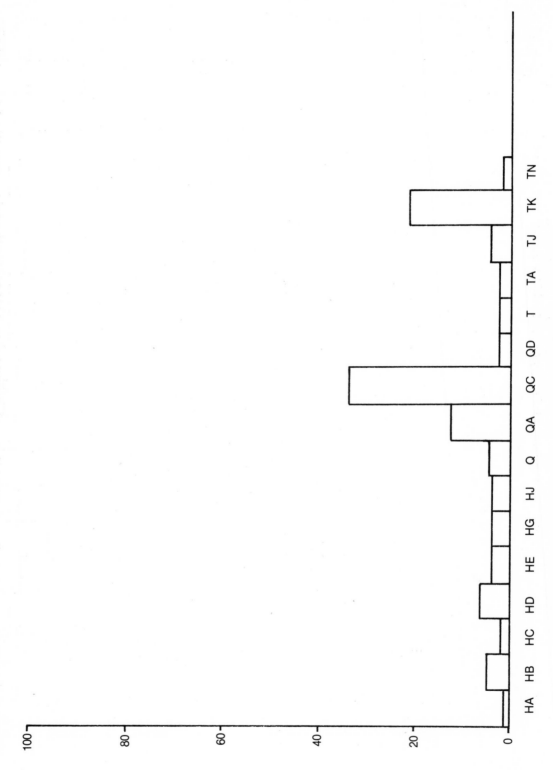

LC categories indicated as a result of mapping from the subject checklist. Each year individual profiles could be updated using both the old profile (attenuated by exponential smoothing, in which the most current year's data is emphasized more than that for previous years) and additions to the profile from the recent year's events. We developed such a profile from our data, as is shown in Figure 7.6.

- - - - - -

While the following chapter provides a framework for library management reporting, Chapter 9 will bring together all of the field trial findings in order to identify practical alternatives for implementing a library decision support system. A strategy will be presented which combines the use of existing technological capabilities with a minimum of additional hardware and software to develop an adequate decision support system for management.

8

Framework for Management Reporting

The three basic components of the library management reporting framework are institutional productivity, resource availability and resource utilization. Reports concerning system status and trends in each of these areas are essential for decision making at all levels of library management. Institutional productivity is manifested by the instructional and/or research thrusts of faculty and research workers. The degree of emphasis in specific subject areas as well as trends in new research and/or instructional programs have bearing on the allocation of library resources. The status of resource availability reflects the current capability of the library to meet both manifest and latent information needs. Finally, manifest demand, as exhibited by resource utilization, must be monitored since this constitutes the ultimate interaction between the library and its users.

DATA BASE COMPONENTS

For each of the three data base components, a pattern or profile may be developed to show the relative degree of emphasis or activity which exists across subject classes. For utilization, the distribution of transactions at the level of user/library interaction is the quantitative basis for developing a profile. For availability, a count of serials and monographs in stock can be classified by subject. However, the counting mechanism for productivity is not naturally determined and many alternatives exist (as discussed in the previous chapter). Nevertheless, a valid, quantitatively based profile is possible.

None of the three information components alone provides a sufficient stimulus for planning or control action. However, by observing deviations or differential trends between the components, problems can be identified and plausible explanations can be formulated. Thus, management action can be stimulated and directed. Let us take a moment to suggest the kinds of management information which might be obtained from comparing patterns of any two out of the three components.

The library should feel a considerable obligation to match the distribution of available resources to the distribution of manifest demand within the context of overall goals and objectives. This applies to both serials and monographs. The distribution of circulation

113

transactions, as well as in-library use and local photocopying, represent user demand that has been satisfied by local resources. When local utilization transactions, classified by subject, do not match the profile of locally available materials, this should be construed as a signal for management attention.

The fact that there is an abundance of resources in an area which has relatively little circulation is not necessarily a reason to reduce support in that subject area. There are many reasons for maintaining a comprehensive collection in an area where there is limited circulation, particularly in a major research library. Justification for the support of such a collection may be found by looking at the productivity profile. Management must also realize that a raw count of transactions is not an entirely valid measure of the relative importance of the circulation in a given area with respect to institutional objectives. These qualifications notwithstanding, there is at least a burden of proof resting on management to justify the mismatch. The existence of a productivity profile can be helpful in supplying the necessary rationale.

In evaluating the availability profile, management must also be aware of the age distribution, by publication date, of the resource materials in a given subject area. Sparse local utilization considering the quantity of available materials may be the result of obsolescence, which might reflect a recent lag in acquisitions. If this proves to be the case, an unmet latent demand might be present. Lancaster (1977) has noted the need for such indicators in evaluating library performance.

A decrease in local use with no matching decrease in productivity may also be an indication of poor selection of materials in the acquisition process. Such a conclusion might be reinforced by an increase in interlibrary loan requests in the same subject area. This would indicate the need for a better liaison between the acquisitions specialist for that subject and the user community. The productivity data base could be examined to identify the key users in the subject for consultation. This can be a more effective, problem-oriented means of keeping in contact with the user community than the customary departmental library representatives or institutional library committee.

Another worthwhile result of comparing use and availability arises when one compares the age distribution of each profile by publication date. A utilization distribution by age of materials will show the rate of obsolescence in a given subject area. Looking, then, at the availability distribution by age, a need for weeding or relocation of materials might be indicated.

The allocation of the periodicals budget is of considerable concern in libraries, particularly in research institutions where this may represent two-thirds of the collection development funds. This decision area is fraught with politics and no strictly objective means exists for making the allocation. The library manager must strive, however, for consistency and objectivity in making and defending decisions. For this purpose, all profile components may be brought to bear on the decisions. Circulation, in-library use and local photocopying demonstrate manifest demand. Substantial numbers of interlibrary loan requests may justify a local subscription if the trend is expected to continue. Sources of such requests may be consulted to discover whether the new demand is a transient one or a trend. Productivity profiles may be reviewed to determine the strength and breadth of activity in the subject area. Decline of activity and use in a subject area can help to identify which serials should be discontinued.

Thus, the objective evidence to direct and defend management decisions can be made available. This is in keeping with the spirit of support for semi-structured decisions. Though no formulas or models exist to prescribe a solution, the availability of relevant, objective information can serve to identify problems and indicate a more appropriate allocation. The quality of decisions can be improved and, of equal importance, the means exist to demonstrate to the institution the rationale for the decisions.

GENERALIZED REPORTING

We have already emphasized that support for semi-structured decisions requires generalized access to management information. The specific information requirements of such decisions cannot be anticipated to the extent that one can identify, in advance, the format and content of a suitable report or set of reports. Attempts to provide comprehensive, formal reports distributed at regular intervals always result in information overload. Compromises in format, timing, detail and scope are, therefore, unavoidable and restrict usefulness in those instances when more data would be helpful.

In short, managers are usually faced with more data than they need or can comprehend, but when they do need support, the structure and content of the information fall far short of what is required. Waiting until a need arises is not practical either. In most instances, the time required to capture and process the appropriate data far exceeds the interval within which the decision must be made. Also, the cost of such a special analysis often exceeds the potential value of the information. Thus, the concept of a generalized report system allows for a very broad area of decision support without the need to identify in advance the needs of a specific decision. When a problem or opportunity does arise, a relevant report can be tailored to the requirement and made available in an inexpensive and timely fashion.

Most management reporting with respect to operations arises as a by-product of transactions processing. In libraries this is evidenced by currently available automated circulation systems, most of which provide periodic statistical summaries of transactions. Such a capability represents little additional system cost. However, the fixed format and timing of these reports yields management information on a take-it-or-leave-it basis. Given the purpose of an automated circulation system, any attempt to do more would increase cost and, perhaps, sacrifice efficiency. Thus, a true decision support system must function as a separate system, receiving data from the circulation system and other sources and storing this information until it is needed by management. The retrieval process can then be tailored to management needs without interfering with transactions processing.

REPORT TYPES

In tailoring reports to management needs, timing and format are critical factors; a means to identify types of reports according to these factors must be established. With respect to timing, there are three types of reports:

- Periodic: Automatically distributed at fixed points in time;

- Intermittent: Automatically distributed upon the occurrence of some prescribed event or upon the attainment of some system state;

- *Ad hoc:* Requested at the discretion of the manager.

Independently of the timing dimension, reports may also be classified by the type of format control that exists; any of the following structures might be employed:

- Fixed report: Both format and data content are prescribed in advance and cannot be altered by the manager at the time of distribution;

- Parametric report: Much of the format is prescribed in advance but the manager may specify the data content and select from a menu of format alternatives;

- Report writer: In this form of computer software program, the manager has virtually complete control over format and data content, including titles, labels, calculations performed on stored data items as well as a choice of tables, graphs, bar charts, pie charts, etc. The report writer enables managers to prescribe their reports without writing a computer program. Once managers develop a report structure, they may catalog this structure for later reuse.

- Query language: In contrast with a report, a query is simply a question requiring a short and prompt answer. The query is formulated by the manager and presented to the computer in an English-like syntax and vocabulary. For example: "How many interlibrary loan requests were initiated by the Physics Department in 1979?" The structure of complex queries may be cataloged and reused.

Given any decision situation, it is possible to specify the ideal report type within the dimensions given above. Periodic reports are often the source of information overload. They should be concise and contain only data which are to be reviewed regularly for some predetermined purpose. Periodic reports are usually only useful as a way of keeping in touch with operations and identifying matters that require attention. Where the scope of surveillance is broad and many details must be monitored, periodic reports can become cumbersome. In such cases, an intermittent report which is triggered by some out-of-control condition would be more appropriate.

Periodic and intermittent reports used for surveillance do not (and should not) contain the degree of detail required for problem-solving. When a need for action is identified, an *ad hoc* report focusing on the problem area in considerable detail should be requested.

Fixed report formats are primarily useful for periodic or intermittent surveillance activities. Analysis and problem-solving require the flexibility to structure a report to fit the needs of the manager in dealing with a specific problem. Parametric reports and query languages are usually sufficient for most tasks where prompt retrieval is required. Despite the fact that programming is not required, report development through a report writer can be time-consuming and requires some skill. However, report writers are very useful where a manager wishes to have a tailored report for surveillance and control activities. The structure may be cataloged and used for periodic or intermittent distribution. Report writers may also be useful for major planning projects where immediate response is not essential.

DIMENSIONS OF DATA REPORTING

In a generalized report structure one cannot anticipate the exact data content of required reports. However, with some careful forethought, it is possible to identify and organize a sufficiently comprehensive data base which should be capable of satisfying most needs. In organizing the storage of such a data base it is important to keep in mind the most likely dimensions which will be employed in constructing tables, graphs and charts, such as by bibliographic subject, department, time, etc.

The various entities included in the data model have been already identified in Chapters 6 and 7. The numbers of volumes held and periodicals under subscription and in stock will be tabulated in the availability portion of the data base. Transactions will be recorded in the utilization portion. For instructional activity in a university setting, the tabulation could include numbers of courses, enrollees, majors or graduates. Research activity in any setting could include the number of LC category citations attributed by publications, projects, research grants, theses, dissertations and bibliographic search profiles. Most library management information concerning library and institutional operations can originate in such a data base.

By far the most important dimension for aggregating the above data is by bibliographic subject. The LC classification has been employed at two levels of aggregation. Of course, any intermediate level of aggregation can be accommodated. In addition, the HEGIS classification of university programs is also available through category-by-category mapping. These and other possible subject dimensions form the basis for profiles showing areas of emphasis in resources, needs, activities, etc.

A second dimension frequently used in reporting is time. For use and productivity, time is recorded as the date of a transaction or activity, respectively. These dates provide a basis for reporting trends, producing forecasts and observing shifts in profiles over time. With respect to availability and utilization, the publication dates of holdings are required to display the currency of the collection and the rate of obsolescence of literature in a given subject area. The rate of growth or decay of the collection over time can also be observed on the time dimension.

Finally, the user community may be partitioned into subsets for various reporting objectives. Department affiliation, faculty or student rank, project teams and research or instructional interest would be the most common attributes used to identify subsets. These subsets may be used to pinpoint utilization by and productivity of any one faction of the user community. They may also be used to identify the portion of the collection which should match a particular subset's profile of interest.

REPORT EXAMPLES

As a demonstration of the potential role of the proposed report structure, an attempt will be made to create a situation in which reports are used for both problem identification and analysis in a university setting. Since no availability data were collected in our field trials, only utilization and productivity data will be employed. In the utilization area, only circulation and interlibrary loan are considered.

In Figure 8.1, a bar graph showing circulation and interlibrary loan activity is typical

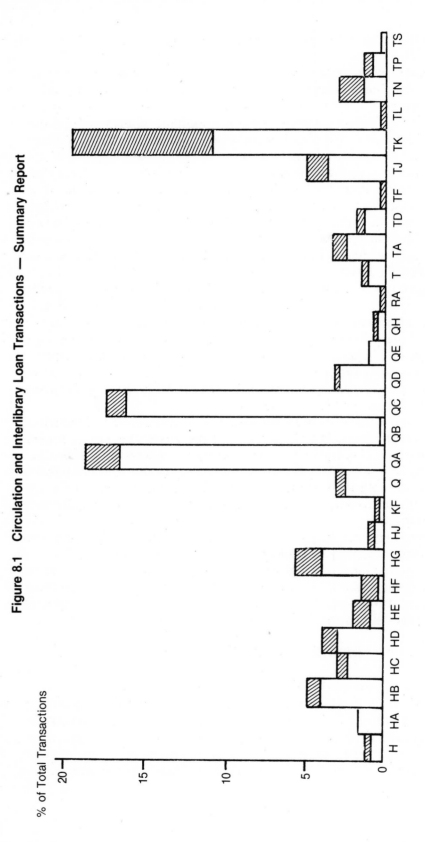

Figure 8.1   Circulation and Interlibrary Loan Transactions — Summary Report

Capital letters denote LC divisions—see Appendix 1 for explanations of codes.

of a periodic surveillance report. All three departments that participated in our field trials are aggregated in this chart, and comparisons between types of utilization across broad LC categories are easily viewed. This chart can be supported by more detailed numeric data if requested by the manager, but a graphic display is usually a more effective means of directing attention to problems.

Examination of Figure 8.1 shows disproportionately heavy use of interlibrary loans in category TK. A high percentage of loan activity with respect to circulation is also observed in categories HF, TN and TP. An explanation for the observed patterns calls for a more intensive exploration of the data pertaining to the LC categories in question. This requires *ad hoc* report generation using either a query language or a parametrically formatted report. Moreover, this report could be circulated periodically in a standard format without risk of information overload.

A closer look at circulation and loan activity within the TK category shows three LC subcategories responsible for virtually all of the loan activity (see Table 8.1). Thus, it is possible to pinpoint the problem within a narrow set of LC ranges. Another intensive view may be taken with respect to the users and types of documents involved. Table 8.2 identifies the users involved in the TK loans including the number of documents requested, department affiliation, years employed and rank. Table 8.3 depicts the type of document borrowed via interlibrary loan by each user. The specific journals involved and what percentage of the loans are monographs in each detailed LC category are readily available. These data may have bearing on subscription decisions and the quality of monograph acquisition decisions. In any case, the specific users have been identified, and a brief interview with those generating large numbers of loans will be helpful.

It is interesting to note that all but one of the loans were requested by users with two or fewer years at the institution and at the rank of Assistant Professor or lower. Typically, newer and younger faculty at an institution tend to be sources of new directions in research and teaching. On the other hand, the stock of monograph and periodical holdings tends to reflect the input and needs of the more established faculty. Thus, this reporting capability has been able to identify a trend through formal rather than informal means.

To bring a broader perspective into the analysis, let us focus on productivity as well as utilization. The bar graph in Figure 8.2 depicts the relative importance of the TK category in teaching and research activities (using measures discussed in Chapter 7) as well as substantial utilization. The vertical axis indicates percent of teaching, research, circulation or interlibrary loan activity, respectively. These four separate activities have been combined into one chart for ease of analysis. The chart indicates that the TK category is most significant of all in both teaching and research. A more intensive view of the TK category alone is shown in Table 8.4. Here the three LC ranges (not including "Other TK") responsible for the bulk of interlibrary loan activity are differentially divided between research and teaching. Conclusions about the adequacy of the collection for these activities require consultation with the faculty identified in Tables 8.2 and 8.3.

The above illustration is intended to demonstrate the value of a reporting capability to deliver support for both surveillance and analysis. The variety of paths that an analysis might take precludes the feasibility of periodic, fixed-format reports playing a significant role. For example, if the TK category had proved to be strictly a teaching area, the analysis might have focused on courses in the area and their support requirements, in which case the loan requests may have been intended for the purpose of producing supplemental readings for students.

Table 8.1   Circulation and Interlibrary Loan Transactions — Detail Report for Category TK

LC Range	Description	Circulations		Interlibrary Loans		Combined Total	
		Number	% of Combined Total	Number	% of Combined Total	Number	% of Combined Total
TK	Electrical Eng. - General	32	25.6%	20	16.0%	52	41.6%
TK 5101-5105	Telecommunications - General	2	1.6	16	12.8	18	14.4
TK 7800-7882	Electronics	13	10.4	11	8.8	24	19.2
Other TK		27	21.6	4	3.2	31	24.8
		74	59.2%	51	40.8%	125	100.0%

Table 8.2   Interlibrary Loan Transactions — Detail Report of Users for Category TK

USERID[1]	Number of Loans	User Name	Dept.	Rank	Number of Years Employed
7	3	Joe Brown	Physics	Asst.	1
17	1	Sam Green	Elec. Eng.	Asst.	6
19	6	Sue White	Elec. Eng.	Asst.	2
31	23	Bill Gray	Elec. Eng.	Asst.	2
38	1	Mary Black	Elec. Eng.	Asst.	1
39	17	Tom Blue	Elec. Eng.	Inst.	2

[1] See Appendix 2 for data base definitions.

Figure 8.2   Distribution of Teaching, Research, Interlibrary Loan and Circulation Activity

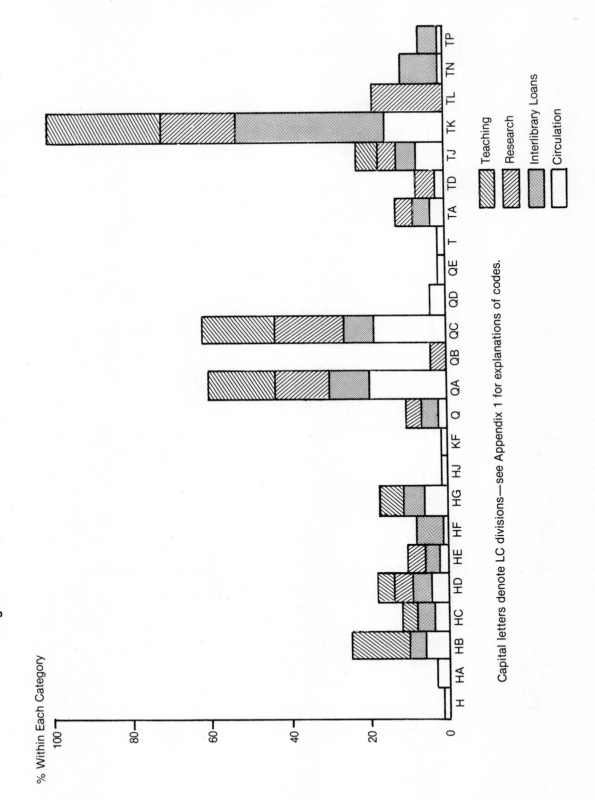

Capital letters denote LC divisions—see Appendix 1 for explanations of codes.

Table 8.3   Interlibrary Loan Transactions — Detail Report of Documents for Category TK

USERID	Number of Loans	Document Requested
7	1	Electrotechnology
	1	Journal of the Institute of Electronics & Communications Engineers of Japan
	1	Book – Electronics
17	1	Telesystems Journal
19	1	Operations Research – Verfahren
	1	Weltwirtschaftliches Archiv (Hamburg)
	1	Asterisque
	2	Environment
	1	Izvestiya Vysshikh Uchebnykh Zuvedenii
31	1	Associazione Elettrotecnica Italiana
	1	Philips Technical Review
	1	Elektrik Mukendisligie
	4	Book – Electrical Engineering – General
	2	Soviet Electrical Engineering
	1	Solar Energy Digest
	1	Proceedings of the IEE, London
	1	Book – Dist. & Trans. of Elec. Power
	1	Electric Power Systems Research
	1	International Journal of Circuit Theory and Applications
	1	Engineering in a Changing Economy
	7	Book – Electronics
	1	Indian Journal of Technology
38	1	Book – Electrical Engineering – General
39	14	Book – Telecommunications – General
	2	Comsat Technical Review
	1	Alta Frequenza
Total	51	

Table 8.4   Circulation, Interlibrary Loans, Research and Teaching — Detail Report for Category TK

LC Range	Component as % of Total TK Circulation	Component as % of Total TK Interlibrary Loans	Component as % of Total TK Research	Component as % of Total TK Teaching
TK	43.2%	39.2%	8.0%	13.9%
TK 5101-5105	2.7	31.4	8.0	11.1
TK 7800-7882	17.6	21.6	44.0	19.4
Other TK	36.5	7.8	40.0	55.6
	100.0%	100.0%	100.0%	100.0%

Ultimately, a response to a problem will require input from faculty. However, the value of the decision support system is in (1) identifying the existence of problems; (2) placing the problems in perspective with regard to the overall productive activities of the institution; (3) setting priorities on the solution of problems involving competition for resources; and (4) identifying specific sources of problems such as faculty, teaching programs and research projects. Such a balanced and comprehensive view is invaluable to rational decision making. All too often the alternative is to allocate resources on the basis of "oiling the squeaky wheel," serving the "important" programs, meeting crises or simply taking an archival approach to the literature. Instead, a decision support system puts library management in close touch with the activities, problems and needs of its users.

9

Implementation Considerations

In Chapter 6 a data base schema was presented of the data elements considered feasible for the purpose of representing the utilization, availability and productivity dimensions of the library and its environment. After evaluating the results of the field trials in Chapter 7 and considering the report requirements of library management in Chapter 8, it is now time to focus on a subset of the original schema. Redundant and unnecessary components have been eliminated. Separate schemata have been developed for academic and special libraries; these are presented in Figures 9.1 and 9.2. (A detailed description of the data content is given in Appendix 2.)

In both schemata the LC-SERIAL file contains the fundamental basis for classifying library documents, institutional activities and users. Any number of intermediate classifications are also possible. In both schemata the NASA file represents the NASA SCAN dissemination service employed in the field study. However, any similar classifications may also be employed to directly relate user interests and the LC-SERIAL file. The mapping of one system of classification onto another is represented in NASA-LC. Users, however, express their interests directly in terms of a familiar classification in the NASA-FAC or NASA-USER files.

In the academic setting, institutional activities are included in the RESEARCH and COURSE files. These are classified indirectly into the LC-SERIAL categorization in the schema. In the case of RESEARCH, the intervening classification will prove useful since users are likely to be required to code their own research endeavors. For the research or special library setting, we have represented a typical research and development institution. In place of the RESEARCH file, we have substituted the designation TASK. USERS are assigned to tasks, and tasks are usually associated with projects (though not necessarily). Both TASK and PROJECT are separately classified within the LC-SERIAL category file.

In both schemata, provision is made to classify departments. The HEGIS code is appropriate for the academic setting, but, for research or special libraries, the ACTIVITY code will probably be unique to the institution. These intervening codes are useful where several departments may be engaging in the same class of activity, and each department may be involved in more than one activity. Finally, all library-related activities are coded directly into the LC-SERIAL classification system in both schemata.

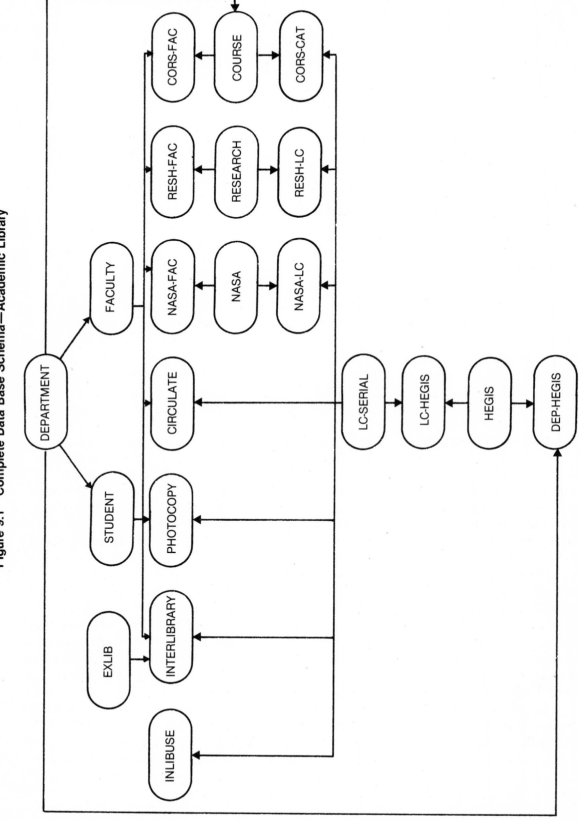

Figure 9.1   Complete Data Base Schema—Academic Library

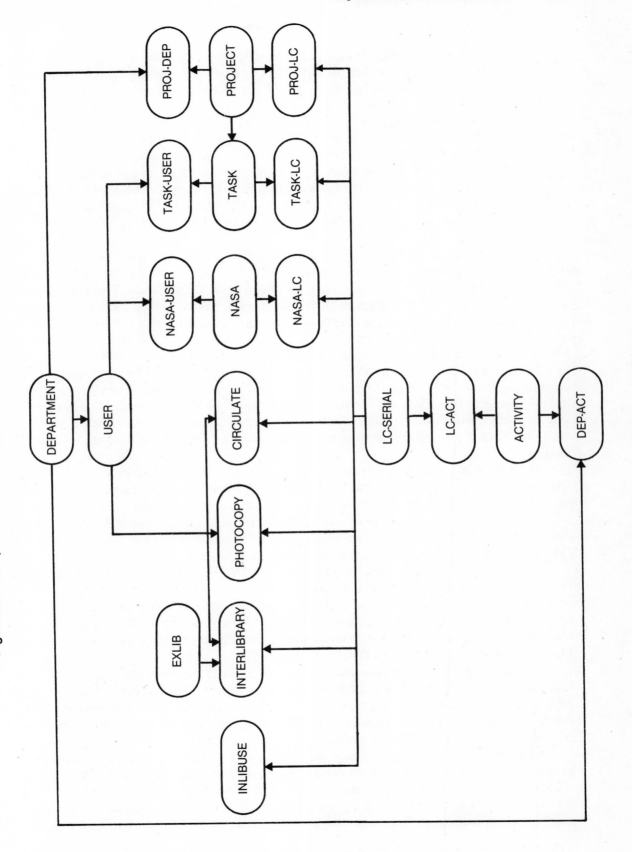

Figure 9.2 Complete Data Base Schema—Research and Development Library

Data concerning individual utilization transactions are recorded as they occur in temporary transaction files. These files are then used as input in a periodic batch update of the management data base. Because of the large volume of these transactions, only summary records are kept in the data base.

Summary records are kept by type of utilization: INTERLIBRARY, CIRCULATE, PHOTOCOPY and INLIBUSE. A separate record occurrence exists for each user and LC category with total number of transactions recorded by year of publication and year of transaction. A quick look at Appendix 2 will indicate that the list of LC categories is extended to include serials by title as separate categories. Linkages exist between the various utilization records and the LC category listing (LC-SERIAL) file. These linkages may be used to assemble the utilization data into profiles by LC, HEGIS or ACTIVITY categories.

Serials not held by the library are also included in the LC-SERIAL file. Statistics may thus be reported concerning potential new subscriptions. Note that the INTERLIBRARY file has record occurrences distinguished by an originating library code. This code provides a linkage to the EXLIB file. Thus, with respect to each source library for loans and photocopies, statistics may be reported concerning amount of activity, average waiting time and average cost. These data are extremely useful to the interlibrary loan clerk who must look for the best source for placing requests as a function of LC-SERIAL category.

For a library that has computer records of its monograph holdings, a second set of summary statistics may be kept for circulation, in-library use and photocopying by individual monograph. This file is not included in the schema diagrams in order to avoid confusion, and this portion of the data base is not crucial to most management needs, but is easily included if monograph catalog records are already available on a computer-readable medium.

Teaching and research productivity in the academic setting are recorded in the data base shown in Figure 9.1. This part of the data base schema and the corresponding file descriptions (see Appendix 2) were derived from the field trial experience. The CORS-CAT file is crucial to classifying teaching activity by subject and this process has already been described. The CORS-FAC file links teaching assignments to individual faculty members. Courses are also linked to the departments offering them.

Research activity has been consolidated into the RESEARCH file. For every research event (publication, funded research project, dissertation or thesis supervised, etc.) a record occurrence is created. It is assumed that the researcher involved will provide a classification of the event from a list of descriptors appropriate to the general subject area (physics, electrical engineering, economics, mathematics, etc.). A mapping of these subject lists onto the LC classification is presumed to exist.

Recording research activities—through annual reports, departmental publication lists, research grants office, etc.—is a common process in almost all universities. The least costly method of data capture is to ask respondents to classify their entries from a pre-defined list of categories. The library then is responsible for assembling these data from the most convenient sources in the institution and key-entering them.

Although the research coding described above is the minimum and most useful source of data concerning research activity, other sources may also exist. Figure 9.1 includes the NASA SCAN as a measure of research interest which can be conveniently recorded. This is typical of the current awareness services which exist at many institutions. To be workable, the classification method must employ a pre-defined, closed list of subject topics.

In a research or special library setting, supporting research and development activities —for example, research projects and tasks—may be coded in a similar fashion. A classification familiar to research workers and project managers must be developed and mapped onto the LC-SERIAL category file. In Figure 9.2 the TASK-LC, PROJ-LC and LC-ACT files represent these pre-defined mappings. The profiles of individual institutional activities are recorded (in the user-oriented classification) in the TASK, PROJECT and ACTIVITY files.

A practical implementation of the above data base schemata is possible not only in a large library that already employs computers in a variety of ways but also in a small library that is only beginning to consider computer applications. The key to successful implementation is staged growth and careful integration with existing and future computer subsystems.

In the following sections we will describe how the decision support system may be implemented as a set of related subsystems. Each subsystem can make a significant contribution to management needs independently of the other. The ability of a given library to implement each subsystem will depend upon the level and kind of technology already in place in that library institution. Subsystems requiring significant additional investment in technology could be delayed, and the decision support system could be introduced in stages. At each stage, the level of information available to support management decisions would be marginally enhanced until a comprehensive system is in place. The subsystem may be identified as productivity, utilization or availability.

PRODUCTIVITY SUBSYSTEM

The productivity subsystem is examined first since this is certainly the most unique component of the proposed decision support system. All libraries have at least a rudimentary, formal means of keeping track of utilization and availability for management purposes. However, surveillance of user needs, with respect to their productive efforts, is seldom addressed in any formal way other than, perhaps, by appointing departmental library representatives or a library committee. Also, in large libraries, subject specialist librarians may be assigned to specific subject areas. Communication and decision making that employ these means are largely unsupported by comprehensive, quantitative information. Thus, of all of the subsystems proposed, the productivity subsystem would likely have the greatest marginal impact on library management.

Data capture for productivity surveillance requires a type of effort not currently in existence in libraries. On the other hand, only a minimal amount of additional technology would be required. Collection of enrollment statistics, project and task data, faculty teaching assignments and classification mapping are labor-intensive. Data entry can be accommodated with a single, conventional terminal linked to the institution's computing system. Similarly, collection of activity data is also labor-intensive, though care should be taken to minimize the classification task for user respondents. Much of the labor is required only at the inception of the productivity subsystem. Classification mapping is predominantly a one-time-only procedure. Likewise, most of the effort associated with capturing activity data lies in the development of appropriate user-oriented subject classification lists. Having accomplished these tasks at one library, the fruit of this effort can be largely duplicated with only minor modification in other similar libraries. This is especially true in academic settings.

While developing the data capture procedures, provision should also be made for processing and reporting these data. These facilities need not be in place for any single subsystem. The existing university computing facility and commonly available statistical software packages would be sufficient initially. Most of the schemata presented above and all of the charts and tables presented in this report were developed using the SAS software.* Some skill is necessary to use this software, and, therefore, this should only be considered as an interim measure. Over the course of time and concurrent with the implementation of other subsystems, more convenient data handling and reporting software can be developed.

UTILIZATION SUBSYSTEM

Successful implementation of this subsystem is highly dependent on technology, and several alternatives are possible. Many libraries already have automated circulation systems which, aside from their primary function of transaction processing, claim to provide a variety of management information. However, all of these systems provide only a limited capability to specify what is reported and the formats employed. Management information is strictly a take-it-or-leave-it by-product of these systems, and most of the reports are intended only to control the circulation process itself.

Tampering with the software in these stand-alone, turnkey systems is not recommended. Improving their reporting capability would still be subject to significant constraints. Furthermore, there is no possibility that such a system could be enhanced to be able to incorporate all of the subsystems being considered here. Moreover, vendors of these systems would disclaim any responsibility for maintaining altered systems.

Rather than trying to turn a transactions processing tool into a management reporting system, the focus should be on the data capture features of automated circulation systems. All of these systems provide a convenient means of identifying the document and the user at the time of the transaction. Users are identified by machine-reading a magnetic strip identification card. Documents are identified by reading a bar code or special printed characters fixed to the document itself. In addition to recording circulation transactions, other reading devices can be employed to record photocopy transactions and reshelving. Having an automated circulation system in place makes the implementation of the utilization subsystem straightforward. The library has already absorbed the cost of tagging documents and installing most of the data capture hardware. Transaction records accumulated by the circulation system can be used as batch input to update the utilization data base. Processing and reporting software requirements would be the same as for the other subsystems.

If an automated circulation system is not in place, there are a number of alternatives. Since each of these alternatives requires expenditure for hardware and a significant implementation effort, it is not recommended they be considered unless there is no prospect of adopting an automated circulation system in the near future. Manual data entry at the circulation station poses the principal clerical burden. A computer terminal similar to that used for entering interlibrary loan transactions could be employed. However, unlike the interlibrary loan station where direct access to the data base is desirable, the circulation

---

*SAS is a software product distributed by SAS Institute, Inc., Cary, NC, and is currently available for use on IBM computers.

station does not require inquiry capability. Circulation transactions could be recorded locally on tape cassette or flexible disk media. These records could then be entered into the data base in batch mode later. Both the identification number of the client and the LC code of the document would be entered. Unless the data is to be used for maintaining a current circulation file, the full LC code need not be entered.

Manual entry of the user identification could be replaced by issuing magnetic strip cards to clients and installing strip readers at the checkout stations. To automatically read document codes will involve using more sophisticated and expensive equipment, which requires that all documents be labeled. Incurring such costs strictly to implement the utilization subsystem of the decision support system is not recommended. However, the manual approach does appear feasible as an interim measure until automated circulation is introduced. In fact, the manual data entry approach and the development of DSS software could be extended to record keeping of circulation transactions. This is not as difficult to accomplish as it might appear at first. Much of the difficulty encountered by libraries introducing automated circulation stems from the cost of labeling documents and the reliability of the sophisticated hardware for automatic reading. The software required in such systems is quite straightforward, easily written in-house and easily adapted to run on any general-purpose university computer.

Data capture for photocopying and interlibrary loan is more easily accomplished manually than it is for circulation data due to the lower volume of activity. In-library use (reshelving) could also be recorded manually with portable recording devices, but the volume of activity may preclude this in some libraries. Portable devices are in common use in industry, for example, in recording inventory in warehouses.

Thus, for the library already equipped with automated circulation, the utilization subsystem is easily implemented with little additional cost. Where no automated circulation system exists, the feasibility of a manual or semiautomatic system depends largely upon the volume of various utilization activities. Low-volume transactions present no problem. However, the investment in a utilization data capture system for decision support alone is not justified. Interim measures would be necessary until an automated circulation system is installed.

AVAILABILITY SUBSYSTEM

Provision has already been made to include an inventory of periodicals held by the library in the LC-SERIAL file, which also includes periodicals frequently requested through interlibrary loan. However, as mentioned earlier, this file would only record the number of monographs held within fairly broad LC categories. As long as these records are maintained accurately, this is certainly a sufficient level of detail for management decisions. No effort to record the existence or circulation of individual monographs is justified from a management information standpoint.

Many libraries, however, already possess a machine-readable file of monograph holdings either through the use of an online card catalog or through their automated circulation system (though some circulation systems do not attempt to maintain such an inventory). If such technology exists, it may easily be integrated into a data base schema.

Maintaining a broadly classified but accurate availability inventory within the LC-SERIAL file will require continuing manual update of the data base as acquisitions and weeding take place. A one-time inventory of documents on hand by publication date as well as periodic verification of the holdings to account for lost documents are also necessary.

PROCESSING AND REPORTING

It is assumed that the library has available the hardware and support services of the institution's computing system. A stand-alone computer system would not be justified solely for the library decision support system. Despite the advances in the microcomputer field, reliable systems capable of handling large files and large volumes of data entry are still about five years away. Furthermore, it is doubtful that hardware available for automated circulation could be successfully adapted to accommodate this additional burden. All data entry, processing, storage and reporting should be feasible on a large, general-purpose machine in either online or batch mode.

If an initial implementation consists of only one subsystem, then an existing data management and statistical software package, such as SAS, should be sufficient for interim processing and reporting. Though not ideal, such a package can be employed as a development tool, and can also give management an opportunity to explore the types of report capabilities which might prove most useful. Later, special software development could focus on these needs.

As the data base grows and new subsystems are added, a true data base management system (DBMS) will be required. This software should provide report writer and query/update components. The report writer would be used to structure both periodic and intermittent reports to be produced. Using this system, the report formats are formally described without the need for programming and then cataloged for reuse as required. The query/update facility enables management to retrieve responses to *ad hoc* questions of fact in a real-time mode. Changes, additions and deletions can also be made to the data base where only a few data items are affected.

Commercially available DBMSs provide the utilities necessary for maintenance and security of stored data. However, some special edit programs would have to be written to validate data entry operations, most of which would be performed in batch mode. Careful attention must be paid to the design of the entire data entry system in order to assure accuracy and consistency in the data base.

Many institutions already have a DBMS in place or are contemplating the addition of such a facility. The library DSS would be but one of many applications which would be able to use this facility. Many of the large DBMSs are quite expensive and acquisition could not be justified by the library application alone. However, a number of packages do exist which are supplied by hardware vendors either free or at modest cost. There are also a few, less sophisticated DBMSs available at reasonable prices but with limited utilities, query/update and report writer capabilities. These would require more programming effort. This programming effort is highly transferable to other implementations, however, since the rudimentary DBMS software available is written in commonly available languages such as FORTRAN, BASIC or PL/1.

The above observations on the cost-benefit of employing DBMS software must be viewed with some reservation. Since technology is rapidly advancing in this area, some impressive DBMS software is available on mini- and even microcomputer systems. It is not unreasonable to forecast that, within a few years, a complete, stand-alone microcomputer system with full data management and reporting software and sufficient data storage capacity will be available to serve as a dedicated library management tool for under $15,000. Thus, many of our statements concerning economic feasibility are very conservative and reflect advice to a library that intends to begin implementation today.

Given the rapid advancement of technology and the likelihood that development of a complete library DSS would take place over a number of years, it is essential that planning for a DSS be focused on the logical design—i.e., the reporting requirements and the underlying data base schema. During this logical design process, existing, general-purpose hardware and software should be employed as much as possible. As the logical design becomes fixed, the issue of choosing the most appropriate hardware and software environment can be addressed. However, the logical system design should never be married to existing technology in the way that circulation and online catalog systems have sometimes been. The DSS should be capable of evolving in a compatible fashion with advances in library operations and changes in management needs.

10

Summary and Conclusions

The need for a clearly defined approach to supporting the decision processes in libraries was well established in Chapters 2 and 3. The most important conclusion derived from that discussion was that the support system must encompass sources of information from the institutional environment in which the academic, research or special library operates. Keeping track of available resources and utilization transactions is simply not enough. The DSS must also be capable of tracking institutional directions and activities.

A second important conclusion arrived at from the discussion in Chapter 3 is that there is no single, consistent pattern of agreement among library managers as to what the important decisions are. Among the many factors that dictate the relative importance of various decision tasks are: size of library, utilization mix, volume of utilization activity, space restrictions, planning for new facilities and budget constraints. In addition, the relative importance of these factors will shift over time in any given library. Thus, library managers are no different than middle managers in other organizations with respect to their need for flexible and evolvable decision support. The DSS must be tailored to meet shifting needs as well as different managerial styles.

Library managers, to make effective plans and decisions, require timely access to relevant information and appropriate tools for information analysis. Managers, however, differ in their requirements for information type, content and form. Educational backgrounds, experiences, personalities, values, perceptions, etc. all affect the manner in which different managers execute their responsibilities. The decision-making process is often informal, with managers collecting and piecing together information until patterns or mental models emerge as a result of using a trial-and-error sequential exploration approach. The experience and judgment of the manager can then be applied to develop effective alternatives and solutions. Highly structured information systems are not helpful in meeting these diverse needs caused by the individuality of judgment and actions on the part of different managers.

A DSS FOR LIBRARY MANAGERS

The types of decisions faced by library managers vary widely along a number of dimensions. Some decisions are highly structured while others are quite unstructured. The degree of structure of a decision depends upon the degree of complexity of the decision and the degree to which salient factors can be identified, measured and related in a coherent fashion. Decision types also vary according to the functional area in which they apply within the organization. Functional areas for libraries might be defined in terms of collection development, technical services, reference and bibliographic service, etc.

The level of decision making in an organization further serves to define and describe the decision process. A convenient system for classifying decisions based on organizational hierarchy is according to the decision levels of strategic planning, management control and operational control. Finally, the decision-making process can be further defined according to the various stages of decision making. Three distinct stages of decision making can be identified as: involvement in intelligence (searching for problems and opportunities); design (defining and analyzing alternative actions); and choice (selecting and implementing a course of action). Again, traditional information systems are not effective in supporting decision making in many of these categories, especially the less structured problems, problems at the management and strategic planning levels, and decisions at the intelligence and design stages. Decisions in these areas represent some of the more important problems facing library management today.

What is needed is a support system which is sufficiently robust and flexible to aid managers with individual mental styles and approaches in making decisions which vary widely in type and makeup. The development of a DSS for library managers would seem to satisfy many of these diverse needs. Decision support systems use the recent advances in computer technology to assist and extend the decision-making capabilities of management; they recognize the unique decision-making styles and preferences of different managers; and they are designed with flexibility sufficient to accommodate these varying needs. This flexibility in design allows different managers to process and retrieve different information according to different dimensions, formats and levels of detail. Classification and graphic analysis comparisons allow contrasts of various information elements to one another and enable them to be viewed in the context of different time periods so trends and relationships can be observed. Unlike the traditional management information system and Operations Research techniques, the emphasis of a DSS is on the decision *process* rather than the decision *product*. A DSS assists managers in all stages of decision making—from problem identification and formulation to choosing a final alternative. The information and analysis tools provided by a DSS allow managers to use more fully their judgment and insights in all phases of the problem-solving process. A DSS is particularly valuable in helping managers use their own problem-solving approach dealing with less structured problems, especially at the management control and strategic planning levels. A capability which allows managers to question, probe, analyze and ultimately choose, using their individual insights and judgments in these areas, is highly desirable.

Identifying Key Decision Tasks

As a first step in developing a Decision Support System, key decision tasks facing library managers were identified and described. Research findings and decision models relating to each task were reviewed with the purpose of providing insight into problem solution and identifying key data elements of value in the decision process. The purpose of this process was to provide a conceptual foundation for the design of a DSS with respect to the decision-making process and potential information elements used in this process. The decision tasks were mapped out according to functional areas of library operation and decision-making organization levels—strategic planning and management control. The functional areas in which key decision tasks were identified include: collection development, technical services, reference and bibliographic service, collection access, access to interlibrary loan and physical facilities.

Interviews with selected library managers were helpful in further defining the identity of the key decision tasks. Although agreement was not reached on specific priorities, as different libraries valued different decision tasks according to their own unique goals and objectives, resource availability, sharing arrangements, etc., there was a high degree of agreement on the key decision tasks identified. These decision tasks were discussed in detail in Chapters 4 and 5.

Using a Data Base Approach

A data base approach was employed in specifying the design of the library decision support system. This procedure was followed for two reasons. First, the objective of the project was not to produce a system for a specific academic library. Second, and more importantly, since few research findings are available on data base compositions and structure in support of library decision-making activities, it is necessary to explore and understand these implications for the design of the decision support system. In designing a DSS it is important to anticipate the variety of requirements expected of a DSS, shifts in emphasis and objectives and differences in managerial styles. Recognizing these factors, it is also important to develop data base capabilities which will meet the broadest range of user requirements. By focusing on data base composition and file structure initially, the greatest degree of breadth and flexibility can be built in to meet a variety of information retrieval, relatability and display needs of a DSS. Once this is accomplished, the necessary data capture and software components can be designed to support the decision tasks of library managers.

The data base approach can be viewed in terms of functional conceptual components. User productivity or activity can be defined as the research and educational activities of an individual student or faculty member, a class, a program or a group of users. User needs can be viewed in terms of problem spaces which define the manner in which users conceptualize a problem or task. Information relevant to problem spaces resides in information bases representing text-format information within or outside of the institution. To identify information relevant to a problem space within these information bases, the problem space must be first characterized in terms of a profile of user needs. These profiles of user needs can be described according to information descriptors which can also be used to structure the manner in which information is classified and cataloged.

Measuring Utilization, Availability and Productivity

Considering the user's set of problem spaces as input to the library system and user productivity or activity as the ultimate objective, other components of the system are then defined. Utilization of service occurs when a user actually receives information from the system. Availability identifies the set of holdings or information bases accessible by the user. The degree to which available resources are used and the ultimate contribution of a library to user productivity should be monitored and reported. This feedback on use and productivity can be used by the library manager in making decisions and allocating resources relevant to the availability of library services and information bases. A key task of this work has been to demonstrate that practical and valid measures of these concepts can be implemented on a cost-effective, operational basis in a library.

Institutional goals and directions as well as environmental opportunities represent important factors of input to library management planning and control activities. Formal indicators of these factors are difficult to develop, and our study only suggests that informal assessments must be given explicit recognition through the assignment of priorities to modulate the aggregate institutional needs profile. Some important institutional classifications of needs under which priorities can be assigned include: educational level (lower division undergraduate, upper division undergraduate, graduate level and continuing education); educational problems (departmental, interdisciplinary, etc.); research and development programs (funded grants, institutes, etc.); and special programs in nonacademic organizations. The degree of institutional emphasis to be placed on these various programs can be assessed subjectively and expressed quantitatively by assigning priorities and selectively adjusting the profiles developed for productivity and utilization.

Users' activities, utilization and interests can be expressed as a profile across a set of categories or classes of subject matter. Similarly, library resources (availability) and aggregate use transactions can be expressed as a profile of relative emphases or strengths across subject categories. In order to relate user profiles with library profiles, the set of subject categories must be identical or a procedure must be available to map the different classification systems on to each other.

Classification, Attributes and Activity Patterns

There appears to be no single, universal, generally accepted subject classification system. After exploring a number of different approaches, the Library of Congress (LC) classification system was decided upon for subject categorization. The principal advantage of the LC system is that most academic, research and special libraries are already using this system for managing and controlling their information resources and to have them monitor and report transactions by any other system of organization would be unacceptable. Adoption of this system requires a mapping process that can relate institutional programs and user profiles to the LC categories for library information availability and utilization transactions. Procedures for accomplishing such a mapping are discussed in Chapter 6.

To maintain a general and evolvable decision support system, the underlying data base must, in effect, be a model of all relevant features and the overall environment of the organization being managed. Components of this model include all relevant entities (e.g., a document, a department, a student, a faculty member) which exist, permanently or temporarily, and all relevant events (e.g., a circulation transaction, an interlibrary loan request, etc.) which take place at various points in time. The scope and detail with which events and entities are described is a design decision based on need and feasibility. Often it is sufficient to describe aggregations of entities of a certain type or of events over a period of time. Entities and events are described by their attributes, which are measurable values of relevant characteristics. Again, the choice of which attributes are worth recording is a design decision. In addition to entities, events and their attributes, it is important to describe the relationships between entities and events. General relatability is often overlooked when designing files and reports to support a specific decision. A general approach to designing a DSS must include a capability to relate data in a flexible fashion.

A number of field trials were conducted in an academic setting to explore the feasibility of data collection, data base devlopment and data base implementation. The focus of the field trials was on developing profiles of faculty activity as manifested by their research and teaching productivity, patterns of utilization and expressions of interests. These profiles reflect the degree of activity as well as its distribution in terms of LC categories.

None of the field trials purported to use a representative sample of faculty across all disciplines or institutions. Rather, the emphasis was placed on identifying efficient and valid data collection procedures. The results of these trials are reported in Chapter 7. While individual patterns of activity may vary from those observed for the specialized fields of study in the trials, the techniques described should be applicable to all fields of study.

USING THE DSS EFFECTIVELY

In general, a support system for less structured decisions requires generalized access to pertinent data. The specific information requirements with regard to content and format of management reports can usually not be identified in advance. Attempts to provide comprehensive, formal reports, distributed at regular intervals, usually result in information overload and are often incompatible with the cognitive style of the manager. Thus, the manager is usually faced with an excess of data when support is not required and a lack of relevant data in terms of desired mode, content and structure when support is required to solve a particular issue or problem. In most cases, the time required to capture and process the appropriate data for an issue or problem exceeds the interval period within which the decision must be made. Also, the cost of such a special analysis often exceeds the potential value of the information.

Thus, the concept of a generalized report support system allows for a very broad area of decision support without having to identify in advance the needs of a specific decision. When a problem or opportunity does arise, a relevant report can be tailored to the need and made available in a timely fashion. Chapter 8 evaluates different report types and methods for extracting relevant information from individual data bases, relating the information using various formats and presenting the data to the manager.

A practical implementation of the data base schema is possible not only in a large library which already employs computers in a variety of functions but also in a small library which is only beginning to consider computer applications. The key to successful implementation is staged growth and careful integration with existing and future computer subsystems. The DSS may be implemented as a set of related subsystems, with each subsystem making a contribution to management needs independently of the others. The ability of a given library to implement each subsystem will depend upon the level and kind of technology already in place in that library. Subsystems requiring significant additional investment in technology could be delayed, with the DSS being introduced in stages. At each stage, the level of information available to support management decisions would be marginally enhanced until a comprehensive system is in place. The subsystems may be identified as productivity, utilization, availability and reporting. This subsystem approach is discussed in Chapter 9.

Essentially, the DSS must be a stand-alone system implemented on a micro or mini mainframe or on the institution's central computer. We do not recommend that an existing automated circulation system or similar systems be adapted to include decision support. However, existing technology should be employed wherever possible to support data capture and transactions processing. To a large extent, the full scope of data capture, processing, storage and retrieval implied by our DSS would not be cost justified if decision support was the only product. The hardware and software requirements are far too costly for this purpose alone. However, much use can be made of existing institutional hardware and software. Details for putting together a DSS at reasonable cost are provided in Chapter 9.

The authors are continuing to explore the implementation process in current work. As computer technology evolves, we will see some of the cost barriers discussed in Chapter 9 begin to dissolve. Ultimately, the most formidable and continuing barrier will be the manpower requirements of data capture. Thus, we have focused our efforts toward a conceptual design which minimizes direct involvement of users and library personnel.

Given the rapid advancement of technology and the likelihood that development of a complete library DSS would take place over a number of years, it is essential that planning for a DSS be focused on the system's logical design, i.e., the reporting requirements and the underlying data base schema. As the logical design becomes fixed, the issue of choosing the most appropriate hardware and software environment can be addressed. However, the logical system design should never be merged with existing technology in the way that many circulation and online catalog systems have been. The DSS should be capable of evolving in a compatible fashion with changes in library operations, changes in management needs and advances in technology.

Appendix 1: Mapping Library of Congress Categories Onto HEGIS Classification

HEGIS CATEGORIES INCLUDED IN STUDY

0504	Banking and Finance	0799	Computer and Information Sciences, Other
0505	Investments and Securities		
0510	Transportation and Public Utilities	0909	Electrical, Electronics and Communications Engineering
0517	Business Economics		
0701	Computer and Information Sciences, General	1901	Physical Sciences, General
		1902	Physics, General (excluding Biophysics)
0702	Information Sciences and Systems		
0703	Data Processing	1903	Molecular Physics
0704	Computer Programming	1904	Nuclear Physics
0705	Systems Analysis	2204	Economics
0798	Computer Structure and Design		

LC DIVISIONS RELEVANT TO STUDY

H	Social Sciences (General)	QE	Geology
HA	Statistics (General and Census)	QH	Natural History
HB	Economic Theory	RA	Public Medicine
HC	Economic History and Conditions	T	Technology (General)
HD	Land, Agriculture, Industry	TA	Engineering (General)
HE	Transportation and Communication	TC	Hydraulic Engineering
		TD	Environmental Technology
HF	Commerce	TE	Highway Engineering
HG	Finance	TF	Railroad Engineering
HJ	Public Finance	TJ	Mechanical Engineering and Machinery
HM	Socioeconomics		
HT	Urban Economics	TK	Electrical Engineering, Electronics, Nuclear Engineering
KF	Banking and Regulation		
Q	Science (General)	TL	Transportation
QA	Mathematics	TN	Mining and Metallurgy
QB	Astronomy	TP	Chemical Technology
QC	Physics	TS	Manufacturing
QD	Chemistry		

LC RANGES APPLICABLE TO EACH HEGIS CATEGORY

0504 BANKING AND FINANCE

HB 531–549	Interest
HC 79.C3	International Finance
HD 39	Corporate Finance—Capital Budgeting
HD 52–52.5	Corporate Finance—Capital Budgeting
HD 2741	Corporate Finance—Mergers & Acquisitions
HD 2951–2968	Cooperatives
HD 2970–3110	Profit Sharing
HD 3120–3575	Cooperatives
HF 5550–5559	Corporate Finance
HF 5564–5585	Credit—General
HF 5568	Credit—Consumer
HG 1–157	Finance—General
HG 171–175	Finance—General
HG 179–188	Finance—Personal
HG 201–1492.5	Money
HG 1501–1720	Banking—General
HG 1725–1811	Banking—Regulation
HG 1766–1768	Banks—Taxation
HG 1776–1798	Banking—Regulation
HG 1811	Central Banking
HG 1851–1873	Banks of Issue
HG 1881–1966	Savings Banking
HG 1968–2031	Banks—Other
HG 2033–2039	Credit Unions
HG 2041–2051	Banks—Other
HG 2121–2351	Banks—Other
HG 2401–2416	Banking—General—U.S.
HG 2421–2445	Banking—Regulation—U.S.
HG 2461	Banking—General—U.S.
HG 2463–2479	Banks—History—U.S.
HG 2481–2493	Banking—General—U.S.
HG 2525–2557	Banks—History—U.S.
HG 2559–2565	U.S. Federal Reserve System
HG 2569	Banking—Foreign
HG 2571–2585	State Banks
HG 2601–2613	Banks—History—U.S.
HG 2624–2626	Savings & Loan Associations
HG 2701–3542.5	Banking—Foreign
HG 3701–3754	Credit—General
HG 3755–3756	Credit—Consumer
HG 3760–3769	Bankruptcy
HG 3811–4000	International Finance
HG 4001–4280.5	Corporate Finance
HG 4028.C4	Corporate Finance—Capital Budgeting
HG 4301–4495	Trusts
HG 4517	International Finance—Developing Countries
HG 4538	International Finance
KF 966–1032	Banking—Regulation
KF 1501–1548.M6	Bankruptcy
Z 7164.F5	Bibliography — Finance, Banking

0505 INVESTMENTS AND SECURITIES

HD 1375–1395	Real Estate
HG 4501–4516	Investments & Securities—General
HG 4519–4527	Investments & Securities—General
HG 4530	Investment Companies
HG 4534	Investment Banking
HG 4537	Investments & Securities—General
HG 4539	Investments and Securities—General
HG 4551–4636	Stocks—Trading
HG 4651	Bonds—General
HG 4655	Real Estate
HG 4661	Stocks—General
HG 4701–4726	Bonds—Public
HG 4751–4841	Bonds—Industrial
HG 4905–4928	Investments & Securities—General
HG 4929	Securities Regulation
HG 4930	Investment Companies
HG 4931–4955	Bonds—Public
HG 4961–5093	Investments & Securities—General
HG 5095	Real Estate
HG 5123	Stocks—General
HG 5123–5129	Investments & Securities—General
HG 5131	Stocks—Trading
HG 5151–5992.5	Investments & Securities—General
HG 6001–6021	Investments & Securities—General
HG 6024	Commodities & Futures
HG 6028–6051	Investments & Securities—General
HG 6041	Stocks—General
HG 6046–6047	Commodities & Futures
HG 8011–9970	Insurance
KF 1066–1086	Securities Regulation
KF 1428–1457	Securities Regulation
Z 7164.C18	Bibliography—Capital Investment
Z 7164.S37	Bibliography—Securities

0510 TRANSPORTATION AND PUBLIC UTILITIES

HD 2763–2768	Public Utilities—General
HD 3840–4420.5	Government Ownership of Industry
HD 4421–4730	Municipal Public Works
HD 4456–4480	Utilities—Water & Sewage
HD 9502	Energy Policy
HD 9580–9581	Public Utilities—Gas
HD 9684–9688	Public Utilities—Electric
HE 1–192.5	Transportation & Communications—General
HE 193–199	Transportation & Public Utilities Regulation
HE 201–328	Transportation & Communications—General
HE 331–377	Roads & Highways
HE 381–971	Transportation—Water
HE 1001–5600	Transportation—Rail
HE 5351–5600	Transportation—Interurban
HE 5601–5720	Transportation—Motor Vehicle
HE 5751–5870	Transportation—Ferries
HE 5880–5999	Express & Delivery Services
HE 6000–7549	Postal Service
HE 7601–8630	Telegraph—Telecommunications
HE 8660–8700.9	Radio & Television Broadcasting
HE 8701–9715	Telephone
HE 9719–9721	Telegraph—Telecommunications
HE 9751–9755	Express & Delivery Services
HE 9761–9900	Transportation—Air
KF 2076–2849	Transportation & Public Utilities Regulation
Z 7164.P85	Bibliography—Postal, Telegraph & Telephone
Z 7164.P96	Bibliography—Public Utilities
Z 7164.S8	Bibliography—Street Railroads
Z 7164.T8	Bibliography—Transportation
Z 7164.U72	Bibliography—Urban Transportation
Z 7164.W2	Bibliography—Waterways
Z 7221–7225	Bibliography—Radio
Z 7231–7236	Bibliography—Railroads
Z 7295	Bibliography—Highways, Roads
Z 7935	Bibliography—Water Supply

0517 BUSINESS ECONOMICS

HB 171–199	Economics—General
HB 201–205	Supply, Demand & Consumption
HB 221–235	Price Theory
HB 236	Price Regulation
HB 241	Production Theory
HB 251	Wealth
HB 301	Labor Economics
HB 401	Economics—Land
HB 601	Profit
HB 601–603	Macroeconomics
HB 771	Distribution
HB 771.5	Macroeconomics
HB 801–805	Supply, Demand & Consumption
HB 821–838	Distribution of Wealth
HB 3711–3729	Economic Conditions—Business Cycles
HB 3730–3840	Economic Forecasting
HC 79.C7	Industrial Costs
HC 79.L3	Labor Economics
HC 79.W24	Price Regulation
HC 80–740	Economic Conditions
HD 41	Competition—Monopoly—Oligopoly
HD 51	Labor Economics
HD 57	Labor Economics
HD 69.C3	Macroeconomics
HD 69.F58	Economic Forecasting
HD 2709–2736	Competition—Monopoly—Oligopoly
HD 2751–2752	Competition—Monopoly—Oligopoly
HD 2769–2930	Competition—Monopoly—Oligopoly
HD 3625–3627	Competition—Monopoly—Oligopoly
HD 4901	Labor Economics
HF 5415.3	Supply, Demand & Consumption
KF 1631–1652	Competition—Monopoly—Oligopoly
KF 1657	Competition—Monopoly—Oligopoly

0701 COMPUTER AND INFO SCI. GENERAL

Q 350–385	Information Theory
QA 76	Computer Science—General
QA 76.15	Computer Science, Dictionaries & Encyclopedias
QA 76.9.066	Computers & Civilization
QA 76.9.P75	Psychological Aspects of Computers
QA 76.9.S8	Computer Standards

0702 INFO SCIENCE AND SYSTEMS

BC 135	Symbolic & Mathematical Logic
Q 350	Information Theory—Serial Works
Q 360	Information Theory—General Works
QA 10.3	Boolean Algebra
QA 76	Computer Science
QA 76.38–.9	Computers
QA 76.8	Special Computers
QA 248.5	Recursive Functions
QA 267–267.5	Machine Theory

QA 268	Coding Theory
QA 268.5	Switching Theory
Z 695.92	Machine Indexing
Z 699	Machine Methods of Information Storage & Retr.
Z 7405.A7	Bibliography—Artificial Intelligence
Z 7405.C9	Bibliography—Cybernetics

0703 DATA PROCESSING

HF 5548.2-6.	Data Processing
HF 5548.3	Real-Time Data Processing
QA 76	Computer Science
QA 76.9.D3	Data Base Management
QA 76.9.D33	Data Compression
QA 76.9.D35	Data Structures
QA 76.9.D6	Documentation
QA 76.9.F5	File Organization
T 57.5	Data Processing
TA 1630-1650	Optical Data Processing

0704 COMPUTER PROGRAMMING

QA 76.6	Programming
QA 76.7	Programming Languages
QA 76.73	Programming Languages

0705 SYSTEMS ANALYSIS

Q 295	System Theory
QA 76.9.C65	Computer Simulation
QA 402	System Analysis
QA 402.2-402.5	Optimization & Control Theory
T 57.6-.97	Systems Analysis
T 57.62	Simulation
T 57.64	Monte Carlo Methods
T 57.7-.84	Mathematical Programming
T 57.85	Network Systems Theory
T 57.9	Queuing Theory
T 57.92-57.97	Game, Decision, Search Theory, etc.
TA 168	Systems Engineering

0798 COMPUTER STRUCT. AND DESIGN

QA 76	Computers—General
QA 76.38	Hybrid Computers
QA 76.4	Analog Computers
QA 76.5	Digital Computers
QA 76.8	Special Computers
QA 76.9.A73	Computer Architecture
QA 76.9.E94	Evaluation of Computer Performance
TA 1630-1650	Optical Data Processing
TK 7885-7895	Computer Engineering—Hardware
TK 7888	Analog Computers

TK 7888.3	Digital Computers
TK 7888.4	Digital Computer Circuits
TK 7889	Special Computers
TK 7895	Special Computer Components

0799 COMPUTER SCI, OTHER

HV 6773	Computer Crime
Q 300-335.5	Cybernetics

0909 ELECTRICAL, ELECTRONICS AND COMMUNICATIONS ENGINEERING

QA 267-268	Machine Theory
QC 501-766	Electricity & Magnetism
TA 1501-1820	Applied Optics—Lasers
TA 2001-2030	Plasma Engineering
TK 1-541	Electrical Engineering—General
TK 1001-1841	Production of Electric Energy or Power
TK 2000-2975	Dynamoelectric Machinery & Auxiliaries
TK 3001-3521	Distribution & Transmission of Electric Power
TK 4001-4102	Applications of Electric Power
TK 4125-4399	Electric Lighting
TK 4500-4661	Infrared Technology—Electric Heating
TK 5101-5105	Telecommunication—General
TK 5107-5865	Telegraph
TK 5981-5990	Electroacoustics
TK 6001-6525	Telephone
TK 6540-6571.5	Radio
TK 6630-6720	Television
TK 7108-7241	Electric Bells & Buzzers
TK 7725	Manufacture of Electrodes
TK 7800-7882	Electronics
TK 7885-7895	Computer Hardware
TK 8300-8360	Photoelectronic Devices
TR 1025-1050	Electrophotography
UG 600-610	Military Telegraph & Telephone
Z 5831-5838	Bibliography—Electricity, Electronics

1901 PHYSICAL SCIENCES, GENERAL

Q 1-295	General Science
QA 273-295	Mathematical Statistics & Probability

1902 PHYSICS, GENERAL—NO BIOPHYSICS

Q 1-101	Science Periodicals & Societies
QA 273-295	Mathematical Statistics & Probability
QC 1-75	Physics—General
QC 81-114	Weights & Measures

QC 120–168	Descriptive & Experimental Mechanics
QC 174.7–176.84	Statistical Physics
QC 177	Theories of Ether
QC 178	Theories of Gravitation
QC 221–246	Acoustics—Sound
QC 251–310.14	Heat—General
QC 310.15–319.7	Thermodynamics
QC 319.8–338.5	Heat Transfer
QC 350–449	Optics & Light—General
QC 450–467	Spectroscopy
QC 474–496.9	Radiation Physics
QC 501–667	Electricity—General
QC 669–675.5	Electromagnetic Theory
QC 676–678.6	Radio Waves
QC 717.6–718.5	Plasma Physics
QC 750–766	Magnetism
Z 5831–5838	Bibliography—Electricity, Electronics
Z 7141–7145	Bibliography—Physics

1903 MOLECULAR PHYSICS

QC 170–171.2	General Molecular Physics
QC 172–173.25	Constitution of Matter & Antimatter
QC 173.28–173.4	Properties of Matter & Antimatter

1904 NUCLEAR PHYSICS

QC 770–789.6	Nuclear Physics—General
QC 789.7–790.8	Nuclear Fission
QC 790.95–791.7	Nuclear Fission
QC 791.9–792	Atomic Energy
QC 793–793.5	Elementary Particle Physics
QC 793.9–794.8	Nuclear Interactions
QC 794.95–796	Radioactivity
Z 5160	Bibliography—Atomic Energy
Z 7144.N8	Bibliography—Nuclear Physics

2204 ECONOMICS

BJ 53	Ethics & Economics
D 635	First World War—Economic Aspects
D 800	Second World War—Economic Aspects
E 441–453	Economic Aspects of Slavery
GN 448–450	Economic Anthropology
HA 1–33	Social Sciences Statistics
HB 1–129	Economic History
HB 131–145	Econometric & Statistical Methods
HB 151–875	Economic Theory
HB 879–3700	Demography
HC 1–730	Economic History
HD 1–91	Production
HD 101–1395	Land
HD 1401–2210	Agricultural Economics
HD 2321–4730	Industries
HD 4801–8942	Labor Economics
HD 9000–9999	Industry Studies
HE	Transportation Economics
HF	Commerce
HG	Finance
HJ	Public Finance
HM 35	Socio-Economics
HQ 1381	Women & Economics
HT 321	City as an Economic Factor
HV 5101–5121	Alcoholism & Economics
N 8600–8675	Economics of Art
QA 273–295	Mathematical Statistics & Probability
T 57.6–.97	Operations Research
Z 5118.E25	Bibliography—Economics, Primitive
Z 7164.E14–.E2	Bibliography—Economics, Economic Policy
Z 7164.07	Bibliography—World & Natural Economy

Appendix 2: Data Base Dictionary

Record/Item Name		Description	Format[1]
FACULTY			
#	USERID	User ID no.	xxxxx[2]
*	DEPID	Department ID no.	xx
	FACNAME	Faculty name	A(20)
	RANK	Full, associate, etc.	x
	YREMPL	Year employment began	99
	DEGREE	Highest degree code	x
	YRDEG	Year degree earned	99
STUDENT			
#	USERID	User ID no.[3]	xxxxx
*	DEPID	Department ID no.	xx
	CLASS	Student class (freshman, graduate, etc.)	x
DEPARTMENT			
#	DEPID	Department ID no.	xx
	DEPNAME	Department name	A(10)
LC-SERIAL			
#	LCID	Code no. for LC category or serial	xxx
	LCALPHA	LC alphabetic category	AA
	LCNUMLO	Lower limit of LC range	9999
	LCNUMHI	Upper limit of LC range	9999
	LCDESC	Description of LC category	A(20)
	DOCTYPE	Document type code (serial, monograph, etc.)	x
	DOCLOC	Document storage location	x
CIRCULATE			
#*	USERID	User ID no.	xxxxx
#*	LCID	Code no. for LC category or serial	xxx
#	CPUBYR	Publication year	99
#	CIRYR	Transaction year	99
	CIRNUM	Accumulated no. of transactions	9999
INTERLIBRARY			
#*	USERID	User ID no.	xxxxx
#*	LCID	Code no. for LC category or serial	xxx
#	LPUBYR	Publication year	99
#	LONYR	Transaction year	99
#*	LIBID	Source library code	xx
	LONNUM	Accumulated no. of transactions	999
	LONPGS	Accumulated no. of pages (photocopy)	9999
	LONCOST	Accumulated cost	999.99
	LONFAIL	Accumulated no. of unfilled requests	99
	LONTIME	Accumulated wait time in days	9999

Record/Item Name		Description	Format[1]
INLIBUSE			
#*	LCID	Code no. for LC category or serial	xxx
#	IPUBYR	Publication year	99
#	INLYR	Transaction year	99
	INLNUM	Accumulated no. of shelvings	9999
PHOTOCOPY			
#*	USERID	User ID no.	xxxxx
#*	LCID	Code no. for LC category or serial	xxx
#	FPUBYR	Publication year	99
#	FOTYR	Transaction year	99
	FOTNUM	Accumulated no. of transactions	999
	FOTPGS	Accumulated no. of pages	9999
EXLIB			
#	LIBID	Source library code	xx
	LIBNAME	Source library name	x(20)
	LIBADDR	Source library address	x(30)
	LIBPHONE	Source library phone no.	xxx-xxx-xxxx
CORS-FAC			
#*	CORID	Course ID no.	xxxxx
#*	USERID	User ID no.	xxxxx
	CORYR	Year taught	99
	ENROLL	Enrollment	999
COURSE			
#	CORID	Course ID no.	xxxxx
*	DEPID	Department ID no.	xx
	CORTITLE	Course title	x(20)
	CORLEVEL	Level code (lower division, graduate, etc.)	x
	CREDIT	Credit awarded	9
CORS-CAT			
#*	CORID	Course ID no.	xxxxx
#*	LCID	Code no. for LC category or serial	xxx
RESEARCH			
#	RESCODE	Code no. for research subject matter	xxx
	RESDESC	Description of research subject matter	x(20)
RESH-FAC			
#*	RESCODE	Code no. for research subject matter	xxx
#*	USERID	User ID no.	xxxxx
	RESTYPE	Activity type code (publication, grant, etc.)	x
	RESYR	Activity year	99
RESH-LC			
#*	RESCODE	Code no. for research subject matter	xxx
#*	LCID	Code no. for LC category or serial	xxx

Record/Item Name		Description	Format[1]
NASA			
#	NASAID	NASA SCAN category code	xx
	NASADESC	Description of NASA SCAN category	x(20)
NASA-FAC			
#*	NASAID	NASA SCAN category code	xx
#*	USERID	User ID no.	xxxxx
	NASAYR	Year of survey	99
NASA-LC			
#*	NASAID	NASA SCAN category code	xx
#*	LCID	Code no. for LC category or serial	xxx
HEGIS			
#	HEGISID	HEGIS category code	xxxx
	HEGISDESC	Description of HEGIS category	x(20)
LC-HEGIS			
#*	LCID	Code no. for LC category or serial	xxx
#*	HEGISID	HEGIS category code	xxxx
DEP-HEGIS			
#*	DEPID	Department ID no.	xx
#*	HEGISID	HEGIS category code	xxxx

[1] x = alphanumeric character
9 = numeric character
A = alphabetic character

[2] User ID format should match code used for institution's personnel files.

[3] Students are not uniquely identified. A separate record is established for each class/department combination.

= primary key for file
* = primary key of owner file

Bibliography

Ackoff, Russell L. *A Concept of Corporate Planning*. New York: Wiley-Interscience, 1970.

Ackoff, Russell L. "Management Misinformation Systems." *Management Science,* vol. 14, December 1967, pp. 147-156.

Allen, Thomas J. *Managing the Flow of Technology: Technology Transfer and the Dissemination of Technological Information Within the R&D Organization*. Cambridge, MA: M.I.T. Press, 1977.

Allen, Thomas J. and Gertsberger, Peter G. *Criteria for Selection of an Information Source*. Cambridge, MA: Sloan School of Management, M.I.T., September 1967.

Allison, Anne Marie and Allan, Ann, eds. *OCLC: A National Library Network*. Short Hills, NJ: Enslow Publishers, 1979.

Allman, Katherine, Wing, Paul and McLaughlin, James. *A Proposed Taxonomy of Postsecondary Education Subject Matter Areas*. (Preliminary Draft). Boulder, CO: National Center for Higher Education Management Systems at Western Interstate Commission for Higher Education, 1975.

Alternative Catalog Newsletter. No. 2. Baltimore, MD: Milton S. Eisenhower Library, Johns Hopkins University, June 1978.

American Library Association. Collection Development Committee, Resources and Technical Services Division. "Guidelines for the Formulation of Collection Development Policies." *Library Resources and Technical Services,* vol. 21, Winter 1977, pp. 40-47.

American Library Association. Library Administration Division. Staff Development Committee. *Staff Development in Libraries: A Directory of Organizations and Activities with a Staff Development Bibliography*. Chicago: American Library Association, 1978.

Anglo-American Cataloging Rules. 2nd edition. Edited by Michael Gorman and Paul W. Winkler. Chicago: American Library Association, 1978.

Angoff, Allan, ed. *Public Relations for Libraries: Essays in Communications Techniques*. Westport, CT: Greenwood Press, 1973.

Anthony, R.N. *Planning and Control Systems: A Framework for Analysis*. Cambridge, MA: Harvard University Graduate School of Business Administration, 1975.

Arms, W.Y. and Walter, T.P. "A Simulation Model for Purchasing Duplicate Copies in a Library." *Journal of Library Automation,* vol. 7, June 1974, pp. 73-82.

Association of Research Libraries. *SPEC Flyer on Staff Development,* no. 18. Washington, DC: Association of Research Libraries, Office of University Library Management Studies, 1975.

Association of Research Libraries. Collection Division. ACRL Joint Committee on University Library Standards. "Standards for University Libraries." *College and Research Libraries News,* April 1979, pp. 101-110.

Atherton, Pauline and Christian, Roger. *Librarians and Online Services.* White Plains, NY: Knowledge Industry Publications, Inc., 1977.

Aveney, Brian and Ghikas, Mary Fischer. "Reactions Measured: 600 Users Meet the COM Catalog." *American Libraries,* vol. 10, February 1979, pp. 82-83.

Baatz, Wilmer, *Collection Development in 19 Libraries of the Association of Research Libraries.* Washington, DC: Council on Library Resources, 1978, ED 153 606.

Bahr, Alice Harrison. *Automated Library Circulation Systems, 1979-80.* 2nd Edition. White Plains, NY: Knowledge Industry Publications, Inc., 1979.

Bahr, Alice Harrison. *Book Theft and Library Security Systems, 1981-82.* White Plains, NY: Knowledge Industry Publications, Inc., 1981.

Bahr, Alice Harrison. *Microforms: The Librarians' View, 1978-79.* White Plains, NY: Knowledge Industry Publications, Inc., 1978.

Baldridge, Victor J. *Power and Conflict in the University: Research in the Sociology of Complex Organizations.* New York: Wiley, 1971.

Bates, Marcia J. "Factors Affecting Subject Catalog Search Success." *Journal of the American Society for Information Science,* vol. 28, May 1977a, pp. 161-169.

Bates, Marcia J. "System Meets User: Problems in Matching Subject Search Terms." *Information Processing and Management,* vol. 13, no. 6, 1977b, pp. 367-368, ED 047 738.

Bates, Marcia J. *User Studies, A Review for Librarians and Information Scientists.* Washington, DC: U.S. Educational Resources Information Center, 1971, ED 047 738.

Battin, P. "Research Libraries in the Network Environment: The Case for Cooperation." *EDUCOM Bulletin,* Summer 1980, pp. 26-31.

Baughman, James. "Toward a Structural Approach to Collection Development." *College and Research Libraries,* vol. 38, May 1977, pp. 241-248.

Baumler, J.V. and Baumler, J.L. "A Simulation of Reserve Book Activities in a College Library Using GPSS/360." *College and Research Libraries,* vol. 36, May 1975, pp. 222-227.

Baumol, W.J. and Marcus, M. *Economics of Academic Libraries.* Prepared for Council on Library Resources by Mathematica, Inc. Washington, DC: American Council on Education, 1973.

Bebout, Lois, Davis, Donald and Oehlerts, Donald. "User Studies in the Humanities: A Survey and a Proposal." *RQ,* vol. 15, Fall 1975, pp. 40-44.

Becker, Joseph. "How Library Automation May Influence New Building Plans." In *Library Buildings: Innovation for Changing Needs.* Edited by A. Trezza. Chicago: American Library Association, 1972, pp. 3-5.

Becker, Joseph. "Telecommunications." *ALA Yearbook.* Chicago: American Library Association, 1977, pp. xxxiv-xxxviii.

Benbasat, Izak. "Cognitive Style Considerations in DSS Design." *Data Base,* vol. 8, Winter 1977, pp. 37-38.

Benford, H.L., et al. "Analysis of Book Reshelving." In *Case Studies in Systems Analysis in a University Library.* Edited by Barton Burkhalter. Metuchen, NJ: Scarecrow Press, 1968, pp. 76-89.

Bernays, Edward L. "Public Relations: Its Origins and Development." In *Public Relations for Libraries.* Edited by A. Angoff. Westport, CT: Greenwood Press, 1973, pp. 1-13.

Blackburn, Robert. "Two Years With a Closed Catalog." *Journal of Academic Librarianship,* vol. 4, no. 6, 1978, pp. 424-429.

Blair, John C. "Measurement and Evaluation of Online Services." In *The Library and Information Manager's Guide to Online Services*. Edited by Ryan E. Hoover. White Plains, NY: Knowledge Industry Publications, Inc., 1980.

Bolgiano, Christina and King, Mary. "Profiling a Periodicals Collection." *College and Research Libraries*, vol. 39, March 1978, pp. 99-104.

Bommer, Michael. "A Decision Model for Purchasing Multiple Copies of Titles in a University Library." *Proceedings of the Eighth Annual AIDS Conference*. San Francisco, November 1976.

Bommer, Michael. *The Development of a Management System for Effective Decision Making and Planning in a University Library*. Ph.D. Dissertation, Philadelphia, University of Pennsylvania, 1971.

Bommer, Michael. "Operations Research in Libraries: A Critical Assessment." *Journal of the American Society for Information Science*, vol. 26, May-June 1975, pp. 137-139.

Bommer, Michael. [Review of] DeProspo, E.R. and others. "Performance Measures for Public Libraries." *Library Quarterly*, vol. 44, July 1974, pp. 273-275.

Bommer, Michael and Ford, Bernard. "A Cost-Benefit Analysis for Determining the Value of an Electronic Security System." *College and Research Libraries*, vol. 35, July 1974, pp. 270-279.

Bonn, George S. "Evaluation of the Collection." *Library Trends*, vol. 22, January 1974, pp. 265-304.

Bookstein, Abraham. "Models for Shelf Reading." *Library Quarterly*, vol. 43, April 1973, pp. 26-37.

Bookstein, Abraham. "Optimal Loan Periods." *Information Processing and Management*, vol. 11, no. 8-12, 1975, pp. 235-242.

Bookstein, Abraham. "Queueing Theory and Congestion of the Library Catalog." *Library Quarterly*, vol. 42, July 1972, pp. 316-328.

Booth, A.D. "On the Geometry of Libraries." *Journal of Documentation*, vol. 25, March 1969, pp. 28-42.

Booz, Allen and Hamilton. *Problems in University Library Management*. A study conducted for the Association of Research Libraries and the American Council on Education. Washington, DC: Association of Research Libraries, 1970.

Booz, Allen and Hamilton. *The Strategic Impact of Information Technology in the 1980s*. A special presentation. New York, 1980.

Boss, Richard. "Circulation Systems: The Options." *Library Technology Reports*, vol. 15, January-February 1979, pp. 7-105.

Bourne, C.P. *Characteristics of Coverage by the Bibliography of Agriculture of the Literature Relating to Agricultural Research and Development*. Palo Alto, CA: Information General Corporation, 1969a, PB 185 425.

Bourne, C.P. *Overlapping Coverage of Bibliography of Agriculture by 15 Other Secondary Sources*. Palo Alto, CA: Information General Corporation, 1969b, PB 185 069.

Bourne, C.P. and Gregor, D. "Planning Serials Cancellations and Cooperative Collection Development in the Health Sciences: Methodology and Background Information." *Medical Library Association Bulletin*, vol. 63, October 1975, pp. 366-377.

Breiting, Amelia. "Staff Development in College and University Libraries." *Special Libraries*, vol. 67, July 1976 , pp. 305-310.

Brock, J.A. *A Program for the Conservation and Preservation of Library Materials in the General Library, University of California, Berkeley*. Berkeley, CA: University of California, 1976.

Brophy, P. et al. *The Library Management Game: A Report on a Research Project*. Lancaster, England: University of Lancaster Library, 1972.

Brown, Maryann Kevin and McHugh, Anita L. *Survey of Costs in Technical Processing and Interlibrary Loan: Summary*. Boulder, CO: Western Interstate Library Coordinating Agency, 1976.

Bruer, J. Michael. "Management Information Aspects of Automated Acquisitions Systems." *Library Resources and Technical Services*, vol. 24, no. 4, Fall 1980, pp. 339-342.

Brutcher, Constance, Gessford, Glen and Rixford, Emmet. "Cost Accounting for the Library." *Library Resources and Technical Services*, vol. 8, Fall 1964, pp. 413-431.

Buckland, Michael. *Book Availability and the Library User*. New York: Pergamon Press, 1975.

Buckland, Michael and Taylor, W.D. "Management Information for Decision-making." *Proceedings of the ASIS Annual Meeting*. Washington, DC: American Society for Information Science, 1976, pp. 88-95.

Burkhalter, B.R. and Race, P.A. "An Analysis of Renewals, Overdues, and Other Factors Influencing the Optimal Charge-Out Period." In *Case Studies in Systems Analysis in a University Library*. Edited by Barton Burkhalter. Metuchen, NJ: Scarecrow Press, 1968, pp. 11-33.

Burns, Robert. "A Generalized Methodology for Library Systems Analysis." *College and Research Libraries*, vol. 32, July 1971, pp. 295-303.

Burton, Robert. "Formula Budgeting: An Example." *Special Libraries*, vol. 66, February 1975, pp. 61-67.

Butler, Brett, Aveney, Brian and Scholz, William. "The Conversion of Manual Catalogs to Collection Data Bases." *Library Technology Reports*, vol. 14, March-April 1978, pp. 109-206.

Butler, Meredith. "Copyright and Reserve Books—What Libraries Are Doing." *College and Research Libraries News*, vol. 39, May 1978, pp. 125-129.

Byrum, John D. and Coe, D. Whitney. "AACR as Applied by Research Libraries for Serials Cataloging." *Library Resources and Technical Services*, vol. 23, Spring 1979, pp. 139-146.

Byrum, John D. and Coe, D. Whitney. "AACR Chapter 6 as Adopted, Applied, and Assessed by Research Libraries." *Library Resources and Technical Services*, vol. 21, Winter 1977, pp. 48-57.

Cabeceiras, James. *The Multimedia Library: Materials Selection and Use*. New York: Academic Press, 1978.

Carlson, Eric D., ed. "Proceedings of a Conference on Decision Support Systems." *Data Base*, vol. 8, Winter 1977, the issue.

Carmon, J.L. "SDI—Where Are We? The Challenge of the Future: The Information Dissemination Center View." Paper presented at the American Society for Information Science Conference, Atlanta, GA, 1974.

Carr, Harry et al. *Regional Interlibrary Loan in New York State: A Comparative Study*. Washington, DC: Checchi & Co., 1976.

Cawkell, A.E. "Cost-Effectiveness and the Benefits of SDI Systems." *The Information Scientist*, vol. 6, December 1972, pp. 143-148.

Cerutti, Elsie and Tucker, Jane C. *Impact of the New Copyright Law on Interlibrary Loan in a Research Library*. Prepared for Library Division, National Bureau of Standards, U.S. Department of Commerce, Washington, DC, 1978, NBS IR 78-1427.

Chabotar, Kent and Lad, Lawrence. *Evaluation Guidelines for Training Programs*. East Lansing, MI: Public Administration Programs, Michigan State University, 1974.

Chait, R. "College Mission Statements." *Science*, vol. 205, September 7, 1979, p. 957.

Chapman, Edward. "Systems Study as Related to Library Operations: Need and Planning." *Library Automation: A State of the Art Review*. Chicago: American Library Association, 1969, pp. 7-12.

Chen, Ching-Chih. *Quantitative Measurement and Dynamic Library Service*. Phoenix, AZ: Oryx Press, 1978.

Chisholm, Margaret. "Selection and Evaluation Tools for Audio and Visual Materials." In *Reader in Media, Technology and Libraries*. Edited by Margaret Chisholm. Englewood, CO: Microcard Editions Books, 1975, pp. 372-384.

Christ, C. West. "Microfiche: A Study of User Attitudes and Reading Habits." *Journal of the American Society for Information Science*, vol. 23, January 1972, pp. 30-35.

Churchman, C. West. "Operations Research Prospects for Libraries: The Realities and Ideals." *Library Quarterly*, vol. 42, January 1972, pp. 6-14.

Churchman, C. West and Schainblatt, A.H. "The Researcher and the Manager: A Dialectic of Implementation." *Management Science*, vol. 11, no. 4, 1975.

Clapp, V.W. and Jordan, R.T. "Quantitative Criteria for Adequacy of Academic Library Collections." *College and Research Libraries*, vol. 26, September 1965, pp. 371-380.

CLENE. Continuing Library Education Network and Exchange. *Continuing Education Courses and Programs for Library, Information and Media Personnel*. Washington, DC: CLENE, 1976.

Cogswell, James A. "On-Line Search Services: Implications for Libraries and Library Users." *College and Research Libraries*, vol. 39, July 1978, pp. 275-280.

Cohen, Michael and March, James, eds. *Leadership and Ambiguity: The American College President*. New York: McGraw-Hill, 1974.

Cole, P.F. "Journal Usage Versus Age of Journal." *Journal of Documentation*, vol. 19, March 1963, pp. 1-11.

Cole, P.F. "A New Look at Reference Scattering." *Journal of Documentation*, vol. 18, June 1962, pp. 58-64.

Connor, J.H. "Selective Dissemination of Information: A Review of the Literature and the Issues." *Library Quarterly*, vol. 37, October 1967, pp. 373-391.

Conroy, Barbara. *Library Staff Development and Continuing Education*. Littleton, CO: Libraries Unlimited, 1978.

Converse, W.R.M. and Standers, O.R. "Rationalizing the Collections Policy: A Computerized Approach." Paper presented at the Canadian Conference on Information Science, Quebec, May 7-9, 1975, ED 105 861.

Cook, J.J. "Increased Seating in the Undergraduate Library: A Study in Effective Space Utilization." In *Case Studies in Systems Analysis in a University Library*. Edited by Barton Burkhalter. Metuchen, NJ: Scarecrow Press, 1968, pp. 142-170.

Cook, Kenneth and Greco, C.M. "The Ugly Duckling Acknowledged: Experimental Design for Decision-Making." Part I. *Journal of Academic Librarianship*, vol. 3, March 1977, pp. 23-28; Part II. *Journal of Academic Librarianship*, vol. 3, May 1977, pp. 85-89.

Cooper, Michael and Dewath, Nancy. "The Effect of User Fees on the Cost of On-Line Searching in Libraries." *Journal of Library Automation*, vol. 10, December 1977, pp. 304-319.

Cooper, Michael and Wolthausen, John. "Misplacement of Books on Library Shelves: A Mathematical Model." *Library Quarterly*, vol. 47, January 1977, pp. 43-57.

Coplen, Ron. "Subscription Agents: To Use or Not to Use." *Special Libraries*, vol. 70, no. 12, December 1979, pp. 519-526.

Corey, James and Bellamy, Fred. "Determining Requirements for a New System." *Library Trends*, vol. 22, April 1973, pp. 533-552.

Coughlin, R.E. et al. *Urban Analysis for Branch Library System Planning*. Westport, CT: Greenwood Press, 1972.

Council on Library Resources. *A National Periodicals Center: Technical Development Plan*. Washington, DC: Council on Library Resources, 1978.

Cox, Carolyn and Juergens, Bonnie. *Microform Catalogs: A Viable Alternative for Texas Libraries*. Dallas, TX: AMIGOS Bibliographic Council, 1977.

Cox, Julius G. *Optimum Storage of Library Material*. Lafayette, IN: Purdue University Libraries, 1964.

Crowley, T. and Childers, T. *Information Service in Public Libraries: Two Studies*. Metuchen, NJ: Scarecrow Press, 1971.

Cuadra, Carlos A. "The Impact of On-Line Retrieval Service." In *On-Line Bibliographic Services—Where We Are, Where We're Going*. Edited by Peter Watson. Chicago: American Library Association, 1977, pp. 2-9.

Darling, Pamela W. "Books in Peril; A Local Preservation Program: Where to Start?" *Library Journal*, vol. 101, November 15, 1976b, pp. 2343-2347.

Darling, Pamela W. "Microforms in Libraries: Preservation and Storage." *Microform Review*, vol. 5, April 1976a, pp. 93-100.

Darling, Pamela W. "Preservation: A National Plan At Last?" *Library Journal*, vol. 102, February 15, 1977, pp. 447-449.

Davenport, Cynthia. *A Study of Document Retrieval Times: An Example of How Data and Evaluation Can Lead to Improved Decision Making in Academic Libraries.* Washington, DC: ERIC Document Reproduction Service, 1977, ED 154 808.

Davis, Charles and Dingle-Cliff, Susan. "Evidence of OCLC's Potential for Special Libraries and Technical Information Centers." *Journal of the American Society for Information Science*, vol. 29, September 1978, pp. 255-256.

Davison, P.S. and Matthews, D.A.R. "Assessment of Information Services." *ASLIB Proceedings*, vol. 21, 1969, pp. 280-283.

Decker, Jean S. "Catalog 'Closings' and Serials." *The Journal of Academic Librarianship*, vol. 5, no. 5, November 1979, pp. 261-265.

DeGennaro, Richard. "Austerity, Technology, and Resource Sharing: Research Libraries Face the Future." *Library Journal*, vol. 100, May 15, 1975, pp. 917-923.

DeGennaro, Richard. "Copyright, Resource Sharing and Hard Times: A View from the Field." *American Libraries*, vol. 8, September 1977, pp. 430-435.

DeGennaro, Richard. "Library Administrators and New Management Systems." *Library Journal*, vol. 103, December 15, 1978, pp. 2477-2482.

Denman, Richard W. "Zero Base Budgeting for Academic Libraries." In *Library Budgeting: Critical Challenges for the Future.* Edited by Sul Lee. Ann Arbor, MI: Pierian Press, 1977.

DeProspo, Ernest R. and Huang, Theodore S. "Continuing Education for the Library Administrator: His Needs." In *Administration and Change: Continuing Education in Library Administration.* Edited by Neal Harlow and others. New Brunswick, NJ: Rutgers University Press, 1969.

DeProspo, Ernest R. et al. *Performance Measures for Public Libraries.* Chicago: Public Library Association/American Library Association, 1973.

Dickinson, Dennis. "Some Reflections on Participative Management in Libraries." *College and Research Libraries*, vol. 39, July 1978, pp. 253-262.

Dillehay, Bette. "Book Budget Allocation; Subjective or Objective Approach." *Special Libraries*, vol. 62, no. 12, December 1971, pp. 509-514.

Dougherty, Richard. "Campus Document Delivery Systems to Serve Academic Libraries." *Journal of Library Automation*, vol. 11, March 1978, pp. 24-31.

Dougherty, Richard and Blomquist, L.L. *Improving Access to Library Resources: The Influence of Organization of Library Collections and of User Attitudes Toward Innovative Services.* Metuchen, NJ: Scarecrow Press, 1974.

Dowell, Arlene Taylor. *Cataloging with Copy: A Decision Maker's Handbook.* Littleton, CO: Libraries Unlimited, 1976.

Downs, Robert B. *Resources of Canadian Academic and Research Libraries.* Ottawa, Ont.: Association of Universities and Colleges of Canada, 1967.

Drage, J.F. "User Preferences in Published Indexes, A Preliminary Test." *Information Scientist*, vol. 2, November 1968, pp. 111-114.

Drake, Miriam A. "Managing Innovation in Academic Libraries." *College and Research Libraries*, vol. 40, no. 6, November 1979, pp. 503-510.

Drake, Miriam A. "Attribution of Library Costs." *College and Research Libraries*, vol. 38, November 1977, pp. 514-519.

Drake, Miriam A. "The Management of Libraries as Professional Organizations." *Special Libraries*, vol. 68, no. 5/6, May/June 1977, pp. 181-186.

Dranov, Paula. *Automated Library Circulation Systems, 1977-78.* White Plains, NY: Knowledge Industry Publications, Inc., 1977.

Dranov, Paula. *Microfilm: The Librarians' View, 1976-77.* White Plains, NY: Knowledge Industry Publications, Inc., 1976.

Drucker, Peter. "Managing the Public Service Institution." *College and Research Libraries*, vol. 37, January 1976, pp. 13-14.

DuMont, Rosemary Ruhig. "A Conceptual Basis for Library Effectiveness." *College and Research Libraries*, vol. 41, no. 2, March 1980, pp. 103-111.

Duncan, Virginia and Parsons, Frances. "Use of Microfilm in an Industrial Research Library." *Special Libraries*, vol. 61, July 1979, pp. 288-290.

Dunlap, C.R. "Organizational Patterns in Academic Libraries 1876-1976. *College and Research Libraries*, vol. 37, September 1976, pp. 395-407.

Dwyer, James R. "Public Response to an Academic Library Microcatalog." *Journal of Academic Librarianship*, vol. 5, July 1979, pp. 132-141.

Dyson, Allan J. "Library Instruction in University Undergraduate Libraries." In *Progress in Educating the Library User*. Edited by John Lubans. New York: Bowker, 1978, pp. 93-103.

Easton, David. *A System Analysis of Political Life*. New York: Wiley, 1965.

Edelman, Franz. "They Went Thataway." *Interfaces*, vol. 7, May 1977, pp. 39-43.

Edelman, Hendrik. "Selection Methodology in Academic Libraries." *Library Resources and Technical Services,* vol. 23, Winter 1979, pp. 33-38.

Eggleton, Richard. "Academic Libraries, Participative Management and Risky Shift." *The Journal of Academic Librarianship,* vol. 5, no. 5, November 1979, pp. 270-273.

Ellsworth, Ralph. *Academic Library Buildings: A Guide to Architectural Issues and Solutions*. Boulder, CO: Colorado Associated University Press, 1973.

Ellsworth, Ralph. *The Economics of Book Storage in College and University Libraries*. Metuchen, NJ: Scarecrow Press, 1969.

Ellsworth, Ralph. *Planning the College and University Library Building*. Boulder, CO: Pruett Press, 1968.

Ellsworth, Ralph. "Some Observations on the Architectural Style, Size and Cost of Libraries." *Journal of Academic Librarianship*, vol. 1, no. 5, 1975, pp. 16-19.

Elton, Martin and Vickery, Brian. "The Scope for Operational Research in the Library and Information Field." *ASLIB Proceedings,* vol. 25, August 1973, pp. 305-319.

Emerson, Katherine. "National Reporting on Reference Transactions, 1976-78." *RQ*, vol. 16, Spring 1977, pp. 199-207.

Euster, J.R. "The Washington Library Network as a Management Information System." *PNLA Quarterly*, vol. 42, Spring 1978, pp. 4-8.

Evans, G. Edward. "Book Selection and Book Collection Usage in Academic Libraries." *Library Quarterly*, vol. 40, July 1970, pp. 297-308.

Evans, Glyn. "The Cost of Information About Library Acquisition Budgets." *Collection Management*, vol. 2, Spring 1978a, pp. 3-23.

Evans, Glyn. *Development of a Responsive Library Acquisition Formula*. Final Report. Washington, DC: U.S. Dept. of Health, Education and Welfare, Office of Education, Office of Libraries and Learning Resources, 1978b.

Evans, Glyn, Gifford, Roger and Franz, Donald. *Collection Development Analysis Using OCLC Archival Tapes*. Final Report. Washington, DC: U.S. Dept. of Health, Education and Welfare, Office of Education, Office of Libraries and Learning Resources, 1977.

Faibisoff, Sylvia and Ely, Donald. "Information and Information Needs." Reprinted in *Key Papers in the Design and Evaluation of Information Systems*. White Plains, NY: Knowledge Industry Publications, Inc., 1978, pp. 270-284.

Falk, Steven. "Reference Service, Statistics, and Status." *RQ*, vol. 18, Winter 1978, pp. 165-167.

Farber, Evan. "Limiting College Library Growth: Bane or Boon?" In *Farewell to Alexandria*. Edited by Daniel Gore. Westport, CT: Greenwood Press, 1976, pp. 34-43.

Ferguson, Anthony W. and Taylor, John R. "What Are You Doing? An Analysis of Activities of Public Service Librarians at a Medium-Size Research Library." *The Journal of Academic Librarianship*, vol. 6, no. 1, March 1980, pp. 24-29.

Fischer, Mary, Sisco, Florence and White, Mark. "Measurement of Productivity for Library Management." In *Information Politics: Proceedings of the 39th ASIS Annual Meeting*, vol. 13. Washington, DC: American Society for Information Science, 1976.

Fishman, Diane and Walitt, Ruth. "Seating and Area Preferences in a College Reserve Room." *College and Research Libraries*, vol. 33, July 1972, pp. 284-297.

Flener, Jane G. "Staff Participation in Management in Large University Libraries." *College and Research Libraries*, vol. 34, July 1973, pp. 275-279.

Force, Ronald and Force, Jo Ellen. "Access to Alternative Catalogs: A Simulation Model." *College and Research Libraries*, vol. 40, May 1979, pp. 234-239.

Ford, Geoffrey. "Research in User Behavior in University Libraries." *Journal of Documentation*, vol. 29, March 1973, pp. 85-112.

Ford, Robert B., Jr. "Help for the Decision-maker: A Decision Process Model." *Bookmark*, vol. 38, no. 3, Spring 1979, pp. 128-134.

Ford, Stephen. *The Acquisition of Library Materials*. Chicago: American Library Association, 1973.

Forrester, J.W. *Principles of Systems*. Cambridge, MA: Wright-Allen Press, 1973.

Friend, J.K. and Jessup. W.N. *Local Government and Strategic Choice: An Operational Research Approach to the Processes of Public Planning*. London: Tavistock, 1969.

Fry, B. and White, H.S. *Publishers and Libraries*. Lexington, MA: Heath/Lexington Books, 1977.

Fussler, Herman and Kocher, Karl. "Contemporary Issues in Bibliographic Control." *Library Quarterly*, vol. 43, July 1977, pp. 237-252.

Fussler, Herman and Simon, Julian. *Patterns in the Use of Books in Large Research Libraries*. Chicago: University of Chicago Press, 1961.

Futas, Elizabeth. *Library Acquisition Policies and Procedures*. Phoenix, AZ: Oryx Press, 1977.

Gabriel, Michael. "Surging Serial Costs: The Microfiche Solution." *Library Journal*, vol. 99, October 1974, pp. 2450-2453.

Gaddy, Dale. *A Microform Handbook*. Silver Spring, MD: National Micrographics Association, 1974.

Gardner, Jeffrey. "CAP: A Project for the Analysis of the Collection Development Process in Large Academic Libraries." In *New Horizons for Academic Libraries*. Edited by Robert D. Stueart and Richard D. Johnson. Papers presented at the First National Conference of the Association of College and Research Libraries, Boston, MA, November 8-11, 1978. New York: K.G. Saur Publishing, Inc., 1979.

Gardner, Jeffrey and Webster, Duane. *The Formulation and Use of Goals and Objectives Statements in Academic and Research Libraries*. Washington, DC: Association of Research Libraries, Office of University Library Management Studies. Occasional Papers #3, April 1974.

Gardner, John and Rowe, Gladys. "Thinking Small in a Big Way." *College and Research Libraries*, vol. 40, no. 6, November 1979, pp. 533-538.

Gertsberger, P.G. and Allen, T.J. "Criteria Used by Research and Development Engineers in the Selection of an Information Source." *Journal of Applied Psychology*, vol. 52, August 1968, pp. 272-279.

Gold, Steven. "Allocating the Book Budget: An Economic Model." *College and Research Libraries*, vol. 36, September 1975, pp. 397-402.

Goldhor, H. "The Effect of Prime Display Location on Public Library Circulation of Selected Adult Titles." *Library Quarterly*, vol. 42, October 1972, pp. 371-389.

Gordon, Harold D. "Open Stacks: A Second Look." *Library Journal*, vol. 94, May 1, 1969, pp. 1844-1845.

Gore, Daniel, ed. *Farewell to Alexandria: Solutions to Space, Growth, and Performance Problems of Libraries.* Westport, CT: Greenwood Press, 1976.

Gore, Daniel. "Let Them Eat Cake While Reading Catalog Cards: An Essay on the Availability Problem." *Library Journal*, vol. 100, January 15, 1975, pp. 93-98.

Gorman, Michael. "Short Can be Beautiful." *American Libraries*, vol. 10, November 1979, pp. 607-608.

Govan, James. "The Better Mousetrap: External Accountability and Staff Participation." *Library Trends*, vol. 26, Fall 1977, pp. 255-267.

Goyal, S.K. "Allocation of Library Funds to Different Departments of a University—An Operational Research Approach." *College and Research Libraries*, vol. 34, May 1973, pp. 219-222.

Goyal, S.K. "Application of Operational Research to Problem of Determining Appropriate Loan Period for Periodicals." *Libri*, vol. 20, no. 1-2, 1970, pp. 94-100.

Grant, R.S. "Predicting the Need for Multiple Copies of Books." *Journal of Library Automation*, vol. 4, June 1971, pp. 64-71.

Greene, Robert. "The Effectiveness of Browsing." *College and Research Libraries*, vol. 38, July 1977, pp. 313-316.

Greene, Robert. "Microform Attitude and Frequency of Microform Use." *Journal of Micrographics*, vol. 8, January 1975, pp. 131-134.

Gross, J. and Talavage, J. "A Multiple-Objective Planning Methodology for Information Service Managers." *Information Processing and Management*, vol. 15, 1979, pp. 155-167.

Halldorsson, Egill and Murfin, Marjorie. "The Performance of Professionals and Nonprofessionals in the Reference Interview." *College and Research Libraries*, vol. 38, September 1977, pp. 385-395.

Hamburg, Morris, Clelland, Richard, Bommer, Michael, Ramist, Leonard and Whitfield, Ronald. *Library Planning and Decision-Making Systems.* Cambridge, MA: M.I.T. Press, 1974.

Hamburg, Morris et al. "A Systems Approach to Library Management." *Journal of Systems Engineering*, vol. 4, January 1976, pp. 117-129.

Hansen, J.V., McKell, L.J., and Heitger, L.E. "Decision Oriented Frameworks for Management Information Systems Design." *Information Processing and Management*, vol. 13, no. 4, 1977, pp. 215-225.

Harris, I.W. *The Influence of Accessibility on Academic Library Use.* Doctoral Dissertation, New Brunswick, NJ: Rutgers, The State University, 1966.

Harvey, L.J. *Managing Colleges and Universities by Objectives.* Littleton, CO: Ireland Educational Corporation, 1976.

Hawkins, Donald. "Impact of On Line Systems on Literature Searching Service." Paper presented at 10th Middle Atlantic Regional Meeting, Philadelphia: American Chemical Society, 1976.

Heilprin, Lawrence. "Economics of 'On Demand' Library Copying." *Proceedings of the National Microfilm Association.* Annapolis, MD: NMA, 1962, pp. 311-339.

Heinlein, William F. "Using Student Assistants in Academic Reference." *RQ*, vol. 15, Summer 1976, pp. 323-325.

Herner, Saul. "System Design, Evaluation and Costing." *Special Libraries*, vol. 58, October 1967, pp. 576-581.

Heyman, Berna L. and Abbott, George L. "Automated Acquisitions: A Bibliography." *Journal of Library Automation*, vol. 13, no. 4, December 1980, pp. 260-264.

Hickey, Doralyn. "Theory of Bibliographic Control in Libraries." *Library Quarterly*, vol. 43, July 1977, pp. 253-273.

Hieber, C.E. *An Analysis of Questions and Answers in Libraries.* Bethlehem, PA: Center for the Information Sciences, Lehigh University, 1966.

Hitchingham, Eileen E. "MEDLINE Use in a University Without a School of Medicine." *Special Libraries*, vol. 67, April 1976, pp. 188-194.

Hitchingham, Eileen E. "Selecting Measures Applicable to Evaluation of On-Line Literature Searching." *Drexel Library Quarterly*, vol. 13, July 1977, pp. 52-67.

Hoffman, Andrea. "Collection Development Programs in Academic Libraries: An Administrative Approach." *Bookmark*, vol. 38, no. 3, Spring 1979, pp. 121-125.

Holler, Frederick L. "Toward a Reference Theory." *RQ*, vol. 14, Summer 1975, pp. 301-309.

Hoover, Ryan E. "Overview of Online Information Retrieval." In *The Library and Information Manager's Guide to Online Services*. Edited by Ryan E. Hoover. White Plains, NY: Knowledge Industry Publications, Inc., 1980.

Horn, Roger. "The Idea of Academic Library Management." *College and Research Libraries*, vol. 36, November 1975, pp. 464-472.

Horny, Karen L. "NOTIS-3 (Northwestern On-Line Total Integrated System): Technical Services Applications." *Library Resources and Technical Services*, vol. 22, Fall 1978, pp. 361-367.

Hulbert, Linda and Curry, Stewart. "Evaluation of an Approval Plan." *College and Research Libraries*, vol. 39, November 1978, pp. 485-491.

Jackson, Eugene B., Jackson, Ruth L. and Kennedy, Robert A. *Industrial Information Systems*. Stroudsburg, PA: Dowden, Hutchinson & Ross, Inc., 1978.

Jacob, MaryEllen L. "A National Interlibrary Loan Network: The OCLC Approach." *American Society for Information Science Bulletin*, vol. 5, June 1979, pp. 24-25.

Jacob, MaryEllen, Dodson, Ann T. and Finnegan, Nancy. "Special Libraries and Databases: A State-of-the-Art Report." *Special Libraries*, vol. 72, no. 2, April 1981, pp. 103-112.

Jahoda, Gerald et al. "The Reference Process: Modules for Instruction." *RQ*, vol. 17, Fall 1977, pp. 7-12.

Jain, A.K. "Sampling and Data Collection Methods for a Book-Use Study." *Library Quarterly*, vol. 39, July 1969, pp. 245-252.

Johns, Claude J. and Peischl, Thomas M. "Management Data Generated by Automated Circulation Systems: Uses and Limitations." In *Proceedings of the ASIS Annual Meeting*, vol. 15. White Plains, NY: Knowledge Industry Publications, Inc., 1978, pp. 171-173.

The Johns Hopkins University. The Milton S. Eisenhower Library. *Management Review and Analysis Program Report*. Baltimore, MD: September 1976.

Jones, W.O. "How Many Reference Librarians Are Enough?" *RQ*, vol. 14, Fall 1974, pp. 16-19.

Jordan, Robert T. "Library Characteristics of Colleges Ranking High in Academic Excellence." *College and Research Libraries*, vol. 24, September 1963, pp. 369-376.

Kantor, Paul B. "Availability Analysis." *Journal of the American Society for Information Science*, vol. 27, September-October 1976b, pp. 311-319.

Kantor, Paul B. "The Library as an Information Utility in the University Context: Evaluation and Measurement of Service." *Journal of the American Society of Information Science*, vol. 27, March/April 1976a, pp. 100-112.

Kaplan, Louis. "On Decision Sharing in Libraries: How Much Do We Know?" *College and Research Libraries*, vol. 38, no. 1, January 1977, pp. 25-31.

Kaplan, Louis. "The Literature of Participation: From Optimism to Realism." *College and Research Libraries*, vol. 36, no. 6, November 1975, pp. 437-479.

Kaser, David. "Evaluation of Administrative Services." *Library Trends*, vol. 22, January 1974, pp. 257-264.

Kaske, N.K. *Effectiveness of Library Operations: A Management Information Systems Approach and Application*. Library Science Dissertation. Norman, OK: The University of Oklahoma, 1973.

Kast, F.E. and Rosenzweig, J.E. *Organization and Management: A Systems Approach*. 2nd Edition. New York: McGraw-Hill, 1974.

Kates, Jacqueline R. "One Measure of a Library's Contribution." *Special Libraries*, vol. 65, no. 8, August 1974, pp. 332-336.

Katz, William A. *Collection Development: The Selection of Materials for Libraries*. New York: Holt, Rinehart and Winston, 1980.

Keen, P.G.W. and Morton, Michael S. Scott. *Decision Support Systems: An Organizational Perspective*. Reading, MA: Addison-Wesley, 1978.

Kent, Allen. "Crystal Gazing into the Future." *Journal of Library Automation*, vol. 11, December 1978, pp. 329-337.

Kilgour, Frederick. "Interlibrary Loans On-Line." *Library Journal*, vol. 104, February 15, 1979, pp. 460-463.

King, D.W., ed. *Key Papers in the Design and Evaluation of Information Systems*. White Plains, NY: Knowledge Industry Publications, Inc., 1978.

King, David N. and Ory, John C. "Effects of Library Instruction on Student Research: A Case Study." *College and Research Libraries*, vol. 42, no. 1, January 1981, pp. 31-41.

King, G.B. and Berry, R. *Evaluation of the University of Minnesota Libraries Reference Department Telephone Information Source, Pilot Study*. Minneapolis: Library School, University of Minnesota, 1973.

Knight, Nancy H. "Theft Detection Systems Revisited: An Updated Survey." *Library Technology Reports*, vol. 15, May-June 1979, pp. 221-409.

Knowles, Malcolm, "Model for Assessing Continuing Education Needs for a Profession." In CLENE: Continuing Library Education Network and Exchange. *Proceedings: First CLENE Assembly*. Washington, DC: CLENE, 1976, pp. 82-98.

Koenig, Michael. "Budgets and Budgeting Parts I & II." *Special Libraries*, vol. 68, July/August 1977, pp. 228-240.

Koenig, Michael. "On-Line Serials Collection Analysis." *Journal of the American Society for Information Science*, vol. 30, May 1979, pp. 148-153.

Kohut, Joseph and Walker, John. "Allocating the Book Budget; Equity and Economic Efficiency." *College and Research Libraries*, vol. 36, 1975, pp. 403-410.

Kornfeld, S. "Exxon Research and Engineering Company's Information Services." *Information Manager*, vol. 1, no. 3, March-April 1979, pp. 22-28.

Kortendick, James and Stone, Elizabeth. *Job Dimensions and Educational Needs in Librarianship*. Chicago: American Library Association, 1971.

Kortendick, James and Stone, Elizabeth. *Post-Masters Education for Middle and Upper Level Personnel in Library and Information Centers*. Washington, DC: U.S. Dept. of Health, Education and Welfare, Office of Education, 1972.

Kountz, John. "Automated Acquisitions Systems: A Survey." *Journal of Library Automation*, vol. 13, no. 4, December 1980, pp. 250-260.

Kraft, Donald and Polacsek, Richard. "A Journal-Worth Measure for a Journal-Selection Decision Model." *Collection Management*, vol. 2,, Summer 1978, pp. 129-139.

Kunkel, Barbara K., Rau, Susan L. and Miller, Betty. "The Use of Computerized Data Bases by Special Libraries." *Bookmark*, vol. 36, no. 2, Winter 1977, pp. 49-54.

Kunz, Arthur. "The Use of Data Gathering Instruments in Library Planning." *Library Trends*, vol. 24, January 1976, pp. 459-471.

Lancaster, F.W. *The Measurement and Evaluation of Library Services*. Washington, DC: Information Resources Press, 1977.

Lancaster, F.W. *Toward Paperless Information Systems*. New York: Academic Press, 1978.

Lancaster, Wilfred. "The Tip of the Iceberg." *Bulletin of the American Society for Information Science*, vol. 4, February 1978, p. 32.

Landram, Christina. "Cataloging: OCLC Terminal Plus Printer." *Library Resources and Technical Services*, vol. 21, Spring 1977, pp. 147-155.

Lantz, Brian E. "Manual Versus Computerized Retrospective Reference Retrieval in an Academic Library." *Journal of Librarianship*, vol. 10, April 1978, pp. 119-130.

Leach, Ronald G. "Finding Time You Never Knew You Had." *The Journal of Academic Librarianship*, vol. 6, no. 1, March 1980, pp. 4-8.

Leggate, Peter, Rossiter, B.N. and Rowland, J.F.B. "Evaluation of an SDI Service Based on the Index Chemicus Registry System." *Journal of Chemical Documentation*, vol. 13, August 1973, pp. 192-203.

Leimkuhler, Ferdinand. "The Bradford Distribution." *Journal of Documentation*, vol. 23, September 1967, pp. 197-207.

Leimkuhler, Ferdinand. "Library Operations Research: A Process of Discovery and Justification." *Library Quarterly*, vol. 42, January 1972, pp. 84-96.

Leimkuhler, Ferdinand and Cooper, Michael. "Cost Accounting and Analysis for University Libraries." *College and Research Libraries*, vol. 32, November 1971, pp. 449-464.

Lemke, Darrell. "Library Networks and the Provision of Management Information." *Catholic Library World*, vol. 49, April 1978, pp. 376-379.

Levine, Jamie J. and Logan, Timothy. *On-Line Resource Sharing: A Comparison of BALLOTS and OCLC—A Guide for Library Administrators*. San Jose, CA: California Library Authority for Systems and Services, 1977.

Lewis, Ralph W. "User's Reactions to Microfiche: A Preliminary Study." *College and Research Libraries*, vol. 31, July 1970, pp. 260-268.

Library Trends. "Personnel Development and Continuing Education in Libraries." Edited by Elizabeth Stone. Vol. 20, July 1971, the issue.

Licklider, J.C.R. *Libraries of the Future*. Cambridge, MA: M.I.T. Press, 1965.

Lincoln, Robert. "Vendors and Delivery." *Canadian Library Journal*, vol. 35, February 1978, pp. 51-57.

Lindgren, Jon. "Seeking a Useful Tradition for Library User Instruction in the College Library." In *Progress in Educating the Library User*. Edited by John Lubans. New York: Bowker, 1978, pp. 71-91.

Line, Maurice. "The Ability of a University Library to Provide Books Wanted by Researchers." *Journal of Librarianship*, vol. 5, January 1973, pp. 37-51.

Line, Maurice and Sandison, Alexander. "Practical Interpretation of Citation and Library Use Studies." *College and Research Libraries*, vol. 36, September 1975, pp. 393-396.

Lipinski, Donna and Almony, Robert. "Library Performance Measurement Through an Automated Circulation System: Attitude and System State Variables." In *Proceedings of the ASIS Annual Meeting*, vol. 15. White Plains, NY: Knowledge Industry Publications, Inc., 1978, pp. 206-208.

Lipon, Anne G. "Library Services to the Graduate Community: The University of California, Berkeley." *College and Research Libraries*, vol. 37, May 1976, pp. 254-255.

Litster, Joyce. *Types of Reference Questions in the Academic Library: An Attempt at Definition*. Toronto: University of Toronto School of Library Science, 1967.

Lubans, John. "Seeking a Partnership Between the Teacher and the Librarian." In *Progress in Educating the Library User*. Edited by John Lubans. New York: Bowker, 1978, pp. 1-11.

Lubans, John, Sr. et al. *A Study with Computer-Based Circulation Data of the Non-Use and Use of a Large Academic Library*. Boulder, CO: University of Colorado Libraries, 1973.

Lucas, Henry C. "An Empirical Study of a Framework for Information Systems." *Decision Sciences*, vol. 5, January 1974, pp. 102-114.

Lucker, Jay K. "Library Resources and Bibliographic Control." *College and Research Libraries*, vol. 40, March 1979, pp. 141-153.

Luhn, H.P. "Selective Dissemination of New Scientific Information with the Aid of Electronic Processing Equipment." *American Documentation*, vol. 12, April 1961, pp. 131-138.

Lyden, Frederick C. "Library Materials Budgeting in the Private University: Austerity and Actions." *Advances in Librarianship*, vol. 10, 1980, pp. 89-154.

Lyden, Frederick C. "Replacement of Hard Copy by Microforms." *Microform Review*, vol. 4, January 1975, pp. 9-14.

Lyders, Richard, Eckels, Diane and Leatherbury, Maurice. "Cost Allocation and Cost Generation." In *New Horizons for*

Academic Libraries. Edited by Robert D. Stueart and Richard D. Johnson. Papers presented at the First National Conference of the Association of College and Research Libraries, Boston, MA, November 8-11, 1978. New York: K.G. Saur Publishing, Inc., 1979.

MacKenzie, A. Graham. "Systems Analysis as a Decision-Making Tool for the Library Manager." *Library Trends*, vol. 21, April 1973, pp. 493-504.

Magrill, Rose and East, Mona. "Collection Development in Large University Libraries." *Advances in Librarianship*, vol. 8, 1978, pp. 2-54.

Mahmoodi, Suzanne. "Assessing Educational Needs of Minnesota Library Personnel: A Proposed Technique." *Minnesota Libraries*, vol. 25, Summer 1976, pp. 51-55.

Maloney, R. Kay, ed. *Personnel Development in Libraries.* New Brunswick, NJ: Graduate School of Library Service, Rutgers University, 1976.

Marchant, Maurice. *Participative Management in Academic Libraries.* Contributions in Librarianship and Information Science, no. 16. Wesport, CT: Greenwood Press, 1976.

Marchant, Maurice. "University Libraries as Economic Systems." *College and Research Libraries*, vol. 36, November 1975, pp. 449-457.

Marcus, Richard, Kugel, Peter and Benenfeld, Alan. "Catalog Information and Text as Indicators of Relevance." *Journal of the American Society for Information Science*, vol. 29, January 1978, pp. 15-30.

Markuson, Barbara. "Library Networks: Progress and Problems." In *The Information Age: Its Development, Its Impact.* Edited by Donald Hammer. Metuchen, NJ: Scarecrow Press, 1976, pp. 34-59.

Marshall, Peter. "How Much, How Often?" *College and Research Libraries*, vol. 35, November 1974, pp. 453-456.

Martell, Charles. "Copyright Law and Reserve Operations—An Interpretation." *College and Research Libraries News*, vol. 39, January 1978, pp. 1-6.

Martell, Charles and Dougherty, Richard. "The Role of Continuing Education and Training in Human Resource Development: An Administrator's Viewpoint." *Journal of Academic Librarianship*, vol. 4, no. 3, 1978, pp. 151-155.

Martin, Jean K. "Impact of Computer-Based Literature Searching on Interlibrary Loan Activity." *Proceedings of the ASIS Annual Meeting.* White Plains, NY: Knowledge Industry Publications, Inc., 1977.

Martin, L.A. *Library Response to Urban Change: A Study of the Chicago Public Library.* Chicago: American Library Association, 1969.

Martin, Susan. *Library Networks, 1981-82.* White Plains, NY: Knowledge Industry Publications, Inc., 1981.

Martin, Susan. "Upgrading 'Brief and Dirty' Data." *American Libraries*, vol. 10, April 1979, pp. 213-214.

Martyn, J. and Slater, M. "Tests on Abstract Journals." *Journal of Documentation*, vol. 20, December 1964, pp. 212-235.

Maslow, A. *Eupsychian Management: A Journal.* Homewood, IL: R.D. Irwin, 1965.

Mason, Ellsworth. "Balbus; or the Future of Library Buildings." In *Farewell to Alexandria.* Edited by Daniel Gore. Westport, CT: Greenwood Press, 1976, pp. 22-33.

Mason, Ellsworth. "Decisions! Decisions!" *Journal of Academic Librarianship*, vol. 1, March 1975, pp. 4-8.

Mason, R.O. and Mitroff, I.I. "A Program for Research on Management Information Systems." *Management Science*, vol. 19, January 1973, pp. 475-487.

Mathews, Frank S. "The Technological Environment." In *The Changing Environment of Libraries.* Edited by John T. Eastlick. Chicago: American Library Association, 1971, pp. 20-29.

Matthews, Joseph R. "The Four Online Bibliographic Utilities: A Comparison." *Library Technology Reports*, vol. 15, no. 6, November-December 1979, pp. 665-838.

McAnally, A.M. and Downs, R.B. "The Changing Role of Directors of University Libraries." *College and Research Libraries*, vol. 34, March 1973, pp. 103-125.

McClelland, David. *Power: The Inner Experience.* New York: Irvington Publishers, 1975.

McClure, Charles R. "Academic Librarians, Information Sources, and Shared Decision Making." *The Journal of Academic Librarianship*, vol. 6, no. 1, March 1980, pp. 9-15.

McClure, Charles R. "The Information Rich Employee and Organizational Decision Making: Review and Comments." *Information Processing and Management*, vol. 14, no. 6, 1979, pp. 381-394.

McClure, Charles R. "The Planning Process: Strategies for Action." *College and Research Libraries*, vol. 39, November 1978, pp. 456-466.

McClure, Charles R. "A Reference Theory of Specific Information Retrieval." *RQ*, vol. 13, Spring 1974, pp. 207-212.

McCullough, Kathleen, Posey, Edwin and Pickett, Doyle. *Approval Plans and Academic Libraries.* Phoenix, AZ: Oryx Press, 1977.

McGeehan, Thomas. *Decision Analysis Technique for Program Evaluation (Goal Programming).* Alexandria, VA: Defense Documentation Center, April 1977, ADO 38800.

McGrath, William. "An Allocation Formula Derived from a Factor Analysis of Academic Departments." *College and Research Libraries*, vol. 30, January 1969a, pp. 51-62.

McGrath, William. "Classifying Courses in the University Catalog." *College and Research Libraries*, vol. 30, November 1969b, pp. 533-539.

McGrath, William. "A Pragmatic Book Allocation Formula for Academic and Public Libraries with a Test for Its Effectiveness." *Library Resources and Technical Services*, vol. 19, Fall 1975, pp. 356-369.

McGregor, D. *The Human Side of Enterprises.* New York: McGraw-Hill, 1960.

Meier, R.L. "Efficiency Criteria for the Operation of Large Libraries." *Library Quarterly*, vol. 31, July 1961, pp. 215-234.

Merchant, Robert C. "Comments on Electronic Systems for Education." In *Library Buildings: Innovation for Changing Needs.* Edited by A. Trezza. Chicago: American Library Association, 1972, pp. 13-17.

Metcalf, Keyes. *Planning Academic and Research Library Buildings.* New York: McGraw-Hill, 1965.

Meyer, R.W. and Panetta, Rebecca. "Two Shared Cataloging Data Bases: A Comparison." *College and Research Libraries*, vol. 38, January 1977, pp. 19-24.

Meyer, Ursula. "New York's Statewide Continuing Professional Education Program: The Early Stages of Development." Paper presented at the First Annual Staff Development Micro-workshop, American Library Association Convention, Detroit, MI, June 28, 1970.

Michael, Mary Ellen. *Continuing Professional Education in Librarianship and Other Fields: A Classified and Annotated Bibliography, 1965-1974.* New York: Garland Publishing Inc., 1975.

Michalko, James and Heidtmann, Toby. "Evaluating the Effectiveness of an Electronic Security System." *College and Research Libraries*, vol. 39, July 1978, pp. 263-267.

Miller, Edward. "User-Oriented Planning." *Special Libraries*, vol. 64, November 1973, pp. 479-482.

Mintzberg, Henry. *The Nature of Managerial Work.* New York: Harper & Row, 1973.

Moran, Robert F. "Improving the Organizational Design of Academic Libraries." *The Journal of Academic Librarianship*, vol. 6, no. 3, July 1980, pp. 140-145.

Morita, Ichiko T. and Gapen, D. Kaye. "A Cost Analysis of the Ohio State College Library On-line Shared Cataloging System in the Ohio State University Libraries." *Library Resources and Technical Services*, vol. 21, Summer 1977, pp. 286-302.

Morse, Philip. *Library Effectiveness: A Systems Approach.* Cambridge, MA: M.I.T. Press, 1968.

Morse, Philip. "Measures of Library Effectiveness." *Library Quarterly*, vol. 42, January 1972, pp. 15-30.

Morton, D.J. "Applying Theory Y to Library Management." *College and Research Libraries*, vol. 36, July 1975, pp. 302-307.

Mosher, Paul H. "Collection Evaluation in Research Libraries: The Search for Quality, Consistency, and System in Collection Development." *Library Resources and Technical Services*, vol. 23, no. 1, Winter 1979, pp. 16-32.

Mosley, Isobel. "Cost-Effectiveness Analysis of the Automation of a Circulation System." *Journal of Library Automation*, vol. 10, September 1977, pp. 240-254.

Mount, Ellis, ed. *Planning the Special Library*. New York: Special Libraries Association, 1972.

Muller, Robert. "Economics of Compact Book Shelving." *Library Trends*, vol. 13, April 1965, pp. 433-447.

Murdock, John and Sherrod, John. "Library and Information Center Management." *Annual Review of Information Science and Technology*, vol. 11, 1976, pp. 381-402.

Murfin, Marjorie E. "The Myth of Accessibility: Frustration and Failure in Retrieving Periodicals." *The Journal of Academic Librarianship*, vol. 6, no. 1, March 1980, pp. 16-19.

Musselman, K. and Talavage, J. "A Managerial Tool for Evaluating Information." Working Paper. Lafayette, IN: Purdue University, August 1978.

Nachlas, Joel and Pierce, Anton. "Determination of Unit Costs for Library Services." *College and Research Libraries*, vol. 40, May 1979, pp. 240-247.

Newell, Allen and Simon, Herbert A. *Human Problem Solving*. Englewood Cliffs, NJ: Prentice-Hall Inc., 1972.

Newman, Wilda B. "Managing a Report Collection for Zero Growth." *Special Libraries*, vol. 71, no. 5/6, May/June 1980, pp. 276-282.

Nutter, Susan K. "Microforms and the User: Key Variables of User Acceptance in a Library Environment." *Drexel Library Quarterly*, vol. 11, October 1975, pp. 17-31.

Oboler, Eli M. "Selling the Academic Library." In *Public Relations for Libraries*. Edited by A. Angoff. Westport, CT: Greenwood Press, 1973, pp. 133-149.

Ohmes, Frances and Jones, J.F. "The Other Half of Cataloging." *Library Resources and Technical Services*, vol. 17, Summer 1973, pp. 320-329.

Olafsen, Tore. "The Demand for Biomedical Periodicals." *Tidskrist Foer Dokumentation*, vol. 35, no. 1, 1979, pp. 3-8.

Orne, Jerrold. "Library Building Trends and Their Meanings." *Library Journal*, vol. 102, December 1, 1977, pp. 2397-2401.

Orr, Richard H. "Measuring the Goodness of Library Services: A General Framework for Considering Quantitative Measures." *Journal of Documentation*, vol. 29, September 1973, pp. 315-332.

Orr, Richard H. "The Scientist as an Information Processor: A Conceptual Model Illustrated with Data on Variables Related to Library Utilization." In *Communication Among Scientists and Engineers*. Edited by C.E. Nelson. Lexington, MA: Heath/Lexington Books, 1970.

Orr, Richard H., Pings, Vern M., Olson, Edwin and Pizer, Irwin. "Development of Methodological Tools for Planning and Manging Library Services. Parts I, II, III." *Bulletin of the Medical Library Association*, vol. 56, July 1968, pp. 235-267; and October 1968, pp. 380-403.

Orr, Richard H. and Schless, A.P. "Document Delivery Capabilities of Major Biomedical Libraries in 1968: Results of a National Survey Employing Standardized Tests." *Bulletin of the Medical Library Association*, vol. 60, July 1972, pp. 382-422.

Ottersen, Signe. "A Bibliography on Standards for Evaluating Libraries." *College and Research Libraries*, vol. 32, March 1971, pp. 127-144.

Packer, Katherine and Soergel, Dagobert. "The Importance of SDI for Current Awareness in Fields with Severe Scatter of Information." *Journal of the American Society for Information Science*, vol. 30, May 1979, pp. 125-135.

Palmour, Vernon E. et al. *A Study of the Characteristics, Costs and Magnitude of Interlibrary Loan in Academic Libraries*. Westport, CT: Greenwood Publishing Co., 1972.

Park, M.K. et al. "Education in the Use of Modern Information Retrieval Techniques." *Journal of Chemical Documentation*, vol. 11, May 1971, pp. 100-102.

Parker, Diane and Carpenter, Eric. "A Zero-Base Budget Approach to Staff Justification for a Combined Reference and Collection Development Department." In *New Horizons for Academic Libraries*. Edited by Robert D. Stueart and Richard D. Johnson. Papers presented at the First National Conference of the Association of College and Research Libraries, Boston, MA, November 8-11, 1978. New York: K.G. Saur Publishing, Inc., 1979.

Patrick, Ruth. *An Annotated Bibliography of Recent Continuing Education Literature*. ERIC Clearinghouse on Information Resources. Stanford, CA: Stanford University, 1976.

Payne, Charles T. "The University of Chicago Library Data Management System." *Library Quarterly*, vol. 47, January 1977, pp. 1-22.

Payne, Charles T. "The University of Chicago Library Data Management System." In *Clinic on Library Applications of Data Processing: Applications of Mini-Computers to Library and Related Problems*. Edited by F.W. Lancaster. Urbana-Champaign, IL: University of Illinois Graduate School of Library Science, 1974.

Perkins, R. *Prospective Teachers' Knowledge of Library Fundamentals*. New York: Scarecrow Press, 1965.

Person, Roland. "Long-Term Evaluation of Bibliographic Instruction: Lasting Encouragement." *College and Research Libraries,*, vol. 42, no 1, January 1981, pp. 19-25.

Pierce, Anton R. and Taylor, Joe K. "A Model for Cost Comparison of Automated Cataloging Systems." *Journal of Library Automation*, vol. 11, March 1978, pp. 6-23.

Pierce, Thomas. "An Empirical Approach to the Allocation of the University Library Book Budget." *Collection Management*, vol. 2, Spring 1978, pp. 39-58.

Piternick, A.B. "Measurement of Journal Availability in a Biomedical Library." *Bulletin of the Medical Library Association*, vol. 60, October 1972, pp. 534-542.

Pizer, Irwin and Cain, Alexander. "Objective Tests of Library Performance." *Special Libraries*, vol. 59, November 1968, pp. 704-711.

Planning for the Future of the Card Catalog. SPEC Kit 46. Washington, DC: Association of Research Libraries, Systems and Procedures Exchange Center, July 1978.

Porter, Lyman W. and Roberts, Karlenett. "Communication in Organization." In *Handbook of Industrial and Organizational Psychology*. Edited by Marvin D. Dunnette. Chicago: Rand McNally, 1976.

Prentice, Ann. *Strategies for Survival: Library Financial Management Today*. LJ Special Report #7. New York: Bowker, 1978.

"The President Views the Campus Library." *Journal of Academic Librarianship*, vol. 3, September 1977, pp. 192-199.

Pritsker, Alan B. and Sadler, J. William. "An Evaluation of Microfilm as a Method of Book Storage." *College and Research Libraries*, vol. 18, July 1957, pp. 290-296.

Project Intrex. *Intrex: Report of a Planning Conference on Information Transfer Experiments*. Cambridge, MA: M.I.T. Press, 1965.

Raffel, Jeffrey. "From Economic to Political Analysis of Library Decision Making." *College and Research Libraries*, vol. 35, November 1974, pp. 412-423.

Raffel, Jeffrey and Shishko, Robert. "Centralization vs. Decentralization: A Location Analysis Approach for Librarians." *Special Libraries*, vol. 63, March 1972, pp. 135-143.

Raffel, Jeffrey and Shishko, Robert. *Systematic Analysis of University Libraries: An Application of Cost-Benefit Analysis to the M.I.T. Libraries*. Cambridge, MA: M.I.T. Press, 1969.

Randall, Gordon. "Budgeting for Libraries." *Special Libraries*, vol. 67, January 1976, pp. 8-12.

Rao, Paladugu V. and Jones, Carole B. "System to Manage Reserve Texts (SMART)." *Journal of Library Automation*, vol. 9, December 1976, pp. 328-334.

Reed, Jutta R. "Cost Comparison of Periodicals in Hard Copy and on Microform." *Microform Review*, vol. 5, July 1976, pp. 185-192.

Reed, Mary Jane Polst. *The Washington Library Networks Computerized Bibliographic System*. Olympia, WA: Washington State University, March 1975, ED 124 187.

Regazzi, John and Hersberger, Rodney. "Queues and Reference Service: Some Implications for Staffing." *College and Research Libraries*, vol. 39, July 1978, pp. 293-298.

Reid, Marion. "Effectiveness of the OCLC Data Base for Acquisitions Verification." *Journal of Academic Librarianship*, vol. 2, January 1977, pp. 303-326.

Reisman, A. et al. "Timeliness of Library Materials Delivery: A Set of Priorities." *Socio-Economic Planning Sciences*, vol. 6, April 1972, pp. 145-152.

Rettig, James. "A Theoretical Model and Definition of the Reference Process." *RQ*, vol. 18, Fall 1978, pp. 19-29.

Rice, Barbara A. "Weeding in Academic and Research Libraries: An Annotated Bibliography." *Collection Management*, vol. 2, Spring 1978, pp. 65-71.

Ricking, Myrl and Booth, Robert. *Personnel Utilization in Libraries: A Systems Approach*. Chicago: American Library Association, 1974.

Robinson, Barbara M. "The Role of Special Libraries in the Emerging National Network." *Special Libraries*, vol. 72, no. 1, January 1981, pp. 8-17.

Rohlf, Robert. "Building-Planning Implications of Automation." In *Library Buildings: Innovation for Changing Needs*. Edited by A. Trezza. Chicago: American Library Association, 1972, pp. 6-10.

Rosenberg, Kenyon C. "Evaluation of an Industrial Library: A Simple-minded Technique." *Special Libraries*, vol. 60, no. 9, November 1969, pp. 635-638.

Rosenberg, Victor. *The Application of Psychometric Techniques to Determine the Attitudes of Individuals Toward Information Seeking*. Bethlehem, PA: Lehigh University, Center for the Information Sciences, 1966a.

Rosenberg, Victor. *Studies in the Man-System Interface in Libraries, Report No. 2: The Application of Psychometric Techniques to Determine the Attitudes of Individuals Toward Information Seeking*. Bethlehem, PA: Lehigh University, Center for the Information Sciences, July 1966b.

Rosenthal, Joseph. "Planning for the Catalogs: A Managerial Perspective." *Journal of Library Automation*, vol. 2, September 1978, pp. 192-205.

Ross, Ryburn. "Cost Analysis of Automation in Technical Services." In *Proceedings of the 1976 Clinic on Library Applications of Data Processing*. Urbana, IL: Graduate School of Library Science, University of Illinois, 1977, pp. 10-27.

Rothstein, Samuel. "The Measurement and Evaluation of Reference Service." *Library Trends*, vol. 12, January 1964, pp. 456-472.

Rouse, Sandra H. and Rouse, William B. "Design of a Model-Based Online Management Information System for Interlibrary Loan Networks." *Information Processing and Management*, vol. 15, no. 2, 1979, pp. 109-122.

Rouse, William B. "A Library Network Model." *Journal of the American Society for Information Science*, vol. 27, March-April 1976, pp. 88-99.

Rouse, William B. "Optimal Resources Allocation in Library Systems." *Journal of the American Society for Information Science*, vol. 26, May-June 1975, pp. 157-165.

Rouse, William B. and Rouse, Sandra H. "Assessing the Impact of Computer Technology on the Performance of Interlibrary Loan Networks." *Journal of the American Society for Information Science*, vol. 28, March 1977, pp. 79-88.

Rouse, William B. and Rouse, Sandra H. "Use of a Librarian/Consultant Team to Study Library Operations." *College and Research Libraries*, vol. 34, September 1973, pp. 242-248.

Rubenstein, Albert and Birr, David. *Designs for Field Experiments on Accessibility, Quality and Use of Sources of Scientific and Technical Information*. A report submitted to NSF. Evanston, IL: The Technological Institute, Northwestern University, 1976.

Runyon, Robert S. "Power and Conflict in Academic Libraries." *Journal of Academic Librarianship*, vol. 3, September 1977, pp. 200-205.

Ryans, Cynthia. "A Study of Errors Found in Non-MARC Cataloging in a Machine-Assisted System." *Journal of Library Automation*, vol. 11, June 1978, pp. 125-132.

Rzasa, Philip and Moriarity, John. "The Types and Needs of Academic Library Users: A Case Study of 6,568 Responses." *College and Research Libraries*, vol. 31, November 1970, pp. 403-409.

Saffady, William. "The Economics of Online Bibliographic Searching: Costs and Cost Justifications." *Library Technology Reports*, vol. 15, September/October 1979, pp. 567-653.

Saffady, William. "Facsimile Transmission for Libraries: Technology and Application Design." *Library Technology Reports*, vol. 15, September/October 1978a, pp. 445-531.

Saffady, William. *Micrographics*. Littleton, CO: Libraries Unlimited, 1978b.

Sage, C.R., Anderson, R.R. and Fitzwater, D.R. "Adaptive Information Dissemination." *American Documentation*, vol. 16, July 1965, pp. 185-200.

St. Clair, Jeffrey W. and Aluri, Rao. "Staffing the Reference Desk: Professionals or Nonprofessionals?" *Journal of Academic Librarianship*, vol. 3, July 1977, pp. 149-153.

Saracevic, T. "Selected Results from an Inquiry into Testing of Information Retrieval Systems." *Journal of the American Society for Information Science*, vol. 22, March-April 1971, pp. 126-139.

Saracevic, T., Shaw, W.M. and Kantor, P.B. "Causes and Dynamics of User Frustration in an Academic Library." *College and Research Libraries*, vol. 38, January 1977, pp. 7-18.

Sargent, Charles. "Zero-Base Budgeting and the Library." *Bulletin of the Medical Library Association*, vol. 66, January 1978, pp. 31-35.

Scales, P.A. "Citation Analysis as Indicators of the Use of Serials: A Comparison of Ranked Title Lists Produced by Citation Counting and From Use Data." *Journal of Documentation*, vol. 32, March 1976, pp. 17-25.

Schad, Jasper. "Allocating Materials Budgets in Institutions of Higher Education." *Journal of Academic Librarianship*, vol. 3, no. 6, 1978, pp. 328-332.

Schmidt, C. James. "Resource Allocation in University Libraries in the 1970's and Beyond." *Library Trends*, vol. 23, April 1975, pp. 643-648.

Schofield, J.L., Cooper, A. and Waters, D.H. "Evaluation of an Academic Library's Stock Effectiveness." *Journal of Librarianship*, vol. 7, July 1975, pp. 207-227.

Scholz, William. "Computer-Based Circulation Systems—A Current Review and Evaluation." *Library Technology Reports*, vol. 13, May 1977, pp. 231-325.

Sellen, Betty-Carol. "Collection Development and the College Library." In *Collection Building: Studies in the Development and Effective Use of Library Resources*. Syracuse, NY: Gaylord Professional Pubs.,1978, pp. 19-24.

Sellers, David Y. "Basic Planning and Budgeting Concepts for Special Libraries." *Special Libraries*, vol. 64, no. 2, February 1973, pp. 70-75.

Shaw, W.M. "Loan Period Distribution in Academic Libraries." *Information Processing and Management*, vol. 12, no. 3, 1976, pp. 157-159.

Shill, Harold B. "Open Stacks and Library Performance." *College and Research Libraries*, vol. 41, no. 3, May 1980, pp. 220-226.

Simon, Herbert A. *Administrative Behavior: A Study of Decision Making Processes in Administrative Organization*. 3rd edition. New York: Free Press, 1976.

Simon, Herbert A. *The New Science of Management Decision*. New York: Harper & Row, 1960.

Simon, Herbert A. *The Shape of Automation for Men and Management*. New York: Harper & Row, 1965.

Singleton, A. "Journal Ranking and Selection: A Review in Physics." *Journal of Documentation*, vol. 32, December 1976, pp. 258-289.

Sinha, Bani and Clelland, Richard. "Application of a Collection-Control Model for Scientific Libraries." *Journal of the American Society for Information Science*, vol. 27, September/October 1976, pp. 320-328.

Slater, M. "Types of Use and User in Industrial Libraries: Some Impressions." *Journal of Documentation*, vol. 19, March 1963, pp. 12-18.

Smith, Patricia and Seba, D.B. "Using the Management Control Process in Information Centers." *Proceedings of the ASIS Annual Meeting*, Washington, DC: American Society for Information Science, 1976, pp. 308-313.

Snyder, Carolyn and Sanders, Nancy. "Continuing Education and Staff Development: Needs Assessment, Comprehensive Program Planning, and Evaluation." *Journal of Academic Librarianship*, vol. 4, July 1978, pp. 144-150.

Soper, M.E. *The Relationships Between Personal Collections and the Selection of Cited References.* Doctoral Dissertation. Urbana, IL: Graduate School of Library Science, University of Illinois, 1972.

Spaulding, F.H. and Stanton, R.O. "Computer-Aided Selection in a Library Network." *Journal of the American Society for Information Science*, vol. 27, September-October 1976, pp. 269-280.

"Special Libraries Assocation/Objectives and Standards for Special Libraries." *Special Libraries*, vol. 55, no. 10, December 1964, pp. 672-680.

Spencer, Carol. "Random Time Sampling with Self-Observation for Library Cost Studies: Unit Costs of Interlibrary Loans and Photocopies at a Regional Medical Library." *Journal of the American Society for Information Science*, May-June 1971, pp. 153-160.

Spicer, Caroline T. "Measuring Reference Service: A Look at the Cornell University Libraries Reference Question Recording System." *Bookmark*, vol. 31, January-February 1972, pp. 79-81.

Sprague, Ralph H., Jr. and Watson, Hugh J. "A Decision Support System for Banks." *Omega*, vol. 4, no. 6, 1976.

Stevens, Norman. "A Hard Look at Reserve." *Journal of Academic Librarianship*, vol. 4, May 1978, pp. 86-87.

Stewart, Blair. "The Costs of Providing Access to Periodical Literature in Academic Libraries." *Catholic Library World*, vol. 49, September 1977, pp. 70-75.

Stokley, Sandra and Reid, Marion. "A Study of Performance of Five Book Dealers Used by Louisiana State University Library." *Library Resources and Technical Services*, vol. 22, Spring 1978, pp. 117-125.

Stone, Elizabeth. "Continuing Education for Librarians in the United States." *Advances in Librarianship*, vol. 8, 1978, pp. 241-331.

Stone, Elizabeth. *Continuing Library Education as Viewed in Relation to Other Continuing Professional Education Movements.* Washington, DC: American Society for Information Science, 1974.

Stone, Elizabeth and Conroy, Barbara. *Continuing Library and Information Science Education: A Final Report to the U.S. National Commission on Libraries and Information Science.* Washington, DC: U.S. Government Printing Office, May 1974.

Strable, Edward G., ed. *Special Libraries: A Guide for Management.* New York: Special Libraries Association, 1975.

Strauss, Lucille J., Shreve, Irene M. and Brown, Alberta L. *Scientific and Technical Libraries: Their Organization and Administration.* New York: John Wiley and Sons, Inc., 1972.

Stuart, M. "Some Effects on Library Users of the Delays in Supplying Publications." *ASLIB Proceedings*, vol. 29, January 1977, pp. 35-45.

Stueart, Robert D. and Johnson, Richard D., eds. *New Horizons for Academic Libraries.* Papers presented at the First National Conference of the Association of College and Research Libraries, Boston, MA, November 8-11, 1978. New York: K.G. Saur Publishing, Inc., 1979.

Summers, F. William. "The Use of Formulae in Resource Allocation." *Library Trends*, vol. 23, April 1975, pp. 631-642.

Swift, D.F., Winn, V.A., Bramer, D.A. and Mills, C.T.R. *A Case Study in Indexing and Clarification in the Sociology of Education: Development of Ideas Concerning the Organization of Materials for Literature Searching.* Milton Keynes, Eng.: Open University, Faculty of Educational Studies, June 1973, 2V (OSTI Report 5171).

Thomas, Kenneth. "Conflict and Conflict Management." In *Handbook of Industrial and Organizational Psychology.* Edited by Marvin D. Dunnett. Chicago: Rand McNally, 1976.

Thomson, S.K. *Interlibrary Loan Involving Academic Libraries.* ACRL Monograph, No. 32. Chicago: American Library Association, 1970.

Thorson, A. Robert. "The Economics of Automated Circulation." In *1976 Clinic on Library Applications of Data Processing.* Urbana, IL: Graduate School of Library Science, University of Illinois, 1977, pp. 28-47.

Tobin, J.C. "A Study of Library 'Use Studies.' " *Information Storage and Retrieval*, vol. 10, March-April 1977, pp. 101-113.

Trow, Martin. "Reflections on the Transition from Mass to Universal Higher Education." *Daedalus*, vol. 12, Winter 1970, p. 99.

Trudell, Libby and Wolper, James. "Interlibrary Loan in New England." *College and Research Libraries*, vol. 39, September 1978, pp. 365-371.

Trueswell, R.W. "User Circulation Satisfaction vs. Size of Holdings at Three Academic Libraries." *College and Research Libraries*, vol. 30, May 1969, pp. 204-213.

Tucker, Jane. "Alternative Models of the Decision-Making Process and Their Implications for Information Packaging." *Proceedings of the ASIS Annual Meeting*. Washington, DC: American Society for Information Science, 1976, pp. 644-653.

Ungarelli, Donald. "The Cost-Benefit of a Book Detection System: A Comparative Study." In *Quantitative Measurement and Dynamic Library Service*. Edited by Ching-Chih Chen. Phoenix, AZ: Oryx Press, 1978, pp. 149-158.

U.S. Library of Congress. Processing Services. "Draft Introductory Statement Concerning 'National Level Bibliographic Record—Books.' " *Library of Congress Information Bulletin*, vol. 37, November 10, 1978, pp. 692-696.

University Library. California State University, Long Beach. *Goals and Objectives of the University Library*. 2nd edition. The Library, March 1978.

University of Massachusetts. *A Management Review and Analysis of the University of Massachusetts at Amherst Libraries*. Amherst, MA, July 1976.

University of Pittsburgh. *A Cost-Benefit Model of Some Critical Library Operations in Terms of Use of Materials: Final Report*. University of Pittsburgh, 1978.

University of Rochester Library. *Management Review and Analysis of the University of Rochester Library: Final Report of the MRAP Study Team*, vol. 1, Rochester, NY, June 1974.

University of Washington. *Report of the Management Study of the University of Washington Libraries*. Seattle, WA, April-November 1973.

Urquhart, Donald. "The National Role in Resource Allocation." *Library Trends*, vol. 23, 1975, pp. 595-601.

Urquhart, John and Schofield, J.L. "Measuring Reader's Failure at the Shelf." *Journal of Documentation*, vol. 27, December 1971, pp. 273-286.

Vavrek, Bernard. "The Nature of Reference Librarianship." *RQ*, vol. 13, Spring 1974, p. 215.

Veaner, Allen. "BALLOTS—The View from Technical Services." *Library Resources and Technical Services*, vol. 21, Spring 1977, pp. 127-145.

Veaner, Allen. "Major Decision Points in Library Automation." *College and Research Libraries*, vol. 31, September 1970, pp. 303-304.

Voos, Henry. "Design of a Management Instrument for Technical Library Information Services." In *Contemporary Problems in Technical Library Information Service*. Edited by Alan Rees. Washington, DC: American Society for Information Science, 1974.

Voth, Sally and Lipp, Mark. "Weeding of a Library Reserve Book Section: A Description of the Kansas State University Library System Using Floppy Diskettes." *Collection Management*, vol. 1, Fall-Winter 1976-77, pp. 79-89.

Waldhart, Thomas J. and Marcum, Thomas P. "Productivity Measurement in Academic Libraries." *Advances in Librarianship*, vol. 6, 1976, pp. 53-78.

Waldron, Helen J. "The Business of Running a Special Library." *Special Libraries*, vol. 62, no. 2, February 1971, pp. 63-70.

Wanger, Judith et al. *Impact of On-Line Retrieval Services: A Survey of Users 1974-1975*. Santa Monica, CA: System Development Corporation, 1976.

Ware, Glenn. "A General Statistical Model for Estimating Future Demand Levels of Data-Base Utilization Within an Information Retrieval Organization." *Journal of the American Society for Information Science*, vol. 24, July-August 1973, pp. 201-264.

Warner, Edward. "Constituency Needs as Determinants of Library Collection and Service Configurations: An Approach to Measurement." *Drexel Library Quarterly*, vol. 13, July 1977, pp. 44-51.

Watson, Paula and Landis, Martha. *Working Paper on Staffing Services and Organization of Reference Departments in Large Academic Libraries*. Urbana, IL: University of Illinois Library, June 1977.

Watson, Peter. "The Dilemma of Fees for Service: Issues and Action for Librarians." *ALA Yearbook*. Chicago: American Library Association, 1978, pp. xv-xxii.

Weber, Hans. "The Librarian's View of Microforms." *IEE Transactions of Professional Communications*, PC-18, 1975, pp. 168-173.

Webster, Duane. "Strategies for Improving the Performance of Academic Libraries." *Journal of Academic Librarianship*, vol. 1, May 1975, pp. 13-18.

Weinberg, Charles B. "The University Library: Analysis and Proposals." *Management Science*, vol. 21, October 1974, pp. 130-140.

Weintraub, D. Kathryn. "The Essentials or Desiderata of the Bibliographic Record as Discovered by Research." *Library Resources and Technical Services*, vol. 23, Fall 1979, pp. 391-405.

Wells, Dorothy. "Coping with Schedules for Extended Hours." *Journal of Academic Librarianship*, vol. 5, March 1979, pp. 24-27.

Wenger, Charles and Childress, Judith. "Journal Evaluation in a Large Research Library." *Journal of the American Society for Information Science*, vol. 28, September 1977, pp. 293-299.

Wessel, C.J. *Criteria for Evaluating the Effectiveness of Library Operations and Services: Phase III Recommended Criteria and Methods for Their Utilization*. Washington, DC: John I. Thompson & Co., 1969.

White, Herbert. "Budgetary Priorities in the Administration of Large Academic Libraries." In *New Horizons for Academic Libraries*. Edited by Robert D. Stueart and Richard D. Johnson. Papers presented at the First National Conference of the Association of College and Research Libraries, Boston, MA, November 8-11, 1978. New York: K.G. Saur Publishing, Inc., 1979a.

White, Herbert "Cost-Effectiveness and Cost-Benefit Determinations in Special Libraries." *Special Libraries*, vol. 70, no. 4, April 1, 1979b, pp. 163-169.

White, Herbert. "Library Management in the Tight Budget Seventies." *Bulletin of the Medical Library Association*, vol. 65, January 1977, pp. 6-12.

Whitlatch, Jo Bell and Kieffer, Karen. "Service at San Jose State University: Survey of Document Availability." *Journal of Academic Librarianship*, vol. 4, September 1978, pp. 196-199.

Wiberley, Stephen. "Sources for the Humanities: Measuring Use and Meeting Needs." In *New Horizons for Academic Libraries*. Edited by Robert D. Stueart and Richard D. Johnson. Papers presented at the First National Conference of the Association of College and Research Libraries, Boston, MA, November 8-11, 1978. New York: K.G. Saur Publishing, Inc., 1979.

Wilkinson, John P. and Miller, William. "The Step Approach to Reference Service." *RQ*, vol. 18, Summer 1978, pp. 293-300.

Williams, G.E. et al. *Library Cost Models: Owning Versus Borrowing Serial Publications*. Chicago: The Center for Research Libraries, 1968.

Wills, Gordon and Oldman, Christine. *A Longitudinal Study of the Costs and Benefits of Selected Library Services: Initial Exploration and Framework*. Cranfield, Bedfordshire: Cranfield School of Management, 1974.

Wilson, Patrick. *Two Kinds of Power: An Essay on Bibliographical Control*. Berkeley, CA: University of California Press, 1968.

Winger, H.W. "Deterioration and Preservation of Library Materials." *Proceedings of the 34th Annual Conference of the Graduate Library School*. Chicago: University of Chicago Press, 1970.

Winstead, P. and Hobson, E. "Institutional Goals: Where to From Here?" *Journal of Higher Education*, vol. 42, November 1971, pp. 669-677.

Wolper, James and Trudell, Libby. "A Model of the NELINET Computerized Interlibrary Loan System: Testing Strategies for Load-Leveling." *Journal of Library Automation*, vol. 11, June 1978, pp. 142-151.

Yagello, Virginia and Guthrie, Gerry. "The Effect of Reduced Loan Periods on High Use Items." *College and Research Libraries*, vol. 36, September 1976, pp. 411-414.

Zipf, G.K. *Human Behavior and the Principle of Least Effort*. Cambridge, MA: Addison-Wesley, 1949.

Subject Index

Author Index

About the Authors

Michael R.W. Bommer is associate professor of management at The School of Management, Clarkson College. His primary interests are in management decision models and information systems. He was project director of a National Science Foundation grant to develop a management information system for academic libraries; this book is an outgrowth of that project. He has also served as a consultant to both government agencies and private industry. Co-author of *Library Planning and Decision-Making Systems* (1974), Professor Bommer has been a contributor to several other books and has published articles in numerous professional journals.

Prior to joining the faculty at Clarkson, Professor Bommer taught at Temple University's School of Business Administration. He was formerly a research associate at the Wharton School, University of Pennsylvania, and a management analyst with the U.S. Army Security Agency. A graduate of Cornell University, he holds an M.S. in industrial engineering from Ohio State University and a Ph.D. in management science from the University of Pennsylvania.

Ronald W. Chorba is associate professor at Clarkson's School of Management. He was co-principal investigator of the National Science Foundation study that led to this book. As a teacher, researcher and consultant on management information systems, he has had a special interest in the applications of computers in management and in information systems for health-care agencies. His articles have appeared in *Management Science, Health Services Research, Decision Sciences* and the *Journal of the American Society for Information Science.*

Professor Chorba was previously associate professor and associate dean of business at the University of Calgary, Canada. He has B.S. and M.S. degrees in mechanical engineering from the Massachusetts Institute of Technology and a Ph.D. in management science from the University of Arizona.